I0415662

September 2010

RECOVERY ACT

Opportunities to Improve Management and Strengthen Accountability over States' and Localities' Uses of Funds

Accountability * Integrity * Reliability

GAO-10-999

September 2010

RECOVERY ACT

Opportunities to Improve Management and Strengthen Accountability over States' and Localities' Uses of Funds

Why GAO Did This Study

This report responds to two ongoing GAO mandates under the American Recovery and Reinvestment Act of 2009 (Recovery Act). It is the latest in a series of reports on the uses of and accountability for Recovery Act funds in 16 selected states, certain localities in those jurisdictions, and the District of Columbia (District). These jurisdictions are estimated to receive about two-thirds of the intergovernmental assistance available through the Recovery Act. This report also responds to GAO's mandate to comment on the jobs estimated in recipient reports. GAO collected and analyzed documents and interviewed state and local officials and other Recovery Act award recipients. GAO also analyzed federal agency guidance and interviewed federal officials.

What GAO Recommends

GAO updates the status of agencies' efforts to implement GAO's 58 previous recommendations and makes 5 new recommendations to improve management and strengthen accountability to the Departments of Transportation (DOT), Housing and Urban Development (HUD), the Treasury, and the Office of Management and Budget (OMB). Agency responses to GAO's new recommendations, as well as to key recommendations that remain open, are shown on the following page.

View GAO-10-999 or key components. For state summaries, see GAO-10-1000SP. For more information, contact J. Christopher Mihm at (202) 512-6806 or mihmj@gao.gov.

What GAO Found

As of September 3, 2010, about $154.8 billion of the approximately $282 billion of total funds made available by the Recovery Act in 2009 for programs administered by states and localities had been paid out by the federal government. Of that amount, over 65 percent—$101.9 billion—had been paid out since the start of federal fiscal year 2010 on October 1, 2009.

Federal Medical Assistance Percentage (FMAP)

As of July 31, 2010, the 16 states and the District had drawn down $43.9 billion in increased FMAP funds. If current spending patterns continue, GAO estimates that these states and the District will draw down $56.2 billion by December 31, 2010—about 95 percent of their initial estimated allocation. Most states reported that, without the increased FMAP funds, they could not have continued to support the substantial Medicaid enrollment growth they have experienced, most of which was attributable to children. Several states also reported that the increased FMAP funds freed up states' funds which helped finance other needs. States and the District remained concerned about the sustainability of their programs without these funds, and most have already reduced or frozen certain provider payment rates or imposed new provider taxes. Congress recently passed legislation to extend the increased FMAP through June 2011, although at lower rates than provided by the Recovery Act. For future program adjustments, states and the District will also need to consider the Patient Protection and Affordable Care Act, which prohibits federal Medicaid reimbursement through 2014 if they apply more restrictive eligibility standards, methods, or procedures.

Education

As of August 27, 2010, the District and states covered in GAO's review had drawn down 72 percent ($18.2 billion) of their awarded State Fiscal Stabilization Fund (SFSF) education stabilization funds; 46 percent ($3.0 billion) for Elementary and Secondary Education Act, Title I, Part A; and 45 percent ($3.4 billion) for Individuals with Disabilities Education Act, Part B. In the spring of 2010, GAO surveyed a nationally representative sample of local educational agencies (LEA) and found that job retention was the primary use of education Recovery Act funds in school year 2009-2010, with an estimated 87 percent of LEAs reporting that Recovery Act funds allowed them to retain or create jobs. Even with Recovery Act funds, one-third of LEAs reported experiencing budget cuts in school year 2009-2010 and nearly 1 in 4 reported losing jobs overall. Because of their budget situations, relatively few LEAs reported making significant progress in advancing the four core education reform areas states are required to address as a condition of receiving SFSF funding. In August 2010, the Education Jobs Fund was created to provide $10 billion to retain and create education jobs nationwide.

Highway Infrastructure Investment and Public Transportation Funding

Nationwide, the Federal Highway Administration (FHWA) obligated $25.6 billion in Recovery Act funds for over 12,300 highway projects, and reimbursed $11.1 billion as of August 2, 2010. The Federal Transit Administration obligated $8.76 billion of Recovery Act funds for about 1,055 grants, and reimbursed $3.6 billion as of August 5, 2010. Highway funds were used primarily for pavement improvement projects, and public transportation funds were used primarily for upgrading transit facilities and improving bus fleets. With emphasis placed on the Recovery Act, many states were slower in obligating regular federal-aid highway funds; FHWA expects all regular funds to be obligated by the end of the fiscal year. Publicly available data likely overstates the number and amount of contracts awarded. GAO recommends that DOT improve the accuracy of these data. DOT has also not corrected previous public information overstating the amount of funds directed to economically distressed areas. GAO recommends that DOT make revised information publicly available. DOT expects to be able to report on Recovery Act outputs, but did not commit to assessing whether transportation investments produced long-term benefits as we recommended in May 2010. GAO believes that understanding the impact of Recovery Act investments continues to be important, plans to continue to monitor DOT's actions, and encourages it to report on long-term benefits.

Energy Efficiency and Conservation Block Grant (EECBG), State Energy Program (SEP), and Weatherization Assistance

The EECBG program provides about $3.2 billion in grants to implement projects that improve energy efficiency; of this amount, approximately $2.8 billion has been allocated directly to recipients. As of August 2010, DOE has obligated about 99 percent of the $2.8 billion in direct formula grants to recipients, who have in turn, obligated about half to subrecipients. The majority of EECBG funds have been obligated for three purposes: energy efficiency retrofits to existing facilities, financial incentive programs, and buildings and facilities. The Recovery Act also provided $3.1 billion to the SEP, which provides funds through formula grants to achieve national energy goals such as increasing energy efficiency and decreasing energy costs. SEP recipients are obligating funds, monitoring, and reporting on project outcomes. The Recovery Act also appropriated $5 billion for the Weatherization Assistance Program. During 2009, DOE obligated about $4.73 billion of the Recovery Act's weatherization funding, while retaining about 5 percent of funds to cover the department's expenses. According to DOE officials, as of June 30, 2010, about 166,000 homes have been weatherized nationwide, or about 29 percent of the 570,000 homes currently planned for weatherization. In May 2010, GAO made several recommendations to DOE, expressing concerns about whether program requirements were being met. DOE generally agreed and has begun to take steps in response to GAO's previous recommendations.

Public Housing Capital Fund, Tax Credit Assistance Program (TCAP), and the Section 1602 Program

As of August 7, 2010, housing agencies had obligated about 46 percent of the nearly $1 billion in Recovery Act Public Housing Capital Fund competitive grants allocated to them for projects such as installing energy-efficient heating and cooling systems in housing units. HUD officials anticipate that some housing agencies may not meet the September 2010 obligation deadline, resulting in those funds being recaptured. GAO believes HUD should continue to closely monitor agencies' progress in obligating remaining funds. As of July 31, 2010, HUD had outlayed about $733 million (32.6 percent) of TCAP funds and Treasury had outlayed about $1.4 billion (25.5 percent) of Section 1602 Program funds. Some state Housing Finance Agencies (HFA) and projects may face challenges meeting upcoming deadlines, including that projects spend 30 percent of Section 1602 Program project costs by December 2010. GAO recommends that Treasury provide guidance to HFAs and plan to deal with the possibility that projects could miss the spending deadline. Treasury said it will monitor project spending and provide additional guidance, if needed. GAO also found that for some TCAP projects, enhanced HUD oversight may be needed. GAO recommends that HUD develop a plan that recognizes the level of oversight others, including HFAs and investors, provide. HUD agrees these projects need additional monitoring.

Accountability and Recipient Reporting

OMB's Single Audit Internal Control Project highlighted areas where significant improvements in the Single Audit process are needed. Most federal awarding agencies did not exercise timely follow-up on action plans to correct internal control deficiencies identified in the project's reports. Since awarding agencies are to approve corrective action plans, untimely follow-up could delay efforts to implement corrective actions. In addition, the Single Audit process timeframes are not conducive to the timely identification and correction of internal control deficiencies. Further, OMB's Single Audit guidance has not been timely, causing inefficiencies related to Single Audits. GAO recommends that the Director of OMB take actions to strengthen the Single Audit and federal follow-up as oversight mechanisms. OMB concurred.

Many recipients reported greater ease in meeting their reporting requirements. GAO's analysis of the data in Recovery.gov shows some improvement, but data quality issues remain, such as the ability to link reports across quarters to follow project progress. OMB, HUD, and Education have implemented all of GAO's earlier recommendations on recipient reporting, including those intended to improve subrecipient reporting. GAO will continue to monitor efforts to improve the quality of reporting.

Contents

Tables

Figures

United States Government Accountability Office
Washington, DC 20548

September 20, 2010

Report to the Congress

In the over 18 months since the American Recovery and Reinvestment Act of 2009 (Recovery Act)[1] was enacted in February 2009, the Department of the Treasury has paid out approximately $154.8 billion in Recovery Act funds for use in states and localities.[2] These funds have been used to support and preserve services in a wide range of areas including health, education, transportation, and housing.

The Recovery Act's recurring mandate specifies several roles for GAO, including conducting bimonthly reviews of how Recovery Act funds are being used in selected states and whether they are achieving the stated purposes of the act.[3] Specifically, the stated purposes of the Recovery Act are to

- preserve and create jobs and promote economic recovery;
- assist those most impacted by the recession;
- provide investments needed to increase economic efficiency by spurring technological advances in science and health;
- invest in transportation, environmental protection, and other infrastructure that will provide long-term economic benefits; and
- stabilize state and local government budgets in order to minimize and avoid reductions in essential services and counterproductive state and local tax increases.

In this report, the seventh in a series in response to the act's mandate, we update and add new information on the following: (1) selected states' and localities' uses of Recovery Act funds, (2) the approaches taken by the selected states and localities to ensure accountability for Recovery Act funds, and (3) states' plans to evaluate the impact of the Recovery Act funds they receive. As in our previous reports, we collected and reported data on programs receiving substantial Recovery Act funds in 16 selected states, certain localities, and the District of Columbia, and made

---

[1]Pub. L. No. 111-5, 123 Stat. 115 (Feb. 17, 2009).

[2]Approximate amount paid out as of September 3, 2010.

[3]Recovery Act, div. A, title IX, § 901, 123 Stat. 191.

recommendations when changes could result in improvements.[4] The selected jurisdictions for our in-depth reviews contain about 65 percent of the U.S. population and are estimated to receive collectively about two-thirds of the intergovernmental assistance available through the Recovery Act.[5] For this report, we visited a nonprobability sample of 167 entities within the 16 states and the District for our program reviews. These entities represented a range of types of governments and the program areas shown in table 1. The local governments also varied by population sizes and economic conditions (unemployment rates greater than or less than the state's overall unemployment rate).

Table 1: GAO's September 2010 Recovery Act Coverage of States and Localities

Number of States Visited	16[a]
Number of Local Governments Visited to Review Overall Use of Funds	24
Number of Entities Visited by Program Area	
Education	19
Transportation	2
State Energy Program	9
Energy Efficiency	41
Weatherization	18
Housing	24
Tax Credit Assistance Program	21
Head Start	9

Source: GAO analysis of states' and localities' use of Recovery Act funds.

[4]GAO, *Recovery Act: States' and Localities' Uses of Funds and Actions Needed to Address Implementation Challenges and Bolster Accountability*, GAO-10-604 (Washington, D.C.: May 26, 2010); *Recovery Act: One Year Later, States' and Localities' Uses of Funds and Opportunities to Strengthen Accountability*, GAO-10-437 (Washington, D.C. Mar. 3, 2010); *Recovery Act: Status of States' and Localities' Use of Funds and Efforts to Ensure Accountability*, GAO-10-231 (Washington, D.C.: Dec. 10, 2009); *Recovery Act: Funds Continue to Provide Fiscal Relief to States and Localities, While Accountability and Reporting Challenges Need to Be Fully Addressed*, GAO-09-1016 (Washington, D.C.: Sept. 23, 2009); *Recovery Act: States' and Localities' Current and Planned Uses of Funds While Facing Fiscal Stresses*, GAO-09-829 (Washington, D.C.: July 8, 2009); and *Recovery Act: As Initial Implementation Unfolds in States and Localities, Continued Attention to Accountability Issues Is Essential*, GAO-09-580 (Washington, D.C.: Apr. 23, 2009).

[5]The selected states are Arizona, California, Colorado, Florida, Georgia, Illinois, Iowa, Massachusetts, Michigan, Mississippi, New Jersey, New York, North Carolina, Ohio, Pennsylvania, and Texas. We also visited the District of Columbia.

GAO-10-999 Recovery Act

Notes: Entities include government officials and agencies, transportation and transit authorities, school districts, charter schools, housing authorities, public utilities, and nonprofit organizations. Appendix IV provides a complete list of the entities visited for this report.

"The District of Columbia is also included in GAO's bimonthly reviews of the use of Recovery Act funds.

As in past reports, the programs we selected for review were chosen primarily because they have begun disbursing funds to states or have known or potential risks. The risks can include existing programs receiving significant amounts of Recovery Act funds or new programs. In some cases, we have also collected data from all states, and from an array of localities, to augment the in-depth reviews. This report focuses on the following programs:

- Federal Medical Assistance Percentage (FMAP);
- State Fiscal Stabilization Fund (SFSF);
- Title I, Part A of the Elementary and Secondary Act of 1965 as amended (ESEA);
- Parts B and C of the Individuals with Disabilities Education Act, as amended (IDEA);
- Federal-Aid Highway Surface Transportation and Transit Capital Assistance Programs;
- State Energy Program (SEP);
- Energy Efficiency and Conservation Block Grant (EECBG) Program;
- Weatherization Assistance Program;
- Public Housing Capital Fund;
- Tax Credit Assistance Program (TCAP); and
- Grants to States for Low-Income Housing Projects in Lieu of Low-Income Housing Credits Program under Section 1602 of division B of the Recovery Act (Section 1602 Program).

The Recovery Act also requires us to comment on the estimates of jobs created or retained reported by recipients.[6] In this report, we provide updated information concerning recipient reporting in accordance with our mandate for quarterly reporting. The Recovery Act requires that nonfederal recipients of Recovery Act funds, including grants, contracts, and loans submit quarterly reports which are to include a list of each project or activity for which Recovery Act funds were expended or obligated and information concerning the amount and use of funds and jobs created or retained by these projects and activities, among other

---

[6]Recovery Act, div. A, § 1512(e), 123 Stat. 288. We will refer to the quarterly reports required by section 1512 as recipient reports.

information. The latest of these recipient reports covered the activity as of the Recovery Act's passage through the quarter ending June 30, 2010.

In this report, we also discuss state and local budget use of Recovery Act funds; federal requirements and guidance; and oversight, transparency, and accountability issues related to the Recovery Act and its implementation. The report provides overall findings, discusses agency actions in response to the open recommendations we made in our prior reports, and presents new recommendations. Our oversight of programs funded by the Recovery Act has resulted in more than 62 Recovery Act related products. See the GAO Related Products section of this report for a list of these products.

Going forward to meet our reoccurring Recovery Act mandates, we will continue to capitalize on the work we have done over the past 18 months in the selected states and the District. However, our focus will shift from reporting on the uses of funds by the selected states and the District for a group of programs funded by the Recovery Act to providing enhanced analysis of the use of Recovery Act funds by states and localities for a single program funded by the Recovery Act in each bimonthly review. We will also shift our review of recipient reporting to focus specifically on implementation within that Recovery Act program. Given that, as of September 3, 2010, more than half—about $154.8 billion of the approximately $282 billion—of total Recovery Act funds for programs administered by states and localities had been paid out by the federal government, evolving to this approach is appropriate and will allow us to provide Congress and other decision makers with more in-depth analyses of programs funded by the Recovery Act and to be responsive to congressional interest in the impact and outcomes of programs as Recovery Act implementation moves forward.

In conducting our work for this report, we analyzed guidance and interviewed officials at the Office of Management and Budget. We also analyzed grant awards—as well as relevant regulations and federal agency guidance on programs selected for this review—and spoke with relevant program officials at the U.S. Departments of Health and Human Services (Centers for Medicare and Medicaid Services), Education, Transportation, Energy, and Housing and Urban Development. In addition, we spoke to entities that play roles in oversight of Recovery Act spending, including federal agency inspectors general, state and local auditors, as well as the

Recovery Accountability and Transparency Board (the Board), which was established by the Recovery Act.[7] We also integrated information from our prior Recovery Act reports into this review where appropriate.

In addition, we continued our review of the use of Recovery Act funds for the 16 selected states, the District, and selected localities. We conducted interviews with state budget officials and reviewed proposed and enacted budgets and revenue forecasts to update our understanding of the use of Recovery Act funds in the 16 selected states and the District. To update our understanding of local governments' use of Recovery Act funds, we met with finance officials and city administrators at the selected localities.

Where statements about state law are attributed to state officials, we did not analyze state legal materials for this report but relied on state officials and other state sources for description and interpretation of relevant state constitutions, statutes, legislative proposals, and other state legal materials. The information obtained from this review cannot be generalized to all states and localities receiving Recovery Act funding. A detailed description of our scope and methodology can be found in appendix I.

We conducted this performance audit from May 27, 2010, to September 20, 2010, in accordance with generally accepted government auditing standards. Those standards require that we plan and perform the audit to obtain sufficient, appropriate evidence to provide a reasonable basis for our findings and conclusions based on our audit objectives. We believe that the evidence obtained provides a reasonable basis for our findings and conclusions based on our audit objectives.

As shown in figure 1, actual federal outlays to states and localities under the Recovery Act totaled approximately $154.8 billion through September 3, 2010. Of that amount, more than 65 percent—$101.9 billion—has been paid out since the start of federal fiscal year 2010 on October 1, 2009.[8] The

---

[7]The Recovery Act established the Board to coordinate and conduct oversight of covered funds to prevent fraud, waste, and abuse. The Board is composed of a chairperson and 12 inspectors general. In addition, the Board established three committees drawn from the 12 inspectors general on the board. Recovery Act, div. A, §§ 1521-1525, 123 Stat. 289-293.

[8]The federal fiscal year runs from October 1 through September 30 of the next calendar year.

figure also shows the estimated federal outlays (in billions of dollars) to states and localities for fiscal years 2009 through 2016.

Figure 1: Estimated vs. Actual Federal Outlays to States and Localities under the Recovery Act

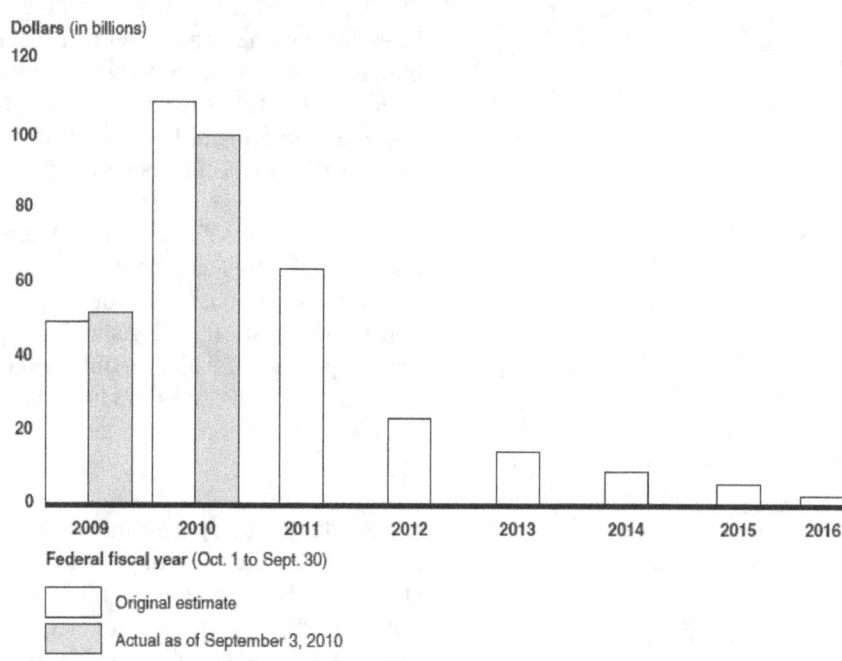

Source: GAO analysis of CBO, Federal Funds Information for States, and Recovery.gov data.

States' and Localities' Uses of Recovery Act Funds Continue

Increased FMAP Continues to Fund Medicaid Enrollment Growth, and States Have Taken Steps to Sustain Their Programs

Medicaid is a joint federal-state program that finances health care for certain categories of low-income individuals, including children, families, persons with disabilities, and persons who are elderly. The federal government matches state spending for Medicaid services according to a formula based on each state's per capita income in relation to the national average per capita income. The rate at which states are reimbursed for Medicaid service expenditures is known as the Federal Medical Assistance Percentage (FMAP), which may range from 50 percent to no more than 83 percent. To obtain federal matching funds for Medicaid, states file a quarterly financial report with the Centers for Medicare and Medicaid Services (CMS) and draw down funds through an existing payment management system used by the Department of Health and Human Services (HHS).

The Recovery Act initially provided eligible states with an estimated $87 billion through increased FMAP rates for 27 months from October 1, 2008, to December 31, 2010.[9] On August 10, 2010, federal legislation was enacted amending the Recovery Act and providing for an extension of increased FMAP funding through June 30, 2011, but at a lower level.[10] On February 25, 2009, CMS made increased FMAP grant awards to states, and states may retroactively claim reimbursement for expenditures that occurred prior to the effective date of the Recovery Act. Generally, for fiscal year 2009 through the third quarter of fiscal year 2011, the increased FMAP is calculated on a quarterly basis and is comprised of three components: (1) a "hold harmless" provision, which maintains states' regular FMAP rates at the highest rate of any fiscal year from 2008 through 2011;[11] (2) a general across-the-board increase of 6.2 percentage points in states' regular FMAPs through the first quarter of fiscal year 2011, which will then be phased down until July 1, 2011;[12] and (3) a further increase in the FMAPs for those states that have a qualifying increase in unemployment rates.

For states to qualify for the increased FMAP, they must pay the state's share of Medicaid costs and comply with a number of requirements, including the following:

---

[9]Recovery Act, div. B, title V, § 5001, Pub. L. No. 111-5, 123 Stat. at 496. CMS made increased FMAP funds available to states on February 25, 2009, and states could retroactively claim reimbursement for expenditures that occurred as of October 1, 2008.

[10]See Pub. L. No. 111-226, § 201, 124 Stat. 2389 (Aug. 10, 2010).

[11]For purposes of this report, the term "regular FMAP" refers to the FMAP as defined in section 1905(b) of the Social Security Act. The term "increased FMAP" refers to the temporary FMAP calculated based on provisions of § 5001 of the Recovery Act, as amended.

[12]Under the amendment to the Recovery Act, states will receive a general across-the-board increase of 3.2 percentage points in their regular FMAPs for the second quarter of federal fiscal year 2011 and a 1.2 percentage point increase in their regular FMAP rates for the third quarter of federal fiscal year 2011. See Pub. L. No. 111-226, § 201, 124 Stat. 2389 (2010). States will continue to be eligible for an unemployment adjustment to their FMAP rates.

- States generally may not apply eligibility standards, methodologies, or procedures that are more restrictive than those that were in effect under their state Medicaid programs on July 1, 2008;[13]
- states must comply with prompt payment requirements;[14,15]
- states cannot deposit or credit amounts attributable (either directly or indirectly) to certain elements of the increased FMAP in any reserve or rainy-day fund of the state;[16] and
- states with political subdivisions—such as cities and counties—that contribute to the nonfederal share of Medicaid spending cannot require the subdivisions to pay a greater percentage of the nonfederal share than would have been required on September 30, 2008.[17]

In addition, CMS requires states to separately track and report on increased FMAP funds. To help states comply with these requirements, CMS provided the funds to states through a separate account in an

---

[13]See Recovery Act, div. B, title V, §5001(f)(1)(A).

[14]Under the Recovery Act, states are not eligible to receive the increased FMAP for certain claims for days during any period in which that state has failed to meet the prompt payment requirement under the Medicaid statute as applied to those claims. See Recovery Act, div. B, title V, §5001(f)(2). Prompt payment requires states to pay 90 percent of clean claims from health care practitioners and certain other providers within 30 days of receipt and 99 percent of these claims within 90 days of receipt. See 42 U.S.C. §1396a(a)(37)(A). A clean claim is a claim that has no defect or impropriety (including any lack of any required substantiating documentation) or particular circumstance requiring special treatment that prevents timely payment from being made on the claim. See Social Security Act section 1816.

[15]States may obtain a waiver from the act's prompt payment requirements if the Secretary of HHS determines that there are exigent circumstances, including natural disasters, which would prevent a state from the timely processing of claims or compliance with reporting requirements A CMS official told us that Maine, Maryland, Massachusetts, North Dakota, and Pennsylvania had received approval for a waiver from the act's prompt payment requirement, and that three states—Idaho, Michigan, and Wisconsin—have requested waivers that are under review.

[16]A state is not eligible for certain elements of increased FMAP if any amounts attributable directly or indirectly to them are deposited in or credited to a state reserve or rainy-day fund. Recovery Act, div. B, title V, §5001(f)(3).

[17]In some states, political subdivisions—such as cities and counties—may be required to help finance the state's share of Medicaid spending. Under the Recovery Act, a state that has such financing arrangements is not eligible for certain elements of the increased FMAP if it requires subdivisions to pay during a quarter of the recession adjustment period a greater percentage of the nonfederal share than the percentage that would have otherwise been required under the state plan on September 30, 2008. See Recovery Act, div. B, title V, § 5001(g)(2). The recession adjustment period is the period beginning October 1, 2008, and ending June 30, 2011.

existing payment management system. CMS also provided guidance in the form of State Medicaid Director letters and written responses to frequently asked questions, and the agency continues to work with states on an individual basis to resolve any compliance issues that may arise.[18]

Despite these restrictions, states are able to make certain adjustments to their Medicaid programs without risking their eligibility for increased FMAP funds. For example, the Recovery Act does not prohibit states from reducing or eliminating optional services, such as dental services, or reducing provider payment rates. States also continue to have flexibility in how they finance the nonfederal share of Medicaid payments, and may implement new financing arrangements or alter existing ones—such as provider taxes, intergovernmental transfers, and certified public expenditures—to generate additional revenues to help finance the nonfederal share of their Medicaid programs.

Increased FMAP Key to States' Continued Efforts to Support Medicaid Enrollment Growth

The FMAP rates in the 16 states and the District increased substantially immediately following enactment of the Recovery Act, and most states' rates continued to increase, albeit at a slower pace, through the fourth quarter of federal fiscal year 2010.[19] During the fourth quarter of federal fiscal year 2010, the increased FMAP averaged about 11 percentage points higher than the regular 2010 FMAP rates, with increases ranging from about 9 percentage points in Iowa to nearly 13 percentage points in Florida. For all states and the District, the largest proportion of the increased FMAP was the component attributable to the across-the-board increase of 6.2 percentage points, followed by qualifying increases in unemployment rates in each of the states.[20] The "hold harmless"

---

[18]For example, CMS's Web site includes State Medicaid Director letters related to the availability or use of increased FMAP funds. See http://www.cms.hhs.gov/SMDL/SMD/list.asp?sortByDID=1a&submit=Go&filterType=none&filterByDID=-99&sortOrder=ascending&intNumPerPage=10.

[19]Immediately following the enactment of the Recovery Act, FMAP rates for the 16 states and the District increased, on average, 9.23 percentage points over their regular 2009 rates. Increased FMAP rates continued to increase through fourth quarter fiscal year 2010—except for California and Florida, whose FMAPs did not increase above their initial first quarter 2009 rates.

[20]Prior to the fourth quarter of fiscal year 2010, the District and all states but Iowa had received the maximum unemployment increase possible. Under the Recovery Act, once a state qualifies for an unemployment increase, the increase is maintained through December 31, 2010. Beginning January 1, 2011, states that experience a sufficient decrease in their unemployment rates could have their increased FMAP rates reduced and HHS is required to provide such states with a 60-day notice of a pending reduction.

component further contributed to the increased FMAP in five sample states, although to a lesser extent. (See table 2.)

Table 2: Regular and Preliminary Increased Fourth Quarter 2010 FMAP Rates and Components of the Increase for 16 States and the District

State	Regular FMAP, fiscal year 2010[a]	Preliminary increased FMAP, fiscal year 2010, fourth quarter[a]	Percentage point FMAP increase	Component and its percentage contribution to the FMAP increase[b]		
				Across the board	Unemployment increase	Hold-harmless
Arizona	65.75	75.93	10.18	61	35	4
California	50.00	61.59	11.59	53	47	0
Colorado	50.00	61.59	11.59	53	47	0
Dist. of Col.	70.00	79.29	9.29	67	33	0
Florida	54.98	67.64	12.66	49	36	15
Georgia	65.10	74.96	9.86	63	37	0
Illinois	50.17	61.88	11.71	53	46	1
Iowa	63.51	72.55	9.04	69	31	0
Massachusetts	50.00	61.59	11.59	53	47	0
Michigan	63.19	73.27	10.08	62	38	0
Mississippi	75.67	84.86	9.19	67	26	7
New Jersey	50.00	61.59	11.59	53	47	0
New York	50.00	61.59	11.59	53	47	0
North Carolina	65.13	74.98	9.85	63	37	0
Ohio	63.42	73.47	10.05	62	38	0
Pennsylvania	54.81	65.85	11.04	56	44	0
Texas	58.73	70.94	12.21	51	34	15
Average			**10.77**	**58**	**39**	**2**

Source: GAO analysis of HHS and data from Federal Funds Information for States, an organization that tracks and reports on the fiscal impact of federal budget and policy decisions on state budgets and programs.

Note: Fiscal year refers to the federal fiscal year, which begins October 1st and ends September 30th. HHS calculates preliminary FMAP rates using Bureau of Labor Statistics unemployment estimates and adjusts these FMAP rates once the final unemployment numbers become available.

[a]The regular fiscal year 2010 FMAP rates were published in the Federal Register on November 26, 2008. The fourth quarter fiscal year 2010 increased FMAP rates are preliminary and were published by Federal Funds Information for States on May 25, 2010.

[b]Average percentage does not add to 100 percent due to rounding.

As of July 31, 2010, the 16 states and the District had drawn down $43.9 billion in increased FMAP funds, which is 75 percent of the total $58.9 billion in increased FMAP that we estimated would be allocated to these states and the District through December 31, 2010.[21] (See table 3.) If current spending patterns continue, we estimate that the 16 states and the District will draw down $56.2 billion by December 31, 2010—about 95 percent of the initial estimated allocation. The national drawdown mirrors the experiences of our sample states, with the 50 states and the District having drawn down 74 percent of their estimated total allocation of nearly $87 billion through the end of 2010.

Table 3: Estimated Allocations and Funds Drawn Down for Recovery Act Increased FMAP for 16 States and the District as of July 31, 2010

Dollars in thousands

State	Increased FMAP estimated allocations to states through December 31, 2010	Total funds drawn down through July 31, 2010	Percentage of estimated allocations drawn down through July 31, 2010
Arizona	$2,031,000	$1,506,593	74.18
California	10,579,000	7,780,020	73.54
Colorado	858,000	665,349	77.55
District Of Columbia	316,000	258,885	81.93
Florida	4,256,000	3,503,359	82.32
Georgia	1,766,000	1,253,713	70.99
Illinois	2,774,000	2,386,470	86.03
Iowa	607,000	415,160	68.40
Massachusetts	3,016,000	2,337,215	77.49
Michigan	2,294,000	1,905,868	83.08
Mississippi	861,000	589,029	68.41
New Jersey	2,134,000	1,653,401	77.48
New York	12,332,000	8,204,506	66.53
North Carolina	2,406,000	1,776,605	73.84
Ohio	3,097,000	2,278,688	73.58
Pennsylvania	4,054,000	2,955,713	72.91

[21]See GAO, *Estimated Temporary Medicaid Funding Allocations Related to Section 5001 of the American Recovery and Reinvestment Act*, GAO-09-364R (Washington, D.C.: Feb. 4, 2009). The Recovery Act provided states and the District with an estimated $87 billion in increased FMAP funds for Medicaid from February 2009 through December 2010. Our estimate was based on funds drawn down by states as of June 30, 2010.

	Dollars in thousands		
State	Increased FMAP estimated allocations to states through December 31, 2010	Total funds drawn down through July 31, 2010	Percentage of estimated allocations drawn down through July 31, 2010
Texas	5,533,000	4,427,624	80.02
Sample total	$58,914,000	$43,898,198	74.51
National total[a]	$86,593,000	$64,071,729	73.99

Source: GAO analysis of HHS data.

[a]The national total includes the 50 states and the District of Columbia.

While the increased FMAP funds are for Medicaid services only, the receipt of these funds may free up funds that states would otherwise have had to use for their Medicaid programs. Similar to their reported uses in fiscal year 2009 and the first half of fiscal year 2010, the 16 states and the District most commonly reported using or planning to use these freed-up funds to cover increased Medicaid caseloads, maintain program eligibility levels, and to finance general budget needs. As with our last survey, most states reported that increased FMAP funding continues to be a major factor in their ability to cover enrollment growth, which has continued to increase since our last Recovery Act report. Between February 2010 and June 2010, overall enrollment across the 16 states and the District grew by an average of nearly 2 percent,[22] with a cumulative increase of 18 percent since October 2007—a rate of increase that is significantly higher than in years prior to the recession.[23] The increase in Medicaid enrollment continues to be attributable primarily to children, a population that is sensitive to economic downturns. However, the highest rate of increase during this period occurred among the nondisabled, nonaged adult population—35 percent, compared to an increase of nearly 19 percent for children.

---

[22]Since October 2007, enrollment growth varied considerably across the 16 states and the District, ranging from 6 percent in Texas to 35 percent in Colorado. Much of Texas's reported enrollment growth occurred between March and June 2010. Prior to March, the state reported flat enrollment from October 2007 through February 2010. Note that the percentages are based on state-reported monthly enrollment data, some of which are preliminary and subject to change.

[23]For example, the Kaiser Family Foundation estimated that national Medicaid enrollment increased by about 1 percent from December 2004 through June 2007. See The Kaiser Commission on Medicaid and the Uninsured, The Henry J. Kaiser Family Foundation, *Medicaid Enrollment in the 50 States June 2008 Data Update* (Washington, D.C., September 2009).

GAO-10-999 Recovery Act

In addition, 10 states and the District reported using freed up funds to maintain benefits and services or to maintain payment rates for practitioners or institutional providers. Six states reported using these funds to meet prompt payment requirements, and five states and the District reporting using the funds to help finance their State Children's Health Insurance Program or other local public health insurance programs. While most states continue to report using freed-up funds for multiple purposes, North Carolina and Ohio again reported that they use these funds exclusively to finance general budget needs.

Despite increases in program enrollment since October 2007, state responses were mixed when asked about changes in the time it takes to process new Medicaid applications. While six states reported an increase in the time it takes to process new applications—most commonly attributing this change to an increase in the volume of new applications and staff cutbacks—nine states and the District reported no change or a decrease in the processing time.[24] Most states and the District reported processing applications, on average, within federally-required time frames.[25]

States Have Taken Actions to Sustain Their Medicaid Programs; Further Adjustments Will Depend on Federal Legislation

When asked about the long-term outlook for their Medicaid programs, the District and all but three of the 16 states reported a concern about sustaining their Medicaid programs once increased FMAP funding is no longer available. When asked about the factors driving their concerns, most states and the District reported (1) the increased share of the state's Medicaid payments in 2011; (2) the current projection of the state's economy and tax revenues; and (3) the current projected growth in the state's Medicaid enrollment for 2011. Mississippi, Ohio, and Texas did not report concerns about their Medicaid programs' sustainability once

---

[24]One state reported it did not know if there had been a change in its application processing time since October 2007. We defined application processing time as the number of days between the date a new application is received and a final eligibility determination is made. States reporting a decrease in processing time most frequently attributed the decrease to streamlined processing procedures, such as use of electronic applications or the automation of citizenship documentation.

[25]CMS generally requires states to process new applications within 45 days from the date of application, or 90 days for individuals applying on the basis of disability.

increased FMAP funds are no longer available.[26] Due to these concerns, most states reported taking actions to adjust their Medicaid programs, including reducing or freezing provider payment rates, implementing new or increasing existing provider taxes, or reducing certain optional benefits. Specifically, 12 states reported reducing or freezing provider payment rates. When given a list of 13 types of providers, these states reported implementing 55 payment rate reductions and 46 payment rate freezes, for a total 101 different rate actions taken since February 2009; on average, these states reduced or froze payment rates for 8 types of providers.[27] States frequently reduced or froze payment rates to nursing facilities, clinics, and home health providers, among others. (See table 4.)

Table 4: Number of States Implementing Payment Reductions or Freezes to Sustain their Medicaid Programs, February 2009 to July 2010

| Providers | Number of states | | |
	Implementing payment reductions	Implementing payment freezes	Total
Nursing facilities	4	6	10
Clinics	7	3	10
Home health providers	7	3	10
Physicians	6	3	9
Inpatient hospitals	4	4	8
Outpatient hospitals	3	4	7
Dental providers	5	3	8
Rehabilitative and therapeutic service providers	4	3	7
Inpatient mental health service providers	3	4	7
Intermediate care facilities for persons with mental retardation	2	5	7
Managed care plans	4	2	6
Targeted case managers	2	3	5

[26]Mississippi previously reported concerns about the sustainability of its program once increased FMAP funds were no longer available; however, a Medicaid official said that more recently, the state decided to use state sources to fully fund the program through 2011. The official added that how the state will fund the Medicaid program in 2012 is not yet known.

[27]The Kaiser Family Foundation recently reported that several Medicaid Directors have expressed concern over the impact that multiple payment cuts to providers may have had on access to services. See The Henry J. Kaiser Family Foundation, *State Medicaid Agencies Prepare for Health Care Reform While Continuing to Face Challenges from the Recession* (Washington, D.C., August 2010).

Providers	Number of states		
	Implementing payment reductions	Implementing payment freezes	Total
Other providers[a]	4	3	7
Total Reductions or Freezes	**55**	**46**	**101**

Source: GAO analysis of state-reported data.

[a]Other providers may include optometrists or providers of medical transportation or durable medical equipment.

In addition, 10 states and the District reported implementing 28 new or increased provider taxes.[28] In contrast to states' changes to provider payment rates, however, states' taxation efforts were concentrated among a handful of provider types. Specifically, 21 of the 28 taxes were imposed on inpatient hospitals, nursing facilities, and outpatient hospitals— providers for which most states reported paying on a cost basis.[29] (See figure 2.)

Figure 2: Number of States Implementing New or Increased Provider Taxes, February 2009 through July 2010

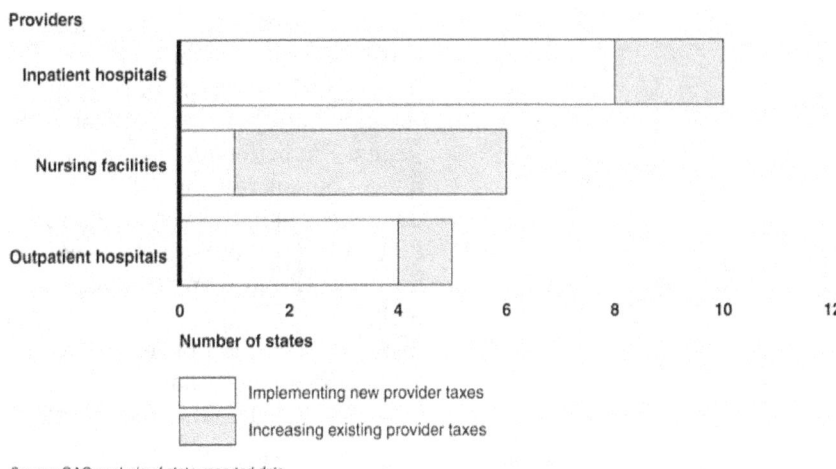

Source: GAO analysis of state-reported data.

---

[28]States reported imposing 15 new provider taxes and increasing 13 existing provider taxes.

[29]States may receive federal matching funds for provider taxes only if such taxes are broad-based, uniformly imposed, and do not result in any taxpayers being held harmless (i.e., receiving state funds to reduce the net payment to the state to below the amount of the tax).

In some cases, states reported implementing payment rate reductions and new taxes on the same providers. For example, at least half of the states that implemented new or increased taxes for inpatient hospitals, nursing facilities, or outpatient hospitals also reduced or froze payments to those same providers. In addition to changes to payment rates and provider taxes, eight states reported making reductions to optional benefits and services, most commonly reducing or eliminating dental services for adults. Several states provided estimates of savings or increased revenue generated by actions they undertook. For example,

- California estimated savings of nearly $600 million from payment rate freezes for long-term care providers and other rate reductions, and the discontinuation of dental and certain other optional services;
- Michigan estimated savings of $152 million from an 8 percent reduction in payment rates for all providers;
- Pennsylvania projected that a new hospital provider tax will generate $498 million in new revenue for the state; and
- New York estimated that increases in various provider taxes will generate an additional $184 million annually.

States were less certain when asked about future program changes that may be necessary to sustain their Medicaid programs after Recovery Act funding ends, and their uncertainty was likely due to questions surrounding a potential extension of the increased FMAP, as well as Patient Protection and Affordable Care Act (PPACA) provisions. At the time of our survey, the legislation amending the Recovery Act to extend the increased FMAP had been proposed but not yet enacted, and the PPACA had just recently been enacted. Despite states' uncertainties, however, 12 states and the District reported on the survey that their 2011 budgets had assumed a full extension of the increased FMAP, and many of these states had not developed a contingency plan in the event that such legislation was not enacted. Nationally, 30 states assumed an extension of increased FMAP in their 2011 budgets.

Under the recent amendments to the Recovery Act, states' increased FMAP rates will decrease by at least 3 percentage points beginning on January 1, 2011, and continue to be phased down to their regular FMAP rates by July 1, 2011. For states that had assumed a full extension of the increased FMAP, the available federal funds will be less than anticipated. The effect of these decreases in states' FMAP rates will vary depending on each state's unique economic circumstances and the size of their Medicaid population.

PPACA also includes several provisions that could affect states' Medicaid programs, and 12 states and the District reported that PPACA will be a major factor in their ability to make future changes to their programs. For example, the maintenance-of-eligibility requirement under PPACA precludes states from receiving federal Medicaid funding if they apply eligibility standards, methods, or procedures under their plan or waiver that are more restrictive than those in effect on the date of PPACA's enactment until the date the Secretary of HHS determines that a health insurance exchange established by the state is fully operational, which must be no later than January 1, 2014.[30] PPACA also requires states to expand Medicaid eligibility by 2014 to cover all persons under age 65 who are not already eligible under mandatory eligibility groups and with incomes up to 133 percent of the federal poverty level, but states have the option to expand eligibility immediately and to receive federal funds for these individuals. While the District has already been approved by CMS to expand eligibility to cover this group prior to 2014, and two other states—California and Colorado—reported that they are planning to do so, it remains to be seen how all the states will respond to this option.[31]

Local Educational Agencies Reported Using Recovery Act Funds for Job Retention and One-Time, Nonrecurring Purchases, While Education Continues Monitoring Efforts

[30]Pub. L. No. 111-148, § 2001(b)(2), 124 Stat. 118, 275. This requirement will continue to apply to children until October 1, 2019. Beginning on January 1, 2011, this provision may have limited applicability if a state certifies to the Secretary that it has a budget deficit or projects to have a budget deficit in the following fiscal year. Pub. L. No. 111-148, § 2001(b)(2). According to CMS, the agency is currently developing guidance on various PPACA provisions.

[31]Connecticut has also obtained approval from CMS to expand eligibility to shift eligible low-income adults from an existing state health care program into Medicaid. Six sample states and the District reported that they currently provide coverage to some adults above 133 percent of the federal poverty level through their Medicaid, State Children's Health Insurance Plan, or other state program.

As Many LEAs Reported Facing Budget Cuts and Fiscal Pressures, Job Retention Was the Primary Use of Recovery Act Education Funds

Our review of states' use of Recovery Act funds covers three programs administered by the U.S. Department of Education (Education)—the State Fiscal Stabilization Fund (SFSF); Title I, Part A of the Elementary and Secondary Education Act of 1965 (ESEA), as amended; and the Individuals with Disabilities Education Act (IDEA), Part B, as amended. As part of this review, we surveyed a nationally representative sample of local educational agencies (LEA)—generally, school districts—about their uses of Recovery Act funds for each of these programs.[32] We also met with program officials at the U.S. Department of Education to discuss ongoing monitoring and technical assistance efforts for Recovery Act funds provided through ESEA Title I, IDEA, and SFSF. At the state level, we spoke with state ESEA Title I officials in five states[33] and the District of Columbia, which had relatively low drawdown rates of ESEA Title I Recovery Act funds. We also interviewed state officials in five states[34] and the District of Columbia about their application for and implementation of the School Improvement Grant program. Finally, we interviewed officials in eight LEAs located in four states[35] to understand how they were using their Recovery Act funds.

Even with Recovery Act Funds, an Estimated One-Third of LEAs Experienced Funding Cuts in School Year 2009-2010 and More Anticipated Cuts in 2010-2011

Education funding in the United States primarily comes from state and local governments. Prior to the influx of Recovery Act funding for education from the federal government, LEAs, on average, derived about 48 percent of their fiscal year 2008 funding from state funds, 44 percent

---

[32]We conducted our survey between March and April 2010, with a 78 percent final weighted response rate at the national level. The results of our sample have a 95 percent confidence interval, with a margin of error of plus or minus 7 percentage points or less, unless otherwise noted. Our survey was conducted prior to the enactment of Pub.L. No. 111-226, which provides $10 billion for the new Education Jobs Fund. As a result, some of the information contained in this report, specifically information related to LEAs' projections for the 2010-2011 school year, does not reflect this additional federal funding.

[33]The five states were Colorado, Massachusetts, Michigan, New Jersey, and New York.

[34]The five states were Colorado, Massachusetts, Michigan, New Jersey, and New York.

[35]The four states were California, Massachusetts, Michigan, and New York.

from local funds, and 8 percent from federal funds.[36] These percentages, however, likely shifted due to increased federal funding through the Recovery Act and reductions in some state budgets for education. While the federal role in financing public education has historically been a limited one, the federal funds appropriated under the Recovery Act provide a significant, but temporary, increase in federal support for education to states and localities, in part, to help them address budget shortfalls. According to the Congressional Research Service, the Recovery Act provided approximately $100 billion for discretionary education programs in fiscal year 2009, which, when combined with regular appropriations for discretionary education programs, represents about a 235 percent increase in federal funding compared to fiscal year 2008.

Over the last 2 years—a time period when many states have dealt with decreasing revenues as a result of the sustained economic downturn—a number of states in our review experienced K-12 education cuts. (See table 5 below for expenditure changes for states in fiscal years 2008 and 2009.) Nationwide, 34 states reported that they cut K-12 education funding in fiscal year 2010, including 12 of the 16 states in our review,[37] according to the Fiscal Survey of States.[38] In some states, such as Arizona and Georgia, these fiscal year 2010 cuts were in addition to expenditure cuts in fiscal years 2009 or 2008. However, other states such as Colorado, Florida, Massachusetts, and Michigan experienced cuts to education expenditures in fiscal year 2009 but did not report cutting K-12 funding in 2010. Looking forward to fiscal year 2011, cuts for K-12 education had been proposed in 10 of the 16 states in our review,[39] according to data presented in the June

---

[36]Zhou, L. (2010). *Revenues and Expenditures for Public Elementary and Secondary Education: School Year 2007-08 (Fiscal Year 2008) (NCES 2010-326)*, report for the National Center for Education Statistics, U.S. Department of Education (Washington D.C., 2010), http://nces.ed.gov/pubsearch/pubsinfo.asp?pubid=2010326 (accessed November 16, 2009).

[37]These states are Arizona, California, Georgia, Iowa, Illinois, Massachusetts, Mississippi, New Jersey, New York, North Carolina, Pennsylvania, and Texas. The fiscal survey of states does not present these data on the District of Columbia.

[38]The number of states reporting K-12 state-level funding cuts to education funding in fiscal year 2010 is based on self-reported data collected by the National Association of State Budget Officers in the spring of 2010. *The Fiscal Survey of States*, "Table 1-A. Fiscal 2010 Program Area Cuts" (page 4), published by the National Governors Association and the National Association of State Budget Officers (June 2010).

[39]These states are Arizona, California, Colorado, Georgia, Illinois, Michigan, Mississippi, New Jersey, New York, and North Carolina.

2010 Fiscal Survey of States report.[40] Given that nearly half of LEA funding, on average, is provided by the states, the impact of state-level cuts to education could significantly affect LEA budgets.

Table 5: Recent Fiscal Year State-Level K-12 Education Expenditure Changes for the States in Our Review

Dollars in millions

State	Changes from fiscal year 2007 Compared to fiscal year 2008		Changes from fiscal year 2008 to fiscal year 2009	
	Expenditure changes	Percentage change	Expenditure changes	Percentage change
Arizona	(175)	(2.9)	(367)	(6.4)
California	2,608	7.1	(7,549)	(19.1)
Colorado	837	13.0	(406)	(5.6)
Florida	25	0.2	(1,280)	(12.1)
Georgia	573	7.8	(459)	(5.8)
Illinois	818	11.1	724	8.8
Iowa	195	8.3	135	5.3
Massachusetts	366	7.4	(238)	(4.5)
Michigan	(176)	(1.5)	(315)	(2.8)
Mississippi	182	7.8	79	3.1
New Jersey	627	6.0	615	5.6
New York	1,839	9.7	1,668	8.0
North Carolina	581	7.7	141	1.7
Ohio	116	1.3	1,643	17.9
Pennsylvania	556	6.3	930	9.9
Texas	3,886	24.7	1,709	8.7

Source: National Association of State Budget Officers, State Expenditure Report, fiscal year 2008 tables 7 and 9.

Notes: State expenditure changes to K-12 education include state general fund and other state funds but do not include Recovery Act or other federal funding or funding from bonds. Numbers in parenthesis are negative. Comparable fiscal year 2010 data were not available at the time of this report. Fiscal years 2007 and 2008 data reflect actual expenditures, while fiscal year 2009 data reflect estimated expenditures because actual expenditures were not available at the time. Data were reported by states and were not compared to actual budget figures.

The funding condition of LEAs across the country is mixed, and districts expected it to worsen in the 2010-2011 school year, even with Recovery Act funding—however, the new Education Jobs Fund created in August 2010 will provide some additional funding. As shown in figure 3, an

[40]*The Fiscal Survey of States*, June 2010, "Table 1-B.Proposed Fiscal 2011 Program Area Cuts" (page 6).

estimated one-third of LEAs faced funding decreases in the 2009-2010 school year, but according to our survey conducted in March and April 2010, more than one-half of LEAs—56 percent—are expecting to face funding decreases in the upcoming 2010-2011 school year.[41] LEA officials we spoke with in California and Massachusetts expect funding declines in 2010-2011 which come on top of cuts made in prior years, indicating that state-level cuts to education have been the primary reason for their large funding declines and continue to provide an uncertain landscape for school funding in coming years. Public Law 111-226, enacted on August 10, 2010 provides $10 billion for the new Education Jobs Fund to retain and create education jobs nationwide.[42] The Fund will generally support education jobs in the 2010-2011 school year and be distributed to states by a formula based on population figures. States can distribute their funding to LEAs based on their own primary funding formulas or LEAs' relative share of federal ESEA Title I funds.

However, while many LEAs reported worsening funding situations, the overall funding levels of many other LEAs increased or remained the same in the 2009-2010 school year; although before the new Education Jobs Fund was created, a smaller proportion reported expecting funding increases in 2010-2011. Specifically, around half of LEAs reported that their overall funding level in the 2009-2010 school year had increased compared to the previous year, and an estimated 12 percent reported that their funding had remained the same. We contacted several school officials who had reported on the survey that their district's funding had increased for the 2009-2010 school year, for the 2010-2011 school year, or during both years. These officials offered a variety of explanations for such funding increases, including increased enrollment numbers due to having added a grade level, having won competitive grant awards, a rebound in state tuition revenue, and having received state aid for a previously approved capital project, including additions to a middle school and high school.

---

[41]Our survey was conducted from March to April 2010, prior to the new $10 billion Education Jobs Fund established in August 2010.

[42]Pub. L. No. 111-226, § 101.

Figure 3: Estimated Percentage of LEAs with Funding-Level Changes in School Year 2009-2010 and Anticipated Changes for School Year 2010-2011, as reported in Spring 2010

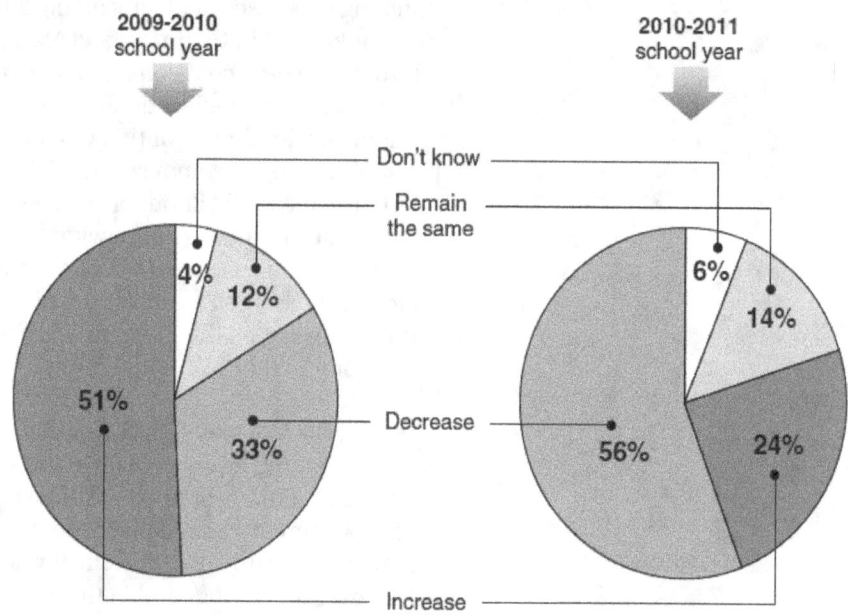

Source: GAO's survey of LEAs.

Note: Percentage estimates have margins of error, at the 95 percent confidence level, of plus or minus 6 percentage points or less.

Moreover, before the creation of the Education Jobs Fund, of those LEAs experiencing funding decreases, the percentage of LEAs that anticipated funding cuts greater than 5 percent is notably higher for the 2010-2011 school year than for the 2009-2010 school year. Specifically, as shown in figure 4, an estimated 31 percent of LEAs expected funding reductions greater than 5 percent in the 2010-2011 school year, compared to 18 percent of LEAs that experienced cuts of this magnitude during the 2009-2010 school year. The percentage of LEAs who anticipated funding cuts of 10 percent or higher is also projected to increase somewhat, from 8 percent in the 2009-2010 school year to 14 percent in the 2010-2011 school year. Officials in some of the school districts we visited in June and July 2010—before the creation of the Education Jobs Fund—noted that their funding situation would likely be more dire in the 2011-2012 school year, when Recovery Act funds are no longer available. For example, Boston Public Schools in Massachusetts, which reported experiencing funding decreases this year and the past 2 years, is already preparing for a decreased budget in fiscal year 2012 and beginning to plan how to address budget shortfalls. Additionally, fewer LEAs anticipate funding increases of more than 5 percent for the 2010-2011 school year than for the 2009-2010 school year. Specifically, as shown in figure 4, only 5 percent of LEAs reported anticipating overall funding levels to increase by more than 5 percent for the 2010-2011 school year compared to 17 percent in the 2009-2010 school year.

Figure 4: Estimated Percentage of LEAs with Sizeable Funding Changes for School Year 2009-2010 and Expected Funding Changes for School Year 2010-2011, as reported in Spring 2010

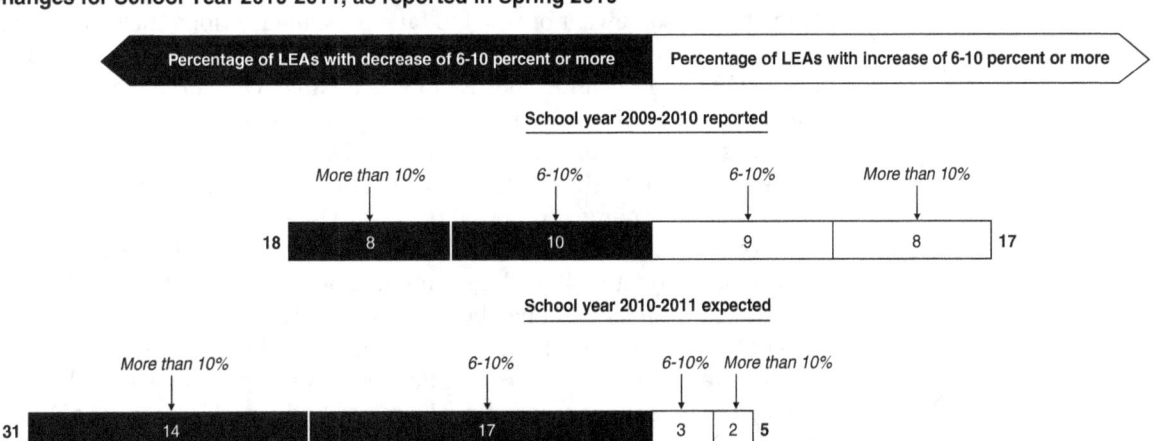

Source: GAO's survey of LEAs.

Note: Percentage estimates have margins of error, at the 95 percent confidence level, of plus or minus 5 percentage points or less.

We also found statistically significant differences between the fiscal situations of urban and rural LEAs and between LEAs of different sizes. For example, significantly more urban LEAs than rural LEAs experienced total funding increases of over 5 percent in the 2009-2010 school year. Specifically, an estimated 32 percent of urban LEAs experienced total funding increases of over 5 percent in the 2009-2010 school year compared to an estimated 8 percent of rural LEAs. We did not find a significant difference between urban and rural LEAs for the 2010-2011 school year, however. While urban LEAs generally fared better than rural LEAs, we found that a larger percentage of the largest LEAs reported expecting a budget decrease for the 2010-2011 school year when compared to all other

LEAs.[43] Specifically, we found that 36 percent of the largest LEAs expected funding to decrease by between 1 and 5 percent in the 2010-2011 school year compared to 26 percent of all other LEAs.

To Address Expected Funding Decreases, in Spring 2010 Many LEAs Reported Being Very Likely to Cut Teachers, Related Staff, and Other Items

Of the 56 percent of LEAs expecting funding decreases, many reported being likely (somewhat or very) to take personnel actions such as cutting positions or freezing pay. However, this information was reported before the $10 billion Education Jobs Fund was created. Our survey results also show that some LEAs also reported being likely to furlough teachers. Specifically, an estimated 76 percent of LEAs that expected funding decreases reported they were likely to cut noninstructional positions and an estimated 70 percent reported they were likely to cut instructional positions. (See fig. 5.) For example, when we met with officials in California's Mountain View-Whisman School District in June 2010, before the Education Jobs Fund had been created, they expected to cut 20 percent of their K-3 teaching staff in the upcoming school year in part due to projected revenue decreases of between 6 to 10 percent. Given these planned reductions in instructional staff, an estimated 70 percent of LEAs reported being likely to increase class size in the coming school year. For example, LEA officials in Mountain View-Whisman School District, Elk Grove Unified School District in California, and Revere Public Schools in Massachusetts said they were increasing class sizes to deal with budget shortfalls. In addition to cutting positions, an estimated 61 percent of LEAs expecting funding decreases are likely to reduce professional development or teacher training. Approximately 55 percent of LEAs expecting funding decreases reported being likely to freeze pay, and around one-third reported being likely to furlough teachers. For example, officials at San Bernardino City Unified School District and Elk Grove Unified School District in California told us they had decided to furlough some employee groups for at least 9 days in the 2010-2011 school year.

---

[43]For our survey, we included a separate strata of the 100 largest LEAs as defined by the number of students. We received a final weighted response rate of 84 percent for this strata.

Figure 5: Likely Personnel Actions for the 2010-2011 School Year Reported by LEAs Anticipating Funding Decreases, as Reported in Spring 2010

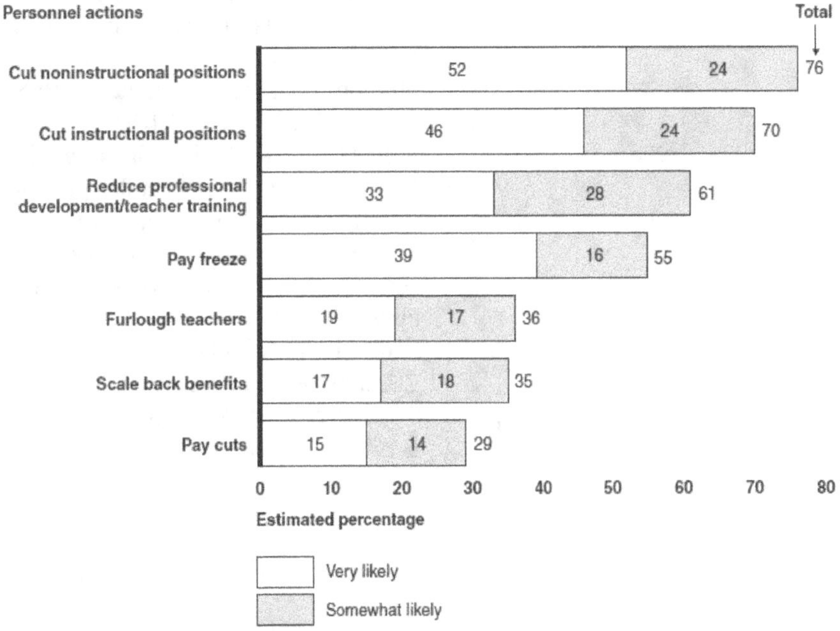

Personnel actions   Total

Cut noninstructional positions   52 | 24   76
Cut instructional positions   46 | 24   70
Reduce professional development/teacher training   33 | 28   61
Pay freeze   39 | 16   55
Furlough teachers   19 | 17   36
Scale back benefits   17 | 18   35
Pay cuts   15 | 14   29

0   10   20   30   40   50   60   70   80
Estimated percentage

☐ Very likely
▨ Somewhat likely

Source: GAO's survey of LEAs.

Note: Percentage estimates have margins of error, at the 95 percent confidence level, of plus or minus 8 percentage points or less.

Similarly, many LEAs expecting funding decreases also reported being likely (somewhat or very) to take nonpersonnel actions, such as reducing instructional supplies and eliminating summer programs. Specifically, an estimated 87 percent of LEAs expecting funding cuts are likely to reduce instructional supplies or equipment, 73 percent are likely to defer maintenance, 71 percent are likely to reduce energy consumption, and 50 percent are likely to reduce custodial services. (See figure 6.) For example, LEA officials in Elk Grove Unified School District said they were very likely to reduce the purchase of instructional supplies—or have already reduced them—and noted that this may result in teachers and parents voluntarily purchasing additional supplies for classrooms. In addition, LEA officials in Kingston Community Schools, Plymouth Educational Center in Michigan, Elk Grove Unified School District, and Boston Public Schools told us they had been deferring maintenance and would continue to defer it, though they would not defer any maintenance that would compromise the safety of children. Examples of deferred maintenance projects included painting rooms, replacing a roof, promptly fixing air conditioners, and resurfacing parking lots. LEA officials in Boston Public Schools and Elk Grove Unified School District said they were very likely to reduce energy consumption through such efforts as lowering the temperature in schools in winter months, offering incentives to schools with lower energy consumption, and using more energy-efficient light bulbs. Officials in Boston Public Schools, San Bernardino City Unified School District, and Elk Grove Unified School District said they had reduced custodial services in their schools and some would likely further reduce them. Smaller proportions of schools reported being likely to reduce transportation, shorten the school year, or close or consolidate schools. A Boston Public Schools official told us the district planned to reduce transportation costs by creating smaller transportation zones, and also hopes to close and consolidate up to 20 schools to reduce costs. In addition, we found that significantly higher percentages of the largest LEAs reported being likely to reduce transportation services. Specifically, 50 percent of large LEAs reported being likely to reduce transportation services, compared to 35 percent of all other LEAs.

Figure 6: Likely Nonpersonnel Actions for School Year 2010-2011 Reported by LEAs Expecting Funding Decreases, as Reported in Spring 2010

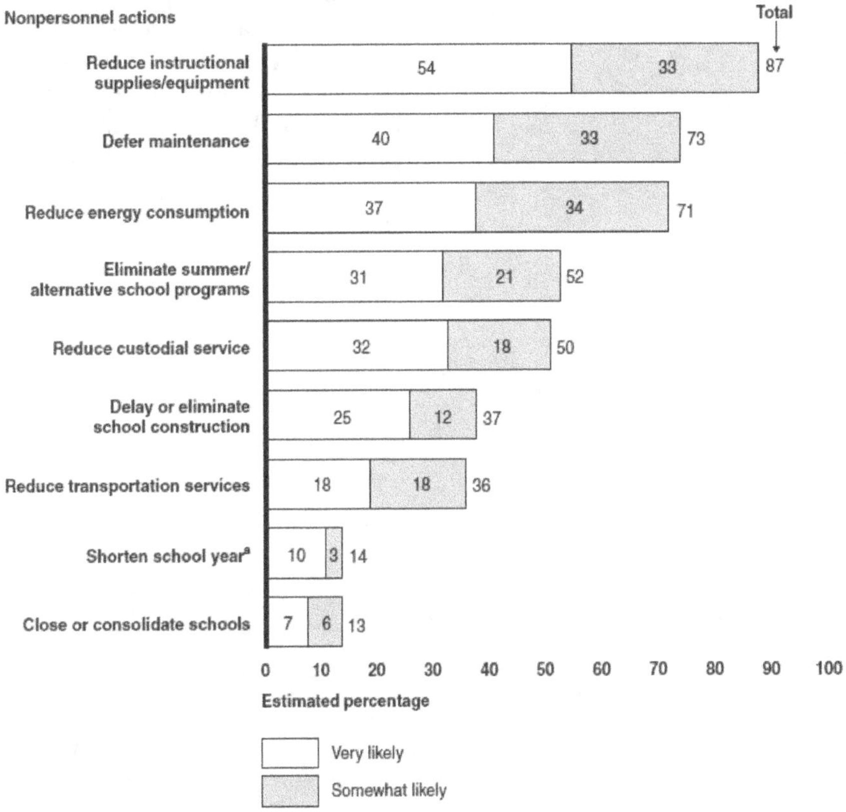

Nonpersonnel actions

Action	Very likely	Somewhat likely	Total
Reduce instructional supplies/equipment	54	33	87
Defer maintenance	40	33	73
Reduce energy consumption	37	34	71
Eliminate summer/alternative school programs	31	21	52
Reduce custodial service	32	18	50
Delay or eliminate school construction	25	12	37
Reduce transportation services	18	18	36
Shorten school year[a]	10	3	14
Close or consolidate schools	7	6	13

Estimated percentage

☐ Very likely
▦ Somewhat likely

Source: GAO's survey of LEAs.

Note: Percentage estimates have margins of error, at the 95 percent confidence level, of plus or minus 8 percentage points or less.

[a]In the case of shortening the school year, due to rounding, the sum of the percentage of LEAs shown as very likely and somewhat likely to take the action is 1 percentage point higher.

Recovery Act Funds Allowed Most LEAs to Retain or Create Teaching Positions and Related Jobs, though Some Still Lost Jobs in School Year 2009-2010

Recovery Act funds for education allowed over three-quarters of LEAs to retain or create teaching positions and related jobs during the 2009-2010 school year, though some LEAs still reported losing jobs even with the additional federal funding. The use of the Recovery Act funding for these purposes is consistent with one of the primary goals of the Recovery Act, which is to save and create jobs in order to help economic recovery. An estimated 87 percent of LEAs across the country reported that Recovery Act funding allowed them to retain or create jobs. Specifically, a higher percentage of LEAs reported retaining staff positions—77 percent—than creating new staff positions —39 percent—for the 2009-2010 school year. In addition, a significantly higher percentage of large LEAs reported that Recovery Act funding allowed them to retain school staff, with nearly all— 98 percent of the largest LEAs in the country—reporting using Recovery Act funding for retention.[44] While most LEAs were able to retain or create jobs with Recovery Act funding, some of these LEAs—nearly 1 in 4—still reported losing jobs overall in their LEA in the 2009-2010 school year. (See fig. 7.)

[44]This difference from the national average is statistically significant.

Figure 7: Estimated Percentage of LEAs Nationally That Reported Recovery Act Funding Allowed Job Creation or Retention Compared to the Estimated Percentage of LEAs That Reported Losing Jobs Even with the Additional Funding in School Year 2009-2010, as Reported in Spring 2010

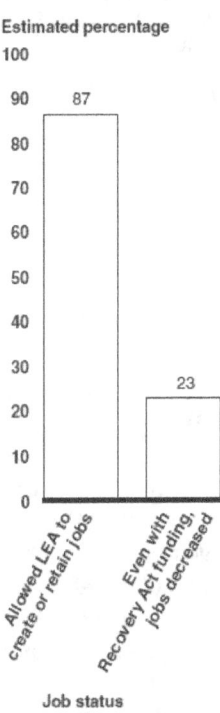

Source: GAO's survey of LEAs.

Notes: Percentage estimates have margins of error, at the 95 percent confidence level, of plus or minus 5 percentage points or less. These columns are not mutually exclusive: almost all LEAs with a net decrease in jobs also retained jobs (92 percent).

Retaining jobs was top use of Recovery Act funds for three education programs: LEAs used large portions of their Recovery Act IDEA Part B; ESEA Title I, Part A; and SFSF education stabilization funds toward staff retention in the 2009-2010 school year. According to our survey, nearly 70 percent of LEAs spent more than half to all of their Recovery Act SFSF education stabilization funds to retain jobs for the 2009-2010 school year. (See fig. 8.) Although a smaller percentage of LEAs reported using half to all of their IDEA Part B and ESEA Title I, Part A Recovery Act funding—25 percent and 27 percent, respectively—for job retention, retaining staff was still the top use cited by LEAs for IDEA Part B and ESEA Title I, Part A Recovery Act funding. For example, LEA officials in Kingston Community School District told us they had used all of their Recovery Act SFSF education stabilization funds and ESEA Title I,

Part A funds, and most of their Recovery Act IDEA Part B, funds to retain staff.

Figure 8: Estimated Percentage of LEAs Nationally That Used More Than Half of SFSF, ESEA Title I, Part A; and IDEA Part B Recovery Act Funding for Retaining Staff in School Year 2009-2010

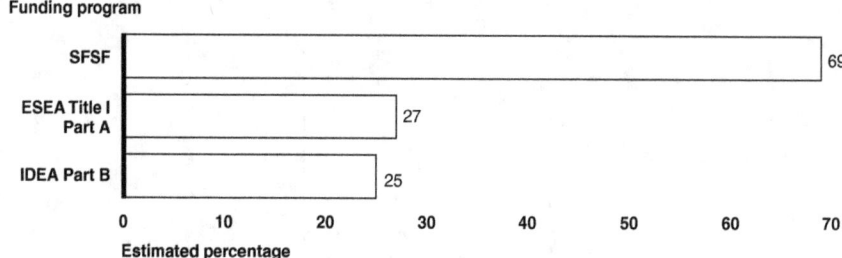

Funding program

Source: GAO's survey of LEAs.

Note: Percentage estimates have margins of error, at the 95 percent confidence level, of plus or minus 6 percentage points or less.

A number of factors may explain why such a large percentage of LEAs spent a significant amount of their Recovery Act funding for job retention. For example, a large portion of school expenditures are employee-related costs—with salaries and benefits accounting for more than 80 percent of local school expenditures, according to Education's most recent data.[45] Also, given the fiscal uncertainty and substantial budget shortfalls facing states, federal funds authorized by the Recovery Act have provided LEAs with additional flexibility to pay for the retention of education staff. Overall, the impact of Recovery Act education funds on job retention may be significant because K-12 public school systems employ about 6.2 million staff, based on Education's estimates, and make up about 4 percent of the nation's workforce.[46] In fact, through the reporting period ending June 30, 2010, nearly two-thirds of full-time equivalent positions reported on Recovery.gov have resulted from Recovery Act education programs.

---

[45]U.S. Department of Education, *The Condition of Education 2010* (June 2010), page 278.

[46]The national estimate of 6.2 million education staff is based on 2007-08 school year data and is taken from Education's *2009 Digest of Education Statistics*, (p.56). The 4 percent of the workforce estimate is GAO's calculation based on Education's 6.2 million staff estimate and employment projections by the U.S. Bureau of Labor Statistics.

Based on our visits to states and LEAs, we were told that Recovery Act SFSF funds, in particular, have provided additional resources and flexibility allowing LEAs to retain staff. For example, one state education official noted that LEAs have more flexibility in spending SFSF funds for general education expenses because ESEA Title I, Part A and IDEA Part B programs target special populations—disadvantaged youth and students with disabilities, respectively. This official said that because funding levels for general education programs in his state have decreased while federal funding levels for ESEA Title I, Part A and IDEA Part B programs have increased, LEAs have used SFSF funds to shore up funding for general education and, in particular, preserve jobs.

Instructional positions were more often retained and created than noninstructional positions: Substantially more LEAs retained or created positions for instructional staff compared to noninstructional staff positions for the 2009-2010 school year. Instructional staff typically includes classroom teachers and paraprofessionals and noninstructional staff can include office support, janitorial staff, and school security staff. Specifically, an estimated 74 percent of LEAs nationally retained jobs for instructional staff, compared to 48 percent that retained them for noninstructional staff. Furthermore, 33 percent of LEAs reported creating new instructional staff positions with Recovery Act funding compared to the 22 percent that created them for noninstructional staff. (See fig. 9). According to a number of LEA officials we interviewed, LEAs often spent Recovery Act funding in ways that would benefit students directly in the classroom, thereby focusing on creating and retaining positions for instructional staff before creating and retaining jobs for noninstructional staff, such as administrative and auxiliary staff. For example, officials from the Plymouth Educational Center said that in order to minimize the impact on students, they have made or would consider making cuts to administration, security guards, and paraprofessionals, and instituting further pay cuts before letting go of teachers.

Figure 9: Estimated Percentage of LEAs Nationally That Retained and Created Instructional and Noninstructional Jobs in School Year 2009-2010

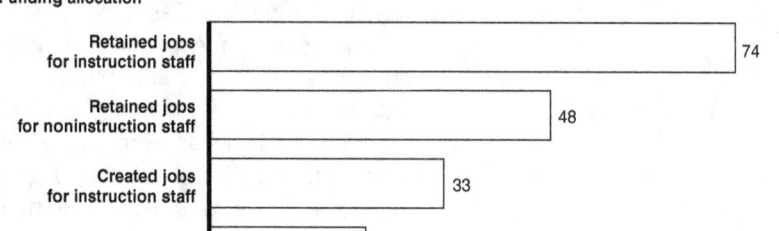

Funding allocation

Source: GAO's survey of LEAs.

Note: Percentage estimates have margins of error, at the 95 percent confidence level, of plus or minus 6 percentage points or less. These categories are not mutually exclusive.

Fewer LEAs Used Large Portions of Their Recovery Act Funding to Hire Staff Than to Retain Staff, although Fund Use for Hiring Varied by Program

Although our survey results indicate that LEAs overall spent a significant amount of their Recovery Act funding from all three programs to retain jobs, LEAs also reported using Recovery Act funding to hire new staff. As indicated in figure 10, the percentage of LEAs that reported using Recovery Act funding to hire new staff varied across the three programs. For example, 4 percent and 6 percent of LEAs reported spending half or more of their Recovery Act IDEA Part B and SFSF funding, respectively, to hire new staff, while 15 percent of LEAs reported the same use for their Recovery Act ESEA Title I, Part A funds. Overall, nearly three-quarters of LEAs did not use any of their Recovery Act SFSF funding to hire new staff, concentrating instead on using that funding for staff retention.

Figure 10: Estimated Percentage of LEAs That Reported Spending Recovery Act Funds to Hire New Staff in the 2009-2010 School Year, by Percent of Recovery Act Funding and Program

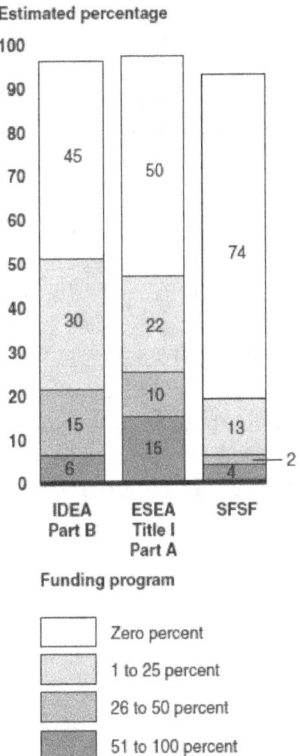

Estimated percentage

	IDEA Part B	ESEA Title I Part A	SFSF
Zero percent	45	50	74
1 to 25 percent	30	22	13
26 to 50 percent	15	10	2
51 to 100 percent	6	16	4

Funding program

Zero percent
1 to 25 percent
26 to 50 percent
51 to 100 percent

Source: GAO's survey of LEAs.

Note: Percentage estimates have margins of error, at the 95 percent confidence level, of plus or minus 7 percentage points or less.

Nearly One in Four LEAs Reported Losing Jobs, Even with Recovery Act Funding, Due to Decreasing Budgets and Other Factors

Even with the additional Recovery Act funding provided to LEAs in school year 2009-2010, nearly one-quarter of LEAs reported losing jobs, primarily due to decreasing overall budgets. Without Recovery Act funds, it is likely that the magnitude of job losses in these LEAs would have been higher, given that nearly all of the LEAs experiencing job loss overall also reported retaining jobs. Specifically, an estimated 92 percent of LEAs where LEA officials indicated the number of teachers had decreased also said that Recovery Act funds had allowed them to retain jobs during the school year. Also, almost 30 percent of LEAs used Recovery Act funds to create new jobs during the 2009-2010 school year, even as their overall number of jobs decreased. For example, according to a Boston Public Schools official, the number of staff in the district had decreased in the 2009-2010 school year, but the district also used Recovery Act funds for both retention and job creation. For example, the district hired 16 new English as a Second Language teachers and specialists with ESEA Title I, Part A Recovery Act funds even as they let go of teachers during school closures.

Decreasing overall budgets at the LEA level was the main reason that LEAs reported losing jobs in School Year 2009-2010. Specifically, 67 percent of LEAs that lost jobs reported that their budget was a factor to a great or very great degree. (See fig. 11.) For example, officials from Elk Grove Unified School District in California told us they laid off about 500 staff at the end of the 2009-2010 school year due to budgetary pressures, after exhausting their reserves and spending Recovery Act funds. In addition to budgetary factors, LEAs lost jobs because of staff attrition and declining enrollment, although to a much lesser extent.

Figure 11: The Factors Affecting a Decrease in the Number of Jobs for the 2009-2010 School Year to a Great or Very Great Degree

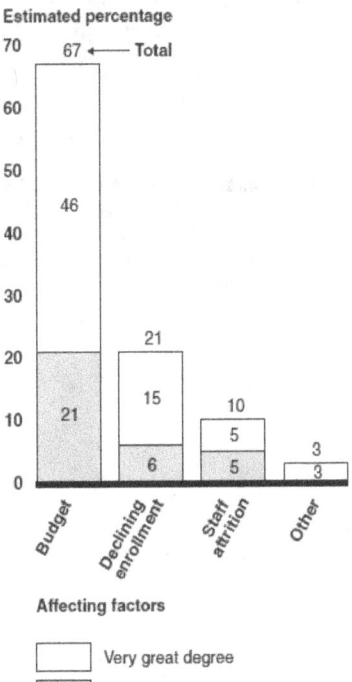

Estimated percentage

Affecting factors

☐ Very great degree
▨ Great degree

Source: GAO's survey of LEAs.

Note: Percentage estimates for totals of very great and great degree have margins of error, at the 95 percent confidence level, of plus or minus 12 percentage points or less.

Recovery Act Funds Were Used by LEAs to Purchase Items That Will Build Capacity without Creating Recurring Costs

In addition to retaining and hiring staff, LEAs spent Recovery Act funds on items that could help build long-term capacity, while also avoiding creating recurring costs for LEAs. Overall, LEAs reported several one-time expenditures such as purchasing computer technology, providing professional development for instructional staff, and purchasing instructional materials as among some of the highest uses of funds after job retention and creation.[47] (See fig. 12.)

Figure 12: Estimated Percentage of LEAs Nationally That Spent More Than 25 Percent of Recovery Act Funds on Providing Professional Development, Purchasing Instructional Materials, and Purchasing Computer Technology in School Year 2009-2010

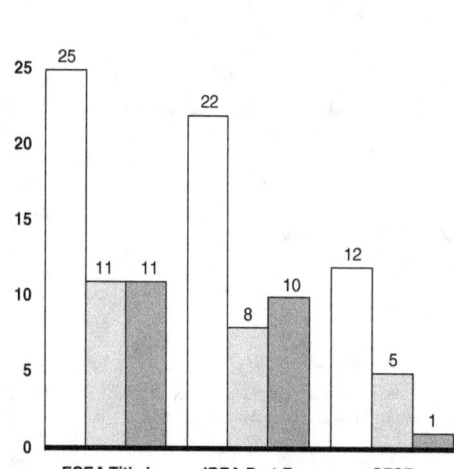

Estimated percentage

Funding program

☐ Purchasing computer technology (example, hardware or software)

▨ Purchasing instructional materials (not including computer software)

▨ Providing professional development for instructional staff

Source: GAO's survey of LEAs.

Note: Percentage estimates have margins of error, at the 95 percent confidence level, of plus or minus 6 percentage points or less.

[47]For Recovery Act SFSF funds, a slightly higher percentage of LEAs reported using the funds to provide transportation (1.8 percent) and school construction/renovation (3.7 percent) than professional development.

LEA officials reported making one-time purchases with Recovery Act funds to enhance district capacity. For example, at Plymouth Educational Center in Michigan, officials told us that Recovery Act funds were used to enhance computer technology for both students and teachers. Further, several LEA officials told us they had used IDEA Part B Recovery Act funds to purchase professional development and assistive technologies that would help build the district's capacity to serve more students with disabilities. These officials told us that they will be able to educate students with disabilities far more affordably within the district than by paying external providers—a benefit they anticipate will continue even after the Recovery Act funds are spent. For example, in rural Michigan, officials told us that IDEA Part B funding has allowed the Kingston Community Schools to build capacity by partnering, along with other schools from the surrounding area, with the University of Kansas to provide coaching and training to teachers who can then provide services to more students with disabilities. In addition, LEA officials in Boston, Massachusetts, said they had used these funds to obtain equipment and provide professional development so they could serve more students with autism within the district.

A Majority of LEAs Maintained the Same Level of Service as the Prior Year, but Some LEAs Reported Not Being Able to Maintain Service Levels

Although more than half of all LEAs reported being able to provide students with the same level of service in 2009-2010 as in 2008-2009, a number of LEAs reported they had not been able to maintain the same level of service at their LEA for the same time frame.[48] Specifically, an estimated 63 percent of LEAs nationally reported that Recovery Act SFSF funds allowed them to maintain the same level of service to students in their LEA in school year 2009-2010 as compared to the previous school year. However, 40 percent of the largest LEAs reported not being able to maintain the same level of service compared to 16 percent of all other LEAs. (See fig. 13.)

---

[48]Our survey asked superintendents' opinions of how Recovery Act SFSF funding affected their LEA's ability to maintain, raise, or decrease their level of service in the 2009-2010 school year. Superintendents and other LEA officials we spoke with explained that "level of service" includes the instructional program provided to students through teaching staff, curriculum, and instructional materials; the noninstructional services provided in school districts such as administrative and janitorial services; and the safety and security of schools.

Figure 13: Reported Changes in LEA Level of Service in School Year 2009-2010 Compared to Level of Service in 2008-2009 among LEAs Receiving SFSF Funds, by Size of LEA

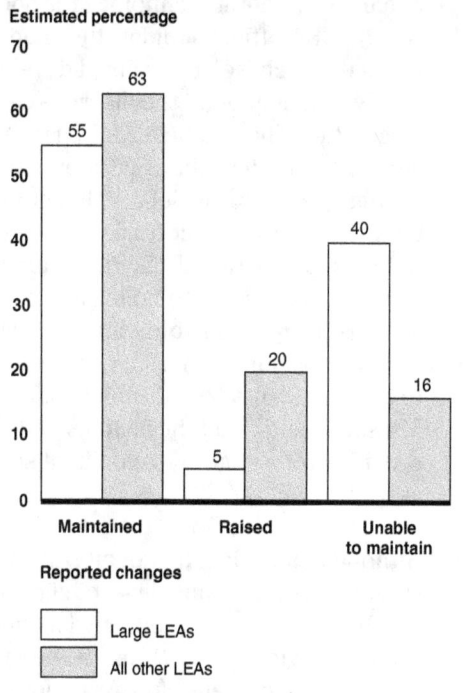

Source: GAO's survey of LEAs.

Note: Percentage estimates have margins of error, at the 95 percent confidence level, of plus or minus 7 percentage points or less.

LEAs reported a range of areas in which there was a great or very great reduction in the level of services, including instructional materials and resources, staff development, and summer school programs. For example, LEA officials from San Bernardino City Unified School District told us they had applied cuts with the intent of having the least impact on children in the classroom, and that these cuts included delay of new textbook adoption, administrative reductions, and reduced maintenance. Further, Boston Public Schools and Revere Public Schools pointed to cuts in programming such as art and music as examples in how their service levels had decreased.

A number of LEAs reported that Recovery Act SFSF funds allowed them to raise their level of service in 2009-2010, with a lower percentage of the largest LEAs reporting raising service levels compared to all other LEAs.

Based on our survey results for the 2009-2010 school year, 20 percent of all LEAs indicated that the additional Recovery Act SFSF funding made it possible to raise the level of services provided to students compared to what the LEA was able to provide in the prior 2008-2009 school year. A significantly lower percentage of the largest LEAs in the country—5 percent—specified that the SFSF funding raised service levels in their schools.

Relatively Few LEAs Report Making Significant Progress in Four Core Education Reforms

Some LEAs report making modest progress in education reform, but relatively few report they are making significant progress in advancing the four core education reform areas states are required to address as a condition of receiving SFSF funding. For example, an estimated 28 percent of LEAs reported making modest progress and just 13 percent of LEAs reported making significant progress in increasing teacher effectiveness—the highest percentage among the four areas. (See fig. 14.) However, some of these goals, such as improving standards and assessments, are more likely to be pursued at the state level than at the local level, while others, such as supporting struggling schools, may not apply to all districts. In order to receive SFSF funding, states had to submit an application to Education that required each state to provide several assurances, including that it would implement strategies to advance four core areas of education reform, as described by Education: (1) increase teacher effectiveness and address inequities in the distribution of highly qualified teachers; (2) establish a pre-K-through-college data system to track student progress and foster improvement; (3) make progress toward rigorous college- and career-ready standards and high-quality assessments that are valid and reliable for all students, including students with limited English proficiency and students with disabilities; and (4) provide targeted, intensive support and effective interventions to turn around schools identified for corrective action or restructuring. Furthermore, in order to receive the remainder of their SFSF allocations (Phase II), states had to agree to collect and publicly report on more than 30 indicators and descriptors related to the four core areas of education reform described above. While states will be responsible for assuring advancement of these reform areas, LEAs were generally given broad discretion in how to spend the SFSF funds. It is not clear how LEA progress in advancing these four reforms will affect states' progress toward meeting their assurances. Education officials noted that they were not surprised that fewer LEAs reported expanding reform efforts in 2009-2010 given their budget situation. Figure 14 depicts the extent to which LEAs reported making modest or significant progress in each of the four reform areas.

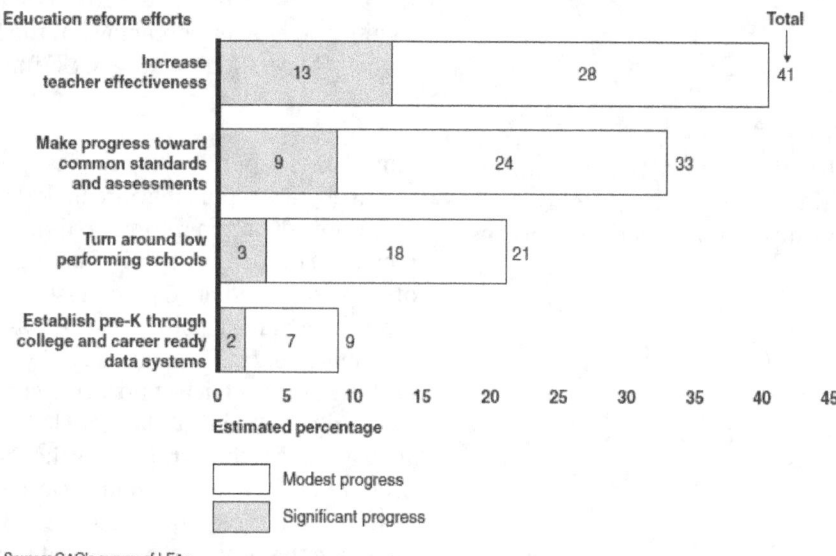

Figure 14: Percentage of LEAs Reporting Significant or Modest Progress toward Education Reform Goals in School Year 2009-2010 Made Possible by Recovery Act Funds

Education reform efforts — Total

- Increase teacher effectiveness: 13 (Significant) + 28 (Modest) = 41
- Make progress toward common standards and assessments: 9 + 24 = 33
- Turn around low performing schools: 3 + 18 = 21
- Establish pre-K through college and career ready data systems: 2 + 7 = 9

Estimated percentage (0, 5, 10, 15, 20, 25, 30, 35, 40, 45)

☐ Modest progress
▨ Significant progress

Source: GAO's survey of LEAs.

Note: Percentage estimates have margins of error, at the 95 percent confidence level, of plus or minus 7 percentage points or less. These categories are not mutually exclusive.

Education Reform Efforts under ESEA Title I, Part A and IDEA Part B Were Maintained or Expanded in the 2009-2010 School Year, but a Small and Growing Number of LEAs Expect Declines in 2010-2011

Almost all LEAs we surveyed stated that ESEA Title I, Part A and IDEA Part B Recovery Act funds allowed their LEAs to either expand or maintain education reform efforts in 2009-2010, but a small and increasing percentage of LEAs expect to reduce reform efforts in 2010-2011 than reduced such efforts in 2009-2010. In addition to retaining and creating jobs, Education officials reported they intended the use of Recovery Act funds to spur education reform in LEAs to improve student achievement.[49] Education provided guidance to states and LEAs on ways to use the

---

[49]In April 2009, Education released guidance that asked LEA officials to consider whether their proposed use of Recovery Act funds would (1) improve results for students, including students in poverty, students with disabilities, and English language learners; (2) increase educators' long-term capacity to improve results for students; (3) advance state, district, or school improvement plans and the reform goals encompassed in the Recovery Act; (4) avoid recurring costs that states, school systems, and schools are unprepared to assume when this funding ends; and (5) include approaches to measure and track implementation and results. See *American Recovery and Reinvestment Act of 2009: Using ARRA Funds to Drive School Reform and Improvement:* U.S. Department of Education: Washington D.C.: April 24, 2009.

Recovery Act funds to stimulate reform, as well as to retain jobs. Because LEAs are required to obligate 85 percent of their Title I, Part A Recovery Act funding by September 30, 2010, unless approved for a waiver, Title I, Part A education reform efforts in districts without waivers could decrease because fewer funds would be available in the upcoming school year.

ESEA Title I, Part A Recovery Act Funding Enhanced Education Reform Efforts at Nearly Half of All LEAs and Helped Enhance or Maintain Reform at Nearly All LEAs

Most LEAs report that Recovery Act funding for ESEA Title I, Part A allowed them to either expand or maintain education reforms for disadvantaged students in both 2009-2010 and 2010-2011, but the percentage of districts that expect to expand reform is lower for 2010-2011 than for the 2009-2010. According to our survey results, an estimated 48 percent of LEAs indicated that the additional ESEA Title I, Part A Recovery Act funding they received allowed their LEA to expand education reform efforts in 2009-2010. For example, officials from one Michigan LEA told us they used the ESEA Title I, Part A Recovery Act funding to enhance a tutoring program for all at-risk students in math and language arts. Officials at another LEA told us the ESEA Title I, Part A Recovery Act funding allowed them to enhance their after-school tutoring program targeted at English language learners. Moreover, an additional 48 percent of LEAs stated that the funding allowed them to maintain reform efforts for ESEA Title I, Part A programs. However, the percentage of districts anticipating ESEA Title I, Part A funding that will allow their district to expand reform efforts is lower for the 2010-2011 school year than for the 2009-2010 school year. (See fig. 15) While an estimated 3 percent of LEAs stated that even with the additional Recovery Act funding provided under ESEA Title I, Part A, education reform efforts decreased in the 2009-2010 school year, this percentage increased to 11 percent when we asked LEAs to look ahead to the 2010-2011 school year. Title I, Part A reform efforts could potentially decrease in the coming school year, in part because LEAs are required to obligate 85 percent of ESEA Title I, Part A Recovery Act funds by September 30, 2010, unless they receive a waiver.

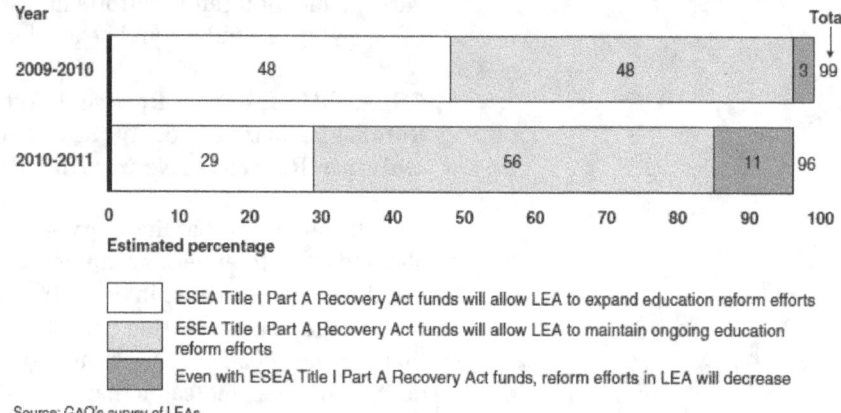

Figure 15: Percentage of LEAs Nationally Reporting ESEA Title I, Part A Recovery Act Funds Have Expanded, Maintained, or Decreased Education Reform Efforts in School Years 2009-2010 and 2010-2011, as Reported in Spring 2010

Year | Total

2009-2010: 48 | 48 | 3 | 99

2010-2011: 29 | 56 | 11 | 96

Estimated percentage (0 to 100)

☐ ESEA Title I Part A Recovery Act funds will allow LEA to expand education reform efforts

☐ ESEA Title I Part A Recovery Act funds will allow LEA to maintain ongoing education reform efforts

☐ Even with ESEA Title I Part A Recovery Act funds, reform efforts in LEA will decrease

Source: GAO's survey of LEAs.

Notes: Percentage estimates have margins of error, at the 95 percent confidence level, of plus or minus 7 percentage points or less.,This figure does not display the percentage of LEAs that chose "Don't Know" as a survey response, and therefore, the percentages do not total to 100 percent.

IDEA Part B Recovery Act Funding Allowed Most LEAs to Either Expand or Maintain Reform Efforts for Special Education Students

Most LEAs report that Recovery Act funding for IDEA Part B allowed them to either expand or maintain education reform efforts for special education students in both 2009-2010 and 2010-2011, but the percentage of districts that expect to expand reform is lower for 2010-2011 than for the previous year. Specifically, in 2009-2010, we estimate that 43 percent of LEAs nationally expanded reform efforts for special education students because of the additional IDEA Part B Recovery Act funding in 2009-2010. (See fig. 16). For example, an official in Boston, Massachusetts, told us that the Boston Public Schools has used some of its IDEA Part B Recovery Act funding to train teachers and purchase equipment to enhance classroom services for autistic students. In addition, 55 percent of LEAs noted that the Recovery Act funding allowed them to maintain ongoing education reform efforts targeted for special education students in the same year. For example, in Michigan, one LEA official we interviewed stated that the LEA had used Recovery Act funding to maintain intervention services for special education students. Looking ahead to the 2010-2011 school year, however, a lower percentage of districts—28 percent—expect to expand reform.

Figure 16: Percentage of LEAs Nationally with IDEA Part B Recovery Act Funds That Reported Expanding, Maintaining, or Decreasing Reform Efforts for Special Education Students in School Years 2009-2010 and 2010-2011, as Reported in Spring 2010

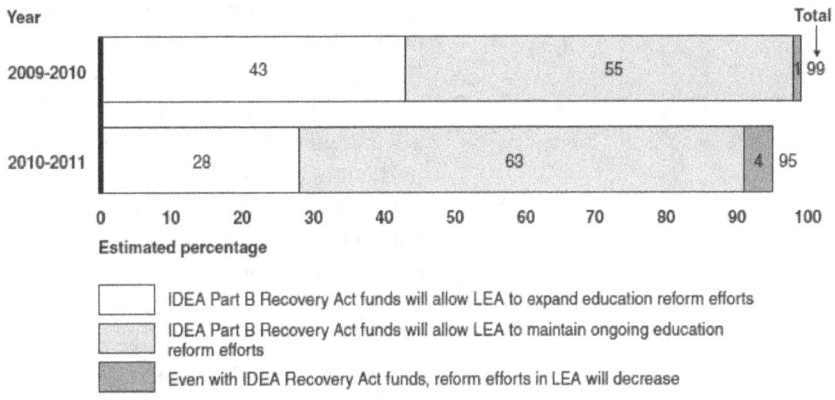

Source: GAO's survey of LEAs.

Notes: Percentage estimates have margins of error, at the 95 percent confidence level, of plus or minus 7 percentage points or less.This figure does not display the percentage of LEAs that chose "Don't Know" as a survey response, and therefore, the percentages do not total to 100 percent.

Given the Increase in IDEA Recovery Act Funding in 2009-2010, about 36 Percent of LEAs Exercised Flexibility to Decrease Local Spending on Special Education, and Primarily Used Funds to Retain Staff

In the 2009-2010 school year, among the 86 percent of LEAs that reported receiving Recovery Act IDEA Part B funds, an estimated 36 percent reported taking advantage of the maintenance-of-effort (MOE) flexibility under IDEA that allows them to reduce their local, or state and local,[50] spending on students with disabilities. IDEA requires LEAs to budget at least the same total or per capita amount of local funds for the education of children with disabilities as the LEA spent in the most recent prior year for which information is available. As provided for in IDEA, in any fiscal year in which an LEA's federal IDEA Part B allocation exceeds the amount

---

[50]Hereafter in this section, "local" will refer to "local, or state and local" funds.

Page 43

GAO-10-999 Recovery Act

the LEA received in the previous year, an eligible LEA[51] may reduce local spending on students with disabilities by up to 50 percent of the amount of the increase, as long as the LEA uses those freed-up funds for activities authorized under ESEA, which supports activities for general education. Because Recovery Act funds for IDEA Part B count as part of an LEA's overall federal IDEA allocation, in fiscal year 2009, the total increase in IDEA Part B funding for LEAs was far larger than the increases in previous years, which provided a greater incentive for many LEAs to take advantage of the MOE flexibility in the 2009-2010 school year. Of the 36 percent of LEAs exercising the flexibility, an estimated 41 percent reported spending more than half of the "freed-up" local funds on retaining staff. Other uses of the freed-up funds included providing professional development for instructional staff, purchasing computer technology, and hiring new staff.

We also found an example of an LEA that planned to take advantage of the MOE flexibility even though it was not eligible to do so. Based on our review of budget documents and local officials' statements, the Syracuse City School District (SCSD) had reduced their 2009-2010 spending by about $2.3 million.[52] We determined, and local officials subsequently agreed, that SCSD was not eligible for the MOE reduction because it was not meeting performance indicators related to graduation and drop-out rates among disabled students and it had a significantly high percentage of students with disabilities being suspended for more than 10 days, among other indicators. When we notified LEA officials of its ineligibility during our visit in March 2010, they attributed their situation to miscommunication among staff in the special education and finance offices and a misunderstanding of the eligibility rules for reducing MOE. LEA officials informed us that they would follow up on this issue and take steps to ensure they met MOE requirements. SCSD subsequently provided documentation showing that they were indeed meeting MOE requirements.

---

[51]To be eligible to exercise this flexibility, the LEA must meet the requirements of IDEA, Part B, including meeting targets in its state's performance plan. In 2009, almost all of the states in our sample had an increase in the number of LEAs that met requirements—and were therefore eligible—compared to the prior year. For more information, see GAO, *Recovery Act: Status of States' and Localities' Use of Funds and Efforts to Ensure Accountability*, GAO-10-231 (Washington, D.C.: Dec. 10, 2009).

[52]SCSD's application to the state for IDEA funds actually reported an increase in funding for the 2009-2010 school year of $125,793. However, this increase was reported in error.

While the decision by LEAs to decrease their local spending can free up funds to address other needs in the current school year, it could also have implications for future local spending on special education. Because LEAs are required to maintain their previous year's level of local spending on special education and related services to continue to receive IDEA Part B funds, LEAs taking advantage of the spending flexibility will only be required to maintain these expenditures at the reduced level in subsequent years. If LEAs that use the flexibility to decrease their local spending do not voluntarily increase their spending in future years, and federal IDEA Part B allocations decrease—specifically by returning to levels comparable to those before the Recovery Act—the total federal, state, and local spending for the education of students with disabilities will decrease compared to overall spending before the Recovery Act. However, while LEAs may maintain the lower level of spending, because of the IDEA requirement that children with disabilities receive a "free appropriate public education," (FAPE) districts may not be able to maintain services for students with disabilities at the lower levels of spending. For example, in Elk Grove Unified School District (California), which reduced local spending in 2009-2010, local officials reported that they have plans to include in their budget for 2010-2011 an amount equal to or greater than their 2008-2009 spending to ensure that services to students with disabilities are maintained. Officials said they needed to do this in order to maintain services for students with disabilities. In contrast, a charter school in Michigan reported that it may not be able to restore funding to previous years' levels, given decreases in state funding, but would make sure it provided services for students with disabilities.

States Vary in the Rate at Which They Draw Down Recovery Act Funds for Education Programs

As of August 27, 2010, states covered by our review had drawn down 72 percent ($18.2 billion) of the awarded SFSF education stabilization funds;[53] 46 percent ($3.0 billion) of Recovery Act funds for ESEA Title I, Part A; and 45 percent ($3.4 billion) of Recovery Act funds for IDEA Part B. Some states had drawn down a much larger portion of their funds than other states. (See table 6.) For example, Arizona, Georgia, Illinois and New Jersey had drawn down all of their SFSF education stabilization funds as of August 27, 2010, while Florida, Mississippi, Pennsylvania, and Texas had drawn down less than 55 percent of these funds.

---

[53]This amount includes both Phase I and Phase II SFSF education stabilization funds.

Table 6: Percentage of Awarded SFSF Education Stabilization, ESEA Title I Part A, and IDEA Part B Recovery Act Funds Drawn Down by Selected States as of August 27, 2010

State	Percentage of awarded Recovery Act funds drawn down		
	SFSF Education Stabilization Funds	ESEA Title I, Part A	IDEA Part B
Arizona	100	48	45
California	87	52	49
Colorado	86	34	36
District of Columbia	82	13	10
Florida	50	46	50
Georgia	100	38	41
Illinois	100	56	52
Iowa	93	95	84
Massachusetts	87	45	46
Michigan	85	40	44
Mississippi	50	41	33
New Jersey	100	34	38
New York	56	36	31
North Carolina	56	49	52
Ohio	56	42	52
Pennsylvania	52	58	49
Texas	42	47	43
Total	**72**	**46**	**45**

Source: U.S. Department of Education.

As noted in a previous report, drawdowns typically lag behind actual expenditures. For example, state officials in New Jersey stated that drawdown figures lag expenditures because funds are only drawn down once districts submit for reimbursement. However, because LEAs are required to obligate 85 percent of ESEA Title I Recovery Act funds by September 30, 2010, a low drawdown rate could indicate either that a large percentage of districts have sought and obtained or will seek and obtain waivers from this requirement or are at risk of not meeting this requirement. To help mitigate the effects of the funding cliff—when Recovery Act funding is no longer available—Education officials are encouraging districts to use carryover waivers to spread ESEA Title I, Part A funds over 2 years. Specifically, in a webinar Education officials hosted on June 15, 2010, Education officials explained how districts could minimize the impact of the funding cliff by strategically using carryover waivers. Also, officials in states we contacted appeared to be following

Education's suggested strategy to encourage the use of carryover waivers. We spoke to state officials in five states and the District of Columbia with relatively low drawdown rates[54] and some of these officials told us they were encouraging districts to spread the funds over the 2-year period rather than try to obligate 85 percent of the funds by September 30, 2010. For example, Massachusetts state officials told us they have encouraged all districts receiving Recovery Act Title I funds to apply for a carryover waiver to allow them the flexibility to use Recovery Act funds throughout the two-year period. Similarly, officials in New York state told us they had requested a blanket waiver for all districts in the state, which was approved by Education.

Education Is Continuing to Provide Technical Assistance and Guidance and Is Monitoring States' Use of Recovery Act Funds

Education has completed 16 of the 18 on site-monitoring visits it scheduled for the 2009-2010 monitoring cycle (including 11 states and the District of Columbia that are in our review),[55] according to department officials. The most frequent monitoring findings related to the Recovery Act had to do with districts failing to follow fiscal and set-aside requirements, such as the requirements to document time and effort of employees paid with Title I, Part A funds and properly calculate how much funding was required to be set aside for specific purposes, according to Education officials. Regarding fiscal requirement findings, the most frequent findings included districts' failure to (1) determine whether services provided in schools receiving ESEA Title I, Part A funding were comparable to those services provided to students in other district schools not receiving ESEA Title I, Part A funding, (2) determine whether federal funding had been used to "supplant" local or state funds by paying for services that had previously been provided using local or state funds, or (3) document that employees funded through multiple funding sources were dedicating the appropriate proportion of their time and effort to serving disadvantaged students. Regarding set-aside calculations, Education officials said that they found that some districts had not included Recovery Act funding in their calculations as required. Education officials provided examples of corrective actions state educational agencies and LEAs with fiscal or set-aside calculation findings could take to resolve these issues. For example, calculations for comparability or set-asides could be corrected to comply with requirements.

---

[54]These states are Colorado, Massachusetts, Michigan, New Jersey, and New York.

[55]These states are Arizona, California, Colorado, Florida, Illinois, Massachusetts, Michigan, North Carolina, New Jersey, New York, and Texas.

For the 2010-2011 monitoring cycle, Education officials plan to conduct on-site visits in 11 states, including 2 in our review,[56] and the Bureau of Indian Education. During each of these 12 monitoring visits, Education officials will assess state and local implementation of the School Improvement Grant program in addition to the implementation of regular and Recovery Act ESEA Title I, Part A requirements. Department officials said that during the upcoming monitoring cycle, they will continue to shift their monitoring focus away from strict audits towards providing technical assistance. Department officials also told us that they will develop state-specific technical assistance for the states reviewed during the 2009-2010 monitoring cycle to help them resolve identified challenges.

Education officials told us they continue to engage state and local officials using a variety of technical assistance efforts. Such efforts include issuing written guidance, hosting webinars, and giving presentations at state ESEA Title I conferences to explain and discuss federal guidance. Education officials also noted that they constantly communicate with state and local officials over the telephone and through email, and issue frequently asked questions to share their answers to questions from state and local officials. Department officials also noted that they have offered state-specific technical assistance to state and local officials in several states, particularly in states with new ESEA Title I leaders. Some of these technical assistance efforts have been initiated as a direct result of the Recovery Act, according to Education officials, who also said that the increased technical assistance efforts have created a strain on their resources and capacity.

Education Continues to Address Recovery Act Issues within Its Ongoing IDEA Monitoring Efforts

Regarding IDEA, in the fall of 2009, Education officials reported that they pursued their regular targeted monitoring visits and technical assistance, which covers 16 states or territories, and in response to the Recovery Act, Education's Office of Special Education Programs (OSEP) is also performing a desk review of all states.[57] According to Education officials,

---

[56]Mississippi and Pennsylvania are scheduled to be monitored in the 2010-2011 monitoring cycle.

[57]OSEP officials indicated that the desk review's content would include questions based on the Department of Education Inspector General's recent findings. See U.S. Department of Education, Office of Inspector General, Final Management Information Report, ED-OIG/X05J0019 (Washington, D.C., June 4, 2010).

the department uses annual performance report information and focused monitoring priorities to determine in which states it will conduct monitoring visits. In the course of its monitoring visits, the department verifies the effectiveness of state systems for general supervision, data collection, and fiscal management, as well as reviews state progress toward the goals from its state performance plan. In conducting site visits, OSEP reviews state records, makes visits to selected LEAs for on-site examination of student records, and assesses state special education systems. Following these visits, Education issues a report on findings and, when noncompliance is found, requires states to demonstrate correction of the noncompliance.

For fall 2010, Education is pursuing some additional monitoring and providing additional support to states in implementing the Recovery Act. Specifically, in addition to its annual monitoring visits, OSEP is planning to visit up to 10 additional states this year. These additional visits will be less intensive than the regular monitoring visits, and will focus more on the Recovery Act than the annual monitoring visits. Also in response to the Recovery Act, the department has assigned four Recovery Act Facilitators, who work with four teams that will provide support and guidance to states regarding their Recovery Act monitoring efforts and the reporting of accurate data for recipient reporting under the Recovery Act.

While they did not have any Recovery Act-specific findings in their most recent monitoring visits, OSEP officials did report some areas on which they will be focusing in their upcoming monitoring. OSEP officials reported that one of the issues they have been focusing on for several years is ensuring timely obligation and expenditure of funds. After finding 10 years ago that states had failed to obligate a total of $32.8 million in IDEA funds before the end of the 27-month timeframe required under the law, the department began to track state-level draw-downs, and now works to remind states that have balances above a certain threshold when the deadlines for obligating funds are approaching. OSEP officials reported that in subsequent years, after they began tracking drawdowns, the expired unobligated funds have declined to about $5.6 million. Also, OSEP officials reported that some states were calculating their state-level MOE spending without including spending on special education from sources outside of the state educational agency. For example, if other state departments are providing counseling or rehabilitation services, that spending must be included. Finally, OSEP officials reported that while state education agencies generally require LEAs to provide a budget for their intended uses of IDEA funds, and require LEAs to attest that they are complying with MOE requirements, states do not always perform monitoring later to ensure that LEAs can document that they spent the funds according to their budgets. In one example, in Iowa, we found equipment purchases under IDEA larger than $5,000 for a single piece of equipment that were not submitted to the state for approval as state officials reported was required.[58] In other examples, we found that the Des Moines Public School District purchased equipment for about $25,000, and the Marshalltown Community School District in Iowa purchased $8,400 in communications equipment and software, without seeking review and approval from the state prior to purchase, as state officials said was required. As we completed our reviews, the LEAs were making changes in their procedures to ensure state approval of IDEA equipment purchases greater than $5,000.

Given State-Level Budget Situations, Education Has Approved Waivers Allowing States to Decrease Their State Spending on Special Education

Because of declines in state-level budgets, Education has approved waiver applications from states to decrease their state-level spending on special education. Under IDEA, the Secretary of Education may waive state-level MOE requirements for equitable purposes due to "exceptional or uncontrollable circumstances such as a natural disaster or a precipitous and unforeseen decline in the financial resources of the State." Education approved a state-level waiver for one state in our review—Iowa[59]—for 2009. Education officials said that the waiver will only apply for 1 year, and, in 2010 Iowa must return its spending on special education to the 2009 level unless the state applies for and receives another waiver.

---

[58] According to guidance issued by Education, in general, to be able to use IDEA funds to purchase equipment, LEAs need to obtain the prior approval of the state. For purposes of this prior approval requirement, "equipment" is defined to mean an article of nonexpendable, tangible personal property having a useful life of more than a year and an acquisition cost which equals or exceeds the lesser of the capitalization level established by the governmental unit for financial statement purposes, or $5,000. See, U.S. Department of Education, Office of Special Education and Rehabilitative Services, *Guidance on Funds for Part B of the Individuals with Disabilities Education Act Made Available Under The American Recovery and Reinvestment Act of 2009* (Washington, D.C., April 2009).

[59] West Virginia's waiver application was also approved. In addition, Kansas received a partial approval. The state requested to decrease spending on special education by $60 million, but Education approved a decrease of $44 million. There is no official appeals process, according to OSEP officials, although Kansas has reapplied, asking for a decrease of $58 million. In addition, Education is currently considering a waiver application for South Carolina.

Education officials said that the department is considering each application individually based on its own merits, and is reminding states in its approval letters that they must provide services to students with disabilities that would still meet the requirement under the law that the state provide a free appropriate public education, despite any cuts. In a June 2010 memorandum, Education said that it was considering the impact of other sources of funding for special education, including those from the Recovery Act, when making waiver decisions.[60] Education officials also told us that they want to ensure that cuts to special education services are equitable when compared to other budget cuts, and therefore they consider the percentage decrease in spending on special education in relation to that of other items in the states' budget, both education-related and other items. Education's guidance also notes that states that receive a waiver may be subject to additional monitoring, and Education officials told us that each of the waiver-approved states will be among the 16 states chosen for full monitoring visits described above and subject to additional monitoring to make sure that free appropriate public education was provided.

Education Has Begun to Monitor SFSF Grantees and Address Initial Challenges Associated with Monitoring Noneducation State and Local Agencies

Education has begun to monitor SFSF grantees, and as of August 30, 2010 had conducted on-site monitoring of 1 state—New York—and Washington, D.C. included in our review[61] as well as desk reviews of two states in our review[62]—Georgia and North Carolina. Education has not yet completed its monitoring reports to states, but department officials told us that its findings were minor and that it would work with states to address any findings. For example, Education officials told us that some of the minor findings included not providing timely certification documents, ensuring that all jobs were reported on required recipient reports, or adhering to

---

[60]U.S. Department Of Education, Office Of Special Education And Rehabilitation Services, *Process And Criteria Used To Evaluate A Request By States To Waive Maintenance Of Effort (MOE) Requirements Under Part B Of The Individuals With Disabilities Education Act (IDEA)* (Washington, D.C., June 2010).

[61]Education has also conducted site visits in three states not included in our review—Maryland, South Carolina and Tennessee.

[62]Education has also conducted desk reviews of three states not included in our review—Alaska, Delaware, and North Dakota.

monitoring schedules of subrecipients. Education has 10 more on-site monitoring visits planned between September and November 2010 and 10 planned for 2011.

Education officials reported some challenges they experienced during their initial monitoring visits because of the differing types of subrecipients and the amount of documentation to review. Education's Office of Elementary and Secondary Education (OESE) is charged with administering and monitoring SFSF funds. While OESE is experienced with monitoring LEAs, SFSF educational stabilization funds may also flow to Institutions of Higher Education, which OESE has little or no experience overseeing. Further, SFSF government services funds provide funding to a broad range of state and local agencies that Education does not normally monitor. For example, SFSF government services funds subrecipients consist of a variety of noneducational entities including state police forces, fire departments, corrections departments, and healthcare facilities and hospitals. Since this is the first SFSF monitoring effort, Education officials told us that it will take time for Education's staff to become familiar with these subrecipients and the types of documentation they provide. In addition, Education officials reported that the amount of information necessary to monitor SFSF funds was voluminous and required more time than was expected, but they are continuing to work to improve the SFSF monitoring process.

In September 2009, we reported that some states faced challenges in developing monitoring plans for SFSF funds, and we recommended that Education take action such as collecting and reviewing documentation of state monitoring plans to ensure that states understand and fulfill their responsibility to monitor subrecipients of SFSF funds. Education acted on our recommendation and required states to submit SFSF monitoring plans to Education by March 12, 2010. Education officials told us they are reviewing the plans to ensure that states planned to adequately monitor SFSF subrecipients.

Given State-Level Budget Situations, Education Has Approved SFSF Waivers Allowing States to Decrease Their State Spending on Education

The Secretary of Education has granted an SFSF MOE waiver to one state in our review—New Jersey—allowing the state to reduce 2009 state support for education below 2006 levels.[63] The department grants these waivers once a state certifies that state education spending did not decrease as a percentage of total state revenues.[64] As we reported in May, the states we reviewed told us they met SFSF MOE levels in fiscal year 2009 or obtained waivers. Because of declines in state-level budgets, two states in our review—Florida and New Jersey—requested a waiver from Education to decrease their 2009 state-level spending on education.[65] After these states' 2009 state education funding figures were finalized, Education officials told us they reviewed waiver applications to ensure that state education funding in 2009 met the requirements for an SFSF waiver. Education officials reported that New Jersey's and Rhode Island's waivers have been approved and that they are currently reviewing South Carolina's and Florida's waivers.

Education Announced Race to the Top Grants and SFSF Phase II Awards

Education has announced that the District of Columbia and 11 states, including Florida, Georgia, Massachusetts, New York, North Carolina, and Ohio, will receive Race to the Top grants.[66] This program is a competitive grant fund created by the Recovery Act as part of SFSF providing $4.35 billion in funding for statewide reform efforts and to develop common academic assessments.[67] In addition, Education officials reported that almost all of the SFSF Phase II funds have been awarded to most states.[68] As such, states now have access to their entire allotment of SFSF funds and all SFSF funds must be obligated by September 30, 2011.

---

[63]Rhode Island was also granted a waiver for 2009 MOE requirements but was not included in our review.

[64]See Pub.L. No. 111-5, § 14012 (2009).

[65]Rhode Island and South Carolina have also requested a waiver from Education to decrease their 2009 state-level spending on education.

[66]Education officials reported that as of August 20, 2010, Tennessee and Delaware have received their Race to the Top grants. Hawaii, Maryland and Rhode Island are the other states that will also receive these grants.

[67]According to Education officials, $4 billion will be provided for statewide reform efforts and $350 million for state consortia to develop common academic assessments. From the time grantees receive their awards, they will have 4 years to spend the grant funds.

[68]Oklahoma's and Puerto Rico's Phase II applications have yet to be approved. Education officials reported they are working with these states and the outlying areas to ensure their plans for using Phase II SFSF funds adhere to applicable requirements.

Education Released New Clarifying Guidance on Recipient Reporting

As in previous reporting periods, FTE positions funded by Education grants accounted for a large proportion of all reported FTEs. Specifically, Education recipients reported around 450,000 FTEs, which represent 60 percent of the nearly 750,000 FTEs reported for the period ending June 30, 2010. To improve the consistency of FTE data collected and reported, in May and March 2010 GAO made several recommendations to Education, including that Education re-emphasize the responsibility of sub-recipients to include hours worked by vendors in their quarterly FTE calculations and that Education provide clarifying guidance to recipients on how to best calculate FTEs for education employees during quarters when school is not in session. Education implemented our recommendations by issuing clarifying guidance on August 26, 2010, that specifies how education sub-recipients are to calculate FTEs for recipient reporting for Education-specific situations, such as how to calculate FTEs for teachers not working during the summer months who are considered full-time employees.

Though the Application Process Has Taken Longer Than Expected, States and LEAs Are Preparing to Implement School Improvement Grants as Soon as Applications Are Approved

Setbacks in issuing final written guidance and resource constraints at Education have slowed the application process for School Improvement Grants (SIG)—competitive awards to help turn around the lowest performing schools—according to department officials. According to Education officials, one reason that the state application process took longer than expected was that the department had to revise the final requirements it initially released in December 2009. According to Education officials, some language in the Consolidated Appropriations Act, 2010 [69] necessitated changes to these requirements. Education officials released revised guidance in late January 2010 and again in June 2010 with a few additional revisions. [70] While the changes to the guidance and other delays created a challenge for some states, Education assisted states in moving their applications forward by responding to questions in a timely manner. In addition, Education extended the application deadline set in the initial guidance document to allow time for the department to

---

[69] Pub. L. No. 111-117 (2009).

[70] U.S. Department of Education, Office of Elementary and Secondary Education, *Final Requirements for School Improvement Grants, As Amended* (Washington, D.C., Jan. 28, 2010); and *Guidance on School Improvement Grants Under Section 103 (g) of the Elementary and Secondary Education Act of 1965* (Washington, D.C., June 29, 2010).

offer technical assistance and for states to revise their applications given the changed requirements.

In addition to the delay caused by issuing revised guidance, department officials said that staffing constraints had limited the department's ability to review state applications, which ranged from 200 to 400 pages in length, and to help state officials revise these applications. They noted that, in some cases, states had to revise the application, sometimes more than once, in order to comply with SIG requirements. Because certain compliance issues related to more than one part of the application (depending on how states put their applications together), Education staff had to reread each application in full after each resubmission to ensure compliance. Overseeing the substantial influx of additional ESEA Title I funds provided through the Recovery Act, including SIG funds, substantially increased staff workload, particularly given that staffing levels did not increase, said a senior Education official. While one staff member works full-time to coordinate the SIG application process at the department, the 17 other staff who were assigned to work on SIG application reviews assumed these responsibilities in addition to their other monitoring, technical assistance, and programmatic duties, according to a senior Education official.

State officials in some states[71] and the District of Columbia told us that they had encountered various challenges in applying for and implementing the School Improvement Grants and that timeframes have been tight. These states were at different stages in the process of selecting LEAs to receive SIG funds, but were taking various steps to address the tight timeframes and work through challenges, and expected that districts would be ready to use the grant funds in the 2010-2011 school year. For example, officials in New York told us in late August that they had nearly completed their review of districts' SIG applications. They also noted encountering challenges in New York City, where school districts are not allowed to replace principals or close schools—steps required by certain school turnaround models—and having to work through two specific collective bargaining issues. In contrast, New Jersey officials said they had completed their review of district applications and selected 12 schools, representing 7 school districts to receive SIG funds, with some districts receiving grants for multiple schools. To ease tight time frames, Michigan officials told us that while awaiting approval from Education, they had

---

[71]These states are Massachusetts and New York.

created an iterative application process for districts, whereby districts were required to submit an initial statement of intent in June, followed by a more detailed initial application in mid-July. State education officials told us they reviewed these initial drafts and gave local officials feedback before the final applications were due. As of late July, Education had approved SIG applications for 48 states and the District of Columbia, including all 16 of the states and the District of Columbia in our review.

Obligations for State Transportation Projects Are Nearly Complete, but Spending from Other Federal Transportation Sources Has Slowed

Use of Transportation Funds

Nationwide, the Federal Highway Administration (FHWA) obligated $25.6 billion in Recovery Act funds for over 12,300 highway projects and reimbursed $11.1 billion as of August 2, 2010. The Federal Transit Administration (FTA) obligated $8.76 billion of Recovery Act funds for about 1,055 grants and reimbursed $3.6 billion as of August 5, 2010.[72] Figure 17 shows FHWA's and FTA's reimbursements during the Recovery Act.

---

[72]Funds are obligated when DOT issues project or grant agreements. Apportioned funds are obligated when DOT issues project or grant agreements to recipients, a process that is typically followed by contractor selection, contract award, and performance. As expenses are incurred, recipients may request and be reimbursed for their expenses following program eligibility guidelines.

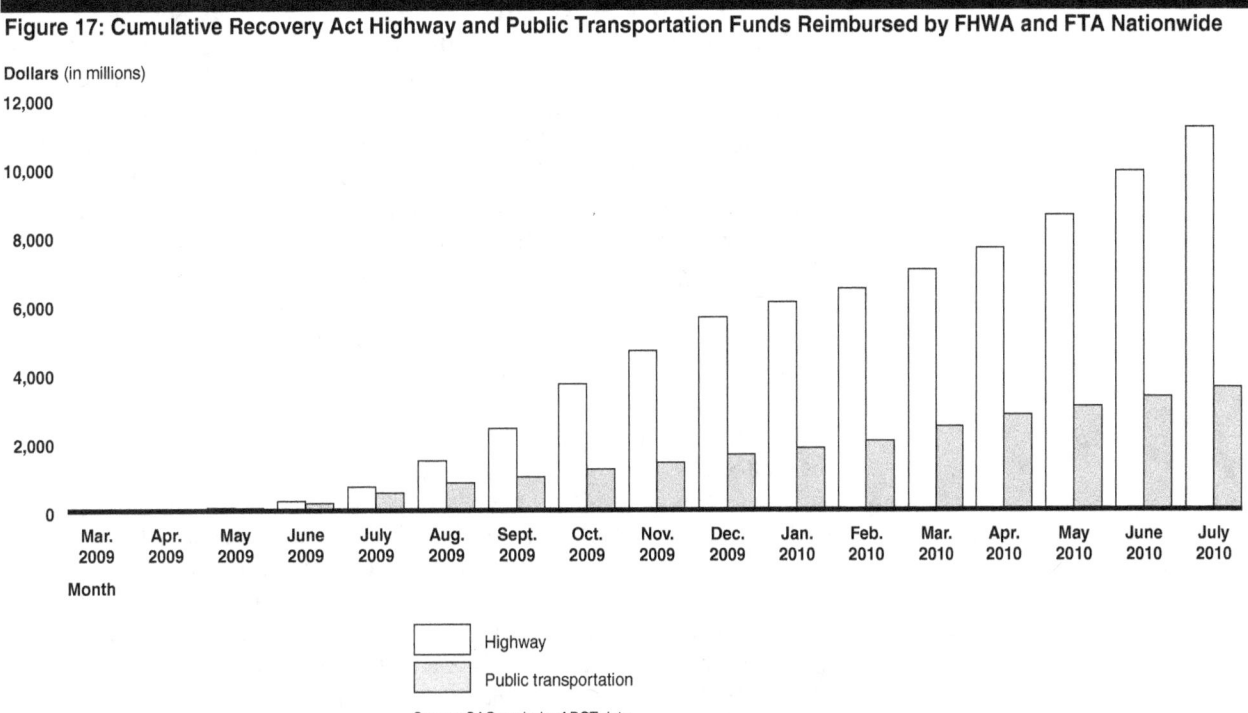

Figure 17: Cumulative Recovery Act Highway and Public Transportation Funds Reimbursed by FHWA and FTA Nationwide

Dollars (in millions)

Month

☐ Highway

☐ Public transportation

Source: GAO analysis of DOT data.

Nationally, 44 percent of funds obligated for highway projects had been reimbursed as of August 2, 2010. Reimbursement rates varied widely among the 16 states and the District—between 23 percent and 77 percent. Illinois, Iowa, and Mississippi had the highest reimbursement rates—each at 65 percent or more. Officials in all 3 states told us that in selecting projects they emphasized projects that could be completed quickly, and each undertook more pavement resurfacing projects—which can be quickly initiated—than any of the other states we reviewed. Five states had reimbursement rates below 30 percent—of particular note, California, which received almost 1 out of every 10 Recovery Act highway dollars apportioned nationwide, had the second lowest reimbursement rate among the 16 states and the District at 26 percent ($633 million). Officials from California noted that the state had undertaken a number of large projects that had the potential to offer long-term benefits but for which construction could not be initiated quickly. For example, California used about $197 million in Recovery Act funds to partially finance the Caldecott Tunnel improvement project (total estimated cost of $420 million). California awarded a contract in November 2009 and began construction of a new tunnel on a congested stretch of highway between Oakland and

Orinda in February 2010, nearly 1 year after the Recovery Act was enacted. California officials also attributed the state's lower reimbursement rates to having a majority of its projects administered by local governments, which are often reimbursed more slowly than state-administered projects. According to California officials, as of June 30, 2010, about 62 percent or $1.5 billion of California's $2.5 billion are obligated for local government projects. California officials stated that locally-administered highway projects take longer to reach the reimbursement phase because of the additional steps required to approve local highway projects and because localities with relatively small projects tend to seek reimbursement in one lump sum at the end of a project to minimize time and administrative costs.

The effect of projects sponsored by local agencies on reimbursements is not limited to California. Among all the 16 states and the District, reimbursement of funds suballocated for metropolitan, regional, and local use lagged behind state projects. Suballocated funds can be administered through local transportation agencies such as city or county agencies that can lack familiarity with federal requirements. As we have previously reported, local agencies have had challenges selecting projects that will meet these requirement and suballocated funds have generally taken longer to obligate than nonsuballocated funds.[73] Data show this pattern extending to reimbursements as well. New Jersey and Arizona had the lowest reimbursement rates on suballocated projects, 10 and 18 percent, respectively. Our past reports have noted that New Jersey and Arizona were among the slowest states to select projects for funding in suballocated areas.

Table 7 shows the total reimbursement rates in the 16 states and the District, as well as the reimbursement rates for state and suballocated projects.

[73]GAO, *Recovery Act: States' and Localities' Uses of Funds and Actions Needed to Address Implementation Challenges and Bolster Accountability,* GAO-10-604 (Washington, D.C.: May 26, 2010).

Table 7: Reimbursement of Recovery Act Funds as a Percentage of Funds Obligated – Ranked by All Funds

State	All funds	Suballocated funds	State funds
District of Columbia	23	29	20
California	26	25	26
Georgia	27	23	29
Ohio	29	35	27
Massachusetts	29	27	30
Florida	31	23	34
Texas	35	32	36
New York	37	37	37
New Jersey	37	10	48
Selected states' average	**39**	**33**	**41**
Arizona	42	18	52
U.S. average	**44**	**37**	**46**
Pennsylvania	47	47	47
North Carolina	47	42	49
Colorado	52	30	61
Michigan	55	53	56
Illinois	65	41	76
Mississippi	69	61	72
Iowa	77	79	76

Source: GAO analysis of FHWA data.

Note: Of the total Recovery Act highway funds available to states, 30 percent is to be directed to suballocated areas and 70 percent is available for use in any area of the state. Percentages based on reimbursements from FHWA to states as of August 2, 2010.

Recovery Act highway obligations were used primarily for pavement improvement projects, such as resurfacing, reconstruction, and rehabilitation of existing roadways. Recovery Act public transportation funds were used primarily for upgrading transit facilities and improving bus fleets (see fig. 18).

Figure 18: Nationwide Recovery Act Highway and Public Transportation Obligations by Project Type

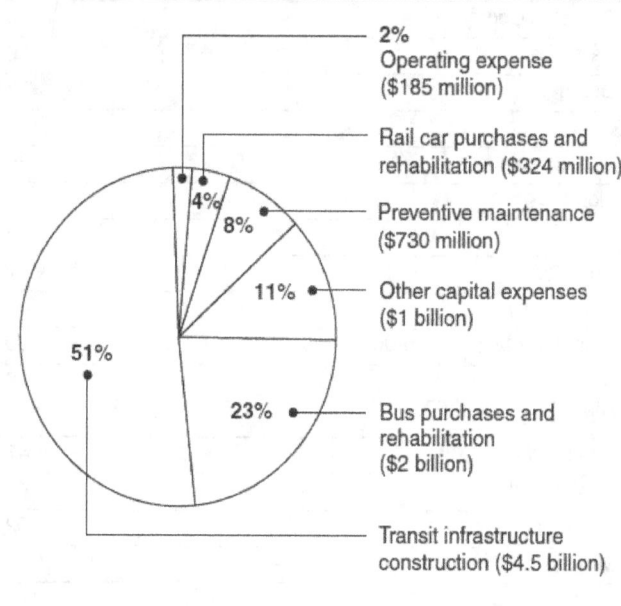

Highway obligations

- Pavement improvement: reconstruction/ rehabilitation ($6.4 billion)
- Pavement improvement: resurface ($5.7 billion)
- Pavement widening ($4 billion)
- New road construction ($1.6 billion)
- Bridge replacement ($1.3 billion)
- Bridge improvement ($1.2 billion)
- New bridge construction ($713 million)
- Other ($4.7 billion)

(22%, 16%, 6%, 5%, 5%, 3%, 18%, 25%)

Public transportation obligations

- 2% Operating expense ($185 million)
- Rail car purchases and rehabilitation ($324 million)
- Preventive maintenance ($730 million)
- Other capital expenses ($1 billion)
- Bus purchases and rehabilitation ($2 billion)
- Transit infrastructure construction ($4.5 billion)

(4%, 8%, 11%, 51%, 23%)

Source: GAO analysis of DOT data.

Notes: Highway and public transportation percentages may not add to 100 because of rounding.

Public transportation obligations include Recovery Act funds that were transferred from FHWA to FTA. The category "other" includes safety projects, such as improving safety at railroad grade crossings, engineering, right-of-way purchases, and transportation enhancement projects, such as pedestrian and bicycle facilities. "Transit infrastructure construction" includes engineering and design, acquisition, construction, and rehabilitation and renovation activities. "Other capital expenses" includes leases, training, finance costs, mobility management project administration, and other capital programs.

Highway data are as of August 2, 2010, and public transportation data are as of August 3, 2010.

States Asked FHWA to Deobligate Funds after the 1-Year Deadline, but Some Suballocated Areas Faced Challenges in Identifying Additional Projects for Funding

As we have previously reported, an economic stimulus package should assure that projects are undertaken quickly to provide a timely stimulus to the economy.[74] The Recovery Act included obligation deadlines to

---

[74]GAO, *Physical Infrastructure: Challenges and Investment Options for the Nation's Infrastructure*, GAO-08-763T (Washington, D.C.: May 8, 2008).

GAO-10-999 Recovery Act

facilitate the timely use of funds, including early March 2010 (1-year) deadlines to obligate Recovery Act highway and transit funds. In our May 2010 report, we reported that the states met these deadlines.

Since the March 2010 deadline for obligating Recovery Act highway funds, states have asked FHWA to deobligate some funds and are subsequently asking FHWA to obligate these funds to new projects. To use states' full apportionments, those funds must be obligated again by September 30, 2010, after which all unobligated highway funds will no longer be available to the states. As of August 2, 2010, about $397 million, or 2.6 percent, of total Recovery Act highway funds remained to be obligated in the 16 states and the District. Nationally, about $565 million remained. These amounts have increased steadily since the March 2010 deadline—for example, in the 1-month period between June 30, 2010, and August 2, 2010, the amount available for obligation increased from about $509 million to $565 million (see fig. 19).

Figure 19: Recovery Act Highway Funds Remaining to Be Obligated Since March 2, 2010

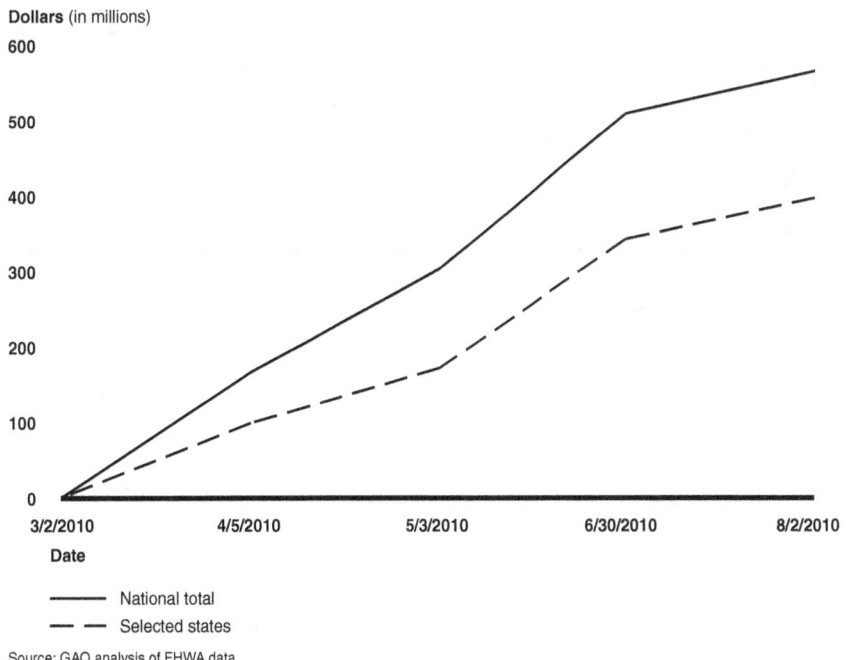

Source: GAO analysis of FHWA data.

Projects supported with suballocated funds generally had higher levels of unobligated funds compared with projects using funds that are not suballocated. As of August 2, 2010, $199 million of the $7.7 billion available to suballocated areas nationwide remained to be obligated before the September 30, 2010, deadline. Also, several of the states we reviewed had unobligated suballocated funds that were roughly three to five times larger than the national average (see table 8). FHWA officials told us that the timely expenditure of funds on projects administered by local public agencies remains an area of concern and that the agency is closely monitoring these projects to ensure, on behalf of the states, that all funds are obligated. These funds will be withdrawn after September 30, 2010, if these funds are not obligated.

Table 8: Percentage of Unobligated Recovery Act Highway Funds

State	Suballocated funds	State funds	All funds
Arizona	12.4	5.6	7.6
California	2.0	3.0	2.7
Colorado	0.0	1.6	1.2
District of Columbia	0.0	12.8	8.9
Florida	5.4	3.6	4.2
Georgia	9.0	7.5	7.9
Illinois	1.4	0.6	0.9
Iowa	0.2	0.9	0.7
Massachusetts	3.2	7.3	6.2
Michigan	1.2	0.9	1.0
Mississippi	1.2	0.0	0.4
New Jersey	1.6	0.4	0.8
New York	0.3	0.5	0.5
North Carolina	8.9	1.8	3.9
Ohio	1.2	4.3	3.4
Pennsylvania	0.0	0.3	0.2
Texas	0.9	1.5	1.3
Selected states' average	2.8	2.5	2.6
U.S. average	2.6	2.0	2.2

Source: GAO analysis of FHWA data.

Note: Of the total Recovery Act highway funds available to states, 30 percent is to be directed to suballocated areas and 70 percent is available for use in any area of the state. Percentages based on obligation of funds by FHWA as of August 2, 2010.

State officials identified several reasons projects might have been delayed in suballocated areas. Officials from the Arizona Department of Transportation, in which 12.4 percent of suballocated funds were unobligated, said that many suballocated areas did not have projects ready for federal-aid funding in part because of limited staff and other resources to move projects through approvals and prepare documentation in a manner consistent with federal requirements. Officials from North Carolina, in which 8.9 percent of suballocated funding was deobligated, told us that local agencies using suballocated funding faced challenges completing environmental documents, acquiring rights-of-way, and finalizing bid documents. As a result, many projects local agencies considered to be "ready-to-go" did not meet various federal standards, and agencies had to find other projects, which created delays.

Among the states we reviewed, most of the funds that the states asked FHWA to deobligate were from contract award savings. From March 2, 2010, to June 7, 2010, the 16 states and the District that we are reviewing requested FHWA to deobligate almost $457 million. About 85 percent of those funds were deobligated due to contracts continuing to be awarded below state cost estimates (see fig. 20).

Figure 20: Deobligations in 16 States and the District from March 2, 2010, to June 7, 2010, by Deobligation Type

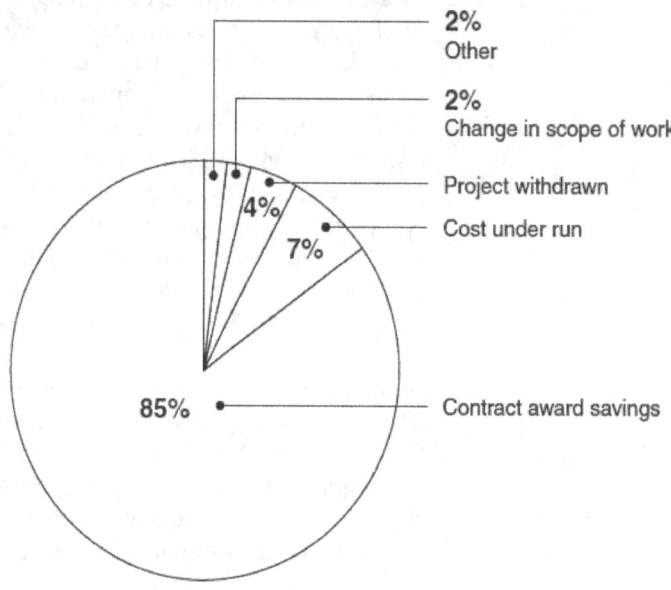

Source: GAO analysis of FHWA data.

Note: "Other" includes obligation reductions due to costs that were found not to be eligible for federal-aid reimbursement, revised estimates for projects, and corrections of data errors.

Withdrawn projects accounted for only about $17 million, or 4 percent, of deobligations from March 2 to June 7, 2010, less than 1 percent of the total $15.2 billion available to the 16 states and the District for highways. Two projects using suballocated funds in California accounted for about $9.7 million of the $17 million in withdrawn projects. In both cases, the project was withdrawn and later established as a new project. California officials told us they withdrew one $1.8 million project because local officials wanted to expand the scope of the project. Another $7.9 million project was withdrawn because it had an incorrect right-of-way certification. Officials told us that the state subsequently resubmitted the project and funding was obligated after correcting the certification.

Contract Data from FHWA's Recovery Act Data System Continues to Be Inaccurate

In May 2010, we reported that while progress has been made in awarding Recovery Act contracts and initiating work, the accuracy of contract data in FHWA's Recovery Act Data System (RADS) is of concern. Among other information, the Recovery Act requires the U.S. Department of Transportation (DOT) to report to Congress on the number of projects for which contracts have been awarded, for which work has begun, and for which work had been completed, and the amount of federal funds associated with these contracts.[75] DOT established RADS because it had not previously collected and reported such information for the regular federal highway formula program. DOT relies on states to enter data into RADS and uses automated data checks and rules, as well as periodic reviews by FHWA Division office officials located in every state, to improve the accuracy of state-reported data.

We continued to find problems with the accuracy of RADS contract data.[76] For example, more than 3,100 contracts were shown as having been awarded on the same date the funds were obligated. We also found that about 1,400 contracts were reported as awarded before FHWA obligated the funds. Because contracts are normally awarded several weeks or months after funds are obligated by FHWA, the numbers and amounts of contracts awarded and work begun is likely overstated. Because FHWA does not have accurate data from states in RADS, it is not able to use RADS to meet the Recovery Act reporting requirements for contracts.

FHWA officials acknowledged that they cannot use data from RADS to provide information on contract award amounts. Officials said they instead use data from FHWA's financial management system to meet the Recovery Act reporting requirements for contracts because this system receives more checks for data accuracy. However, using FHWA's financial management system can also overstate the amount of funds under contract. FHWA reports data at the project level, not at the contract level; this is important because one project can include several contracts. When reporting at the project level, FHWA reports the entire project as being under contract once one contract is awarded, even if several more remain to be awarded. FHWA provided project-level data in its report to Congress dated May 7, 2010,[77] but these data were labeled in the report as contract data. As noted above, the Recovery Act requires DOT to report not only the number of projects, but also the total amount of federal funds

---

[75]Recovery Act, div. A, title XII, § 1201(c).

[76]We reviewed data in RADS as of June 18, 2010, for all 50 states and the District.

[77]DOT Secretary of Transportation, *Section 1201(c) One-Year Report*, (Washington, D.C.: May 7, 2010).

associated with contracts that have been awarded, work has begun, and work is completed.

FHWA has taken some steps to improve data accuracy in RADS, but officials said that there was no date for when they would implement changes. These officials said they have assembled a state advisory group to look at the challenges that exist in RADS and make recommendations on improvements. FHWA officials said they have not had sufficient resources to incorporate additional data checks into the software that would check for errors. Such checks could ensure that milestones are sequentially entered, thereby improving the accuracy of these data.

Many States Requested That FHWA Transfer Funds to FTA for Public Transportation Projects and Many States and Transit Agencies Elected to Use Some Funds for Operating Expenses, Although Data on Operating Expenses Is Limited

As we reported in our prior Recovery Act work, states have the option to request that FHWA transfer Recovery Act highway funds to FTA for use in public transportation programs, just as they do in the regular Federal Aid Highway Program.[78] While most states transfer some funds each year to address transit priorities, data from Recovery Act funds indicated that 21 states requested FHWA transfer some Recovery Act funds to the states' public transportation program. Many states transferred funds shortly after Recovery Act funds became available in February 2009. For example, Caltrans transferred almost $2 million in July 2009. Caltrans officials told us that their state has a robust transfer program because of the state's extensive public transportation system and the system's many needs. Caltrans' subrecipients used this funding for two large projects identified in the state's transportation improvement plan but for which sufficient funding had not been available. Specifically, one subrecipient is purchasing two buses for a rural transit agency, and the second is constructing a new intermodal transit hub that will serve the north Lake Tahoe area. Caltrans officials said that the Recovery Act funding was sufficient to complete these programs.

---

[78]Generally, FHWA has authority pursuant to 23 U.S.C. § 104(k)(1) to transfer funds made available for transit projects to FTA.

According to FTA data, many state departments of transportation (DOT) and transit agencies[79] also used a portion of Recovery Act funds for public transportation operating expenses. In June 2009, Congress gave urbanized areas and states the authority to use a maximum of up to 10 percent of certain Recovery Act transit funds for operating expenses.[80] Data provided by FTA indicated that, nationwide, urbanized areas and states used about $190 million, or about 2 percent of Recovery Act funding for public transportation, toward operating expenses as of August 25, 2010. FTA officials told us that urbanized areas and states determine how much Recovery Act funds they spend on operating expenses. According to FTA data, 169 grantees throughout the U.S. chose to use a portion of public transportation funds for operating expenses. This represented approximately 25 percent of total Recovery Act public transportation grantees. These 169 grantees ranged from major urban transit agencies in San Francisco and St. Louis to transit agencies in smaller cities such as Charlottesville, Virginia, and Pocatello, Idaho. In addition, 18 states used a portion of their Recovery Act funding to pay for operating expenses for rural public transportation.

FTA provided us data on the dollar amounts that urbanized areas and states obligated for operating expenses, but noted that they did not begin to track at a national level the percent of funds each state or urbanized area was using for operating expenses until August 2010. FTA officials also said that they rely on FTA's regional offices—as part of the grant approval and review process—to ensure that urbanized areas and states plan to spend no more than the 10 percent threshold. However, they are considering instituting a control in its electronic grants management system so that staff could not award a grant if an urbanized area or state was over the 10 percent threshold. FTA officials also noted that there is no reporting requirement to make publicly available the percent of funds that urbanized areas and states are using for operating expenses but that they are considering placing summary information on the use of Recovery Act transit funds for operating expenses on the FTA Web site.

We spoke with several states and transit agencies about whether they used Recovery Act funds for operating expenses. For example, officials from Michigan's Department of Transportation, after asking nonurban transit agencies for input, found that funding for operating expenses was a

---

[79]Located in Urbanized Areas; these areas may cross state lines.

[80]Supplemental Appropriations Act, 2009, Pub. L. No. 111-32, § 1202 (June 24, 2009).

priority. According to Michigan Department of Transportation officials, the majority of nonurban transit systems in Michigan are demand response—meaning that passengers are picked up and dropped off where they want to go within a defined service area—and officials told us that expenses for these services have been increasing annually. As a result, officials said the state used the maximum 10 percent of Recovery Act transit funds for this purpose.

Officials from Caltrans told us that they used 1.1 percent of their Recovery Act funds for the operating expenses of their paratransit program.[81] They added that these expenses were already allowable as capital expenses under both the Recovery Act as originally enacted and the regular federal transit programs. Caltrans officials told us that if they had the option to use transit funds for public transportation operating expenses when the Recovery Act was first enacted, they would have used the full 10 percent. However, because California had already identified and requested that funds be obligated for capital projects prior to when the option to use these funds for operating expenses became available, they chose to adhere to their initial plan rather than risk that the funds be deobligated and applied for another purpose.

Transit officials from Illinois and New Jersey said their states chose not to use Recovery Act funds for operating expenses. Illinois DOT officials told us they decided early in the process to devote all Recovery Act funds to capital projects, so that the use of these funds was evident to the public. Illinois also chose to use state funds to cover all administrative expenses related to managing Recovery Act funds both to ensure maximum impact on capital projects and minimize paperwork needed to clear administrative charges for payments. New Jersey Transit officials told us they used Recovery Act funds for preventive maintenance—such as bus mechanical maintenance—which they said was considered a capital expense but did not produce new infrastructure. Officials noted that this reduced pressure on the transit agency's budget, which freed up state funds for operating expenses.

As we reported in May 2010, a portion of the highway money that was transferred was not obligated by the Recovery Act's March 2010 1-year obligation deadline for highways and transit. We noted that the U.S.

---

[81]Caltrans' paratransit program is a curb-to-curb shared ride service for the disabled who are unable to use fixed bus or rail routes.

Department of Transportation (DOT) did not treat these funds as subject to the Recovery Act obligation deadline for either FHWA or FTA because it concluded that once Recovery Act highway funds were transferred to FTA, they were subject to the provisions of the law that apply generally to the transfer of highway funds to FTA. At the time, we expressed no opinion on DOT's determination but stated that we were exploring this issue further.[82] On further review, we have no objection to DOT's interpretation of the applicability of the Recovery Act's 1-year obligation deadlines.[83]

Impact of Transportation Funds

Obligation and Reimbursement of Regular FHWA Formula Funds Slowed during the Recovery Act, Raising Questions about Whether Recovery Act Funds Had the Full Economic Stimulative Effect Intended

While states have been working to have FHWA obligate funds for constructing Recovery Act projects, we found that, compared with previous years, many states were slower in obligating and expending regular federal highway formula funds. FHWA officials stated that with the emphasis placed on the economic benefits to be gained, the obligation of Recovery Act funds and meeting the act's statutory deadlines have taken priority. States are facing drastic fiscal conditions, and FHWA officials

---

[82]GAO, *Recovery Act: States' and Localities' Uses of Funds and Actions Needed to Address Implementation Challenges and Bolster Accountability*, GAO-10-604 (Washington, D.C.: May 26, 2010), 35.

[83]As DOT pointed out, section 104(k) requires that funds transferred under that authority are to be administered in accordance with the provisions of chapter 53 of title 49, United States Code, which does not include a withdrawal and redistribution procedure. 23 U.S.C. § 104(k)(1); 49 U.S.C. § 5334(i)(1). When specific and general statutes appear to conflict and a general provision is "broad enough to include the subject to which the specific provision relates, the specific provision should be regarded as an exception to the general provision so that both may be given effect, the general applying only where the specific provision is inapplicable." B-255979, Oct. 30, 1995, *quoting* B-163375, Sept. 2, 1971. Section 104(k) specifically prescribes the disposition of funds transferred under authority of the section—namely, that funds transferred under section 104(k) are to be administered under chapter 53 of title 49. As such, the Recovery Act's 1-year obligation deadline for FHWA's Highway Infrastructure Investment appropriation does not apply.

Furthermore, because the transferred funds were not originally appropriated to FTA's Transit Capital Assistance or Fixed Guideway Infrastructure Investment Programs, and they were not merged with those funds upon transfer to FTA, they are not subject to FTA's distribution formula for transit capital assistance and fixed guideway infrastructure and, therefore, are not subject to the 1-year obligation deadline applicable to FTA's Recovery Act appropriations. Instead, the funds were transferred after identification of specific ready-to-work projects.

noted economic and budget difficulties in many states have led to staffing shortages. FHWA officials also suggested that uncertainty about future program funding levels may have slowed spending because a long-term reauthorization of federal programs has not yet been enacted.

Nationally, as of June 30, 2010 (the end of the third quarter of the fiscal year), states had $19.7 billion remaining to be obligated, 63 percent more funds than they did at the same time for the 3 previous years[84] (see fig. 21).

Figure 21: Regular Federal Highway Formula Funds Nationwide Remaining to Be Obligated at the End of the Third Quarter of Fiscal Year 2010

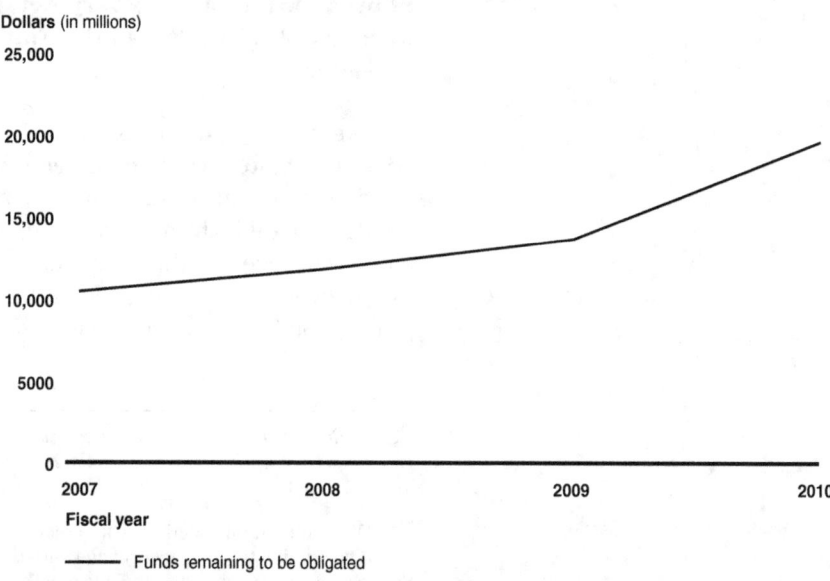

Source: GAO analysis of FHWA data.

In addition, while funding available to states for highways has increased in each of the last 3 fiscal years, we found that as of July 31, 2010, the reimbursement of regular federal highway formula program funds were lower compared with the reimbursement at the same point in the 3 previous fiscal years (see fig. 22).

---

[84]The average of funds remaining to be obligated on June 30 for federal fiscal years 2007, 2008, and 2009 was $12.1 billion.

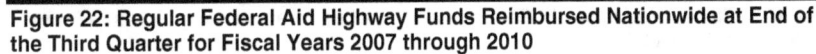

Figure 22: Regular Federal Aid Highway Funds Reimbursed Nationwide at End of the Third Quarter for Fiscal Years 2007 through 2010

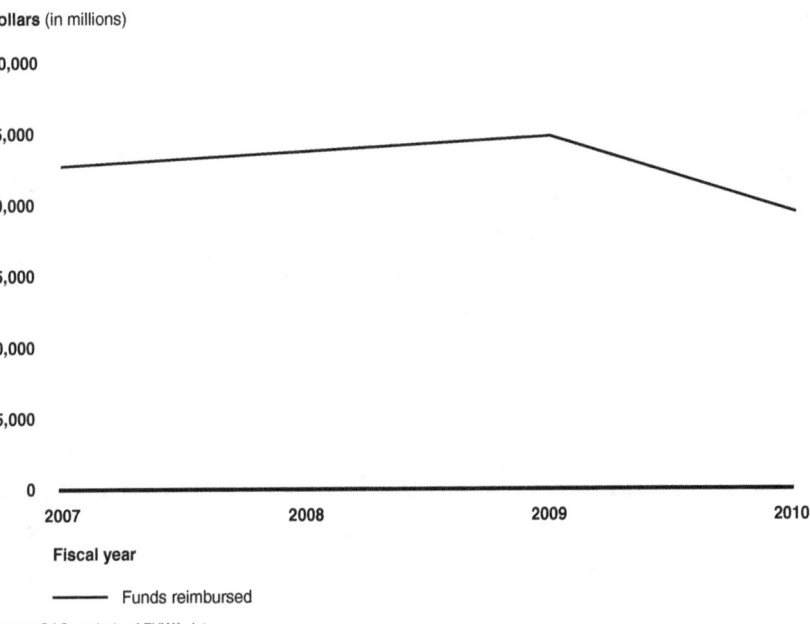

Source: GAO analysis of FHWA data.

As Figure 23 shows, this trend was also true on a monthly average basis. Specifically, the reimbursement of regular federal highway formula funds for the first 10 months of fiscal year 2010 has been almost 18 percent (or about $4.3 billion) less than the average reimbursement in the previous 3 fiscal years.

Figure 23: Nationwide Monthly Reimbursement of Federal Highway Formula Funds for Fiscal Year 2010 and the Average for Fiscal Years 2007-009

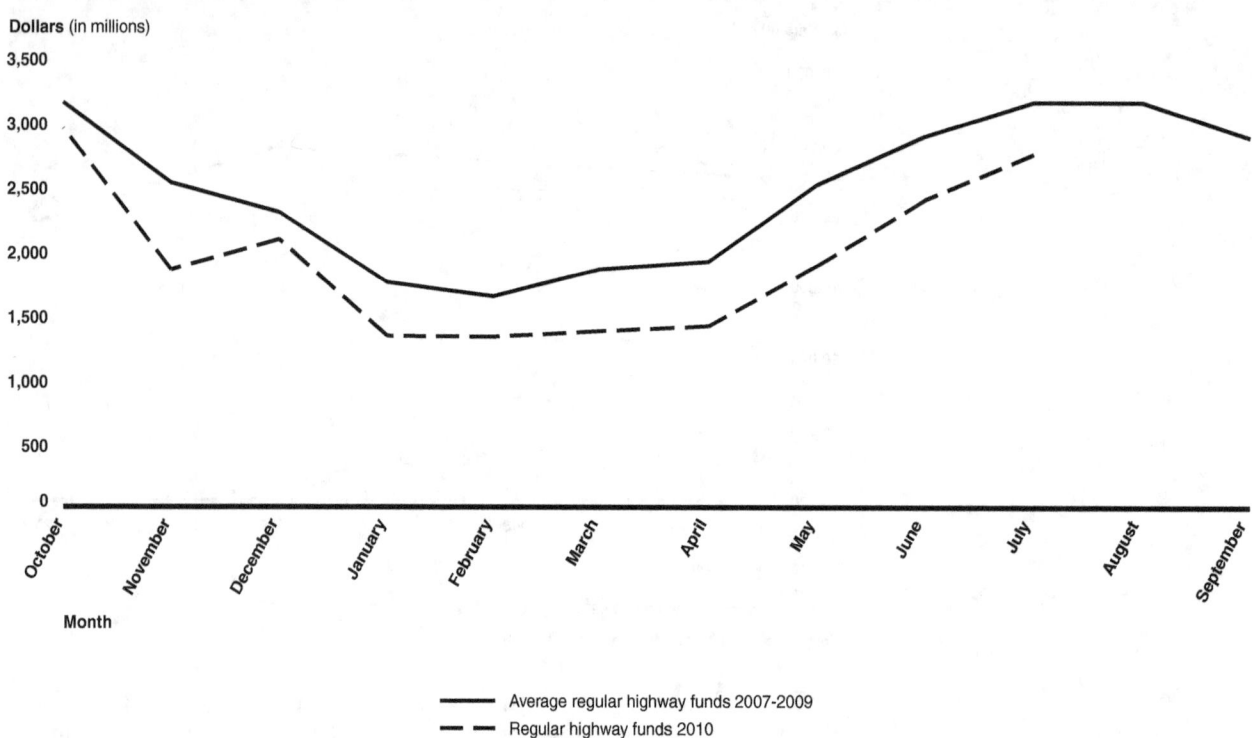

Dollars (in millions)

—— Average regular highway funds 2007-2009
- - - Regular highway funds 2010

Source: GAO analysis of FHWA data.

In the last 3 months of fiscal year 2010, state highway agencies not only have to request FHWA obligate over $500 million in remaining Recovery Act funds, but also $19.7 billion of regular federal highway formula funds. The amount of unobligated regular federal highway formula funds varied among states. For example, Illinois had none as of June 30, 2010, while Utah had $178.4 million—almost 6 times as much compared with its average balance of unobligated funds over the 3 previous years. Nationally, we found 16 states with over twice the amount of unobligated funds, while 5 states had fewer unobligated funds than in the past. Some state officials told us they had not been obligating regular federal highway formula funds as quickly because they had been focusing on meeting the

Recovery Act obligation deadlines and did not have the resources to do both.[85]

Because states did not spend regular federal highway formula funds at the same pace as in previous years, while also spending Recovery Act funds, the full economic benefits of Recovery Act funds are likely to be delayed. Specifically, if states had awarded contracts and begun expending those regular federal highway formula funds at the same rate as in previous years and in conjunction with spending Recovery Act funds, states would have experienced an earlier stimulus effect.[86] Funding being obligated now for projects will need up to several months to award contracts and initiate construction, and the effect on the economy comes when construction is initiated and workers are employed.

FHWA officials said they expect all regular program funds to be obligated by the end of the fiscal year. To ensure that all authorized funds are obligated nationally each year, FHWA redistributes obligation authority from states that are not able to obligate their funds to other states that are. Despite projects being obligated at a slower rate than in previous years, in August 2010, when we completed our review, the 16 states and the District all reported to FHWA that they would fully obligate fiscal year 2010 highway formula funds. We will continue to monitor the relationship of obligations and reimbursements in both the regular federal highway formula program and Recovery Act in future reviews.

DOT Is Developing Plans to Assess the Impact of the Recovery Act but Has Not Committed to Assessing Long-Term Benefits

The goals of the Recovery Act were not only to promote economic recovery and to preserve and create jobs but also to make investments in transportation and other infrastructure that would provide long-term

---

[85]For this report, GAO interviewed officials in California, Florida, Illinois, Massachusetts, Mississippi, North Carolina, and Texas regarding expenditures of their regular federal-aid highway program funds.

[86]The Highway Infrastructure Investment, Transit Capital Assistance and the Fixed Guideway Infrastructure Investment Programs are formula grant programs, which apportion funds to states or their subdivisions by law. Apportioned funds are obligated when DOT issues project or grant agreements to recipients, a process that is typically followed by contractor selection, contract award, and performance. As expenses are incurred, recipients may request and be reimbursed for their expenses following program eligibility guidelines.

economic benefits. However, the Recovery Act did not include requirements that DOT or states measure the impact of funding on highway and transit projects to assess whether these projects ultimately produced long-term benefits. In our May 2010 report, we noted that, although DOT developed performance plans to measure the impact of Recovery Act transportation programs, these plans generally did not contain an extensive discussion of specific goals and measures needed to assess the impact of Recovery Act projects. As we have reported, it is important for organizations to measure performance to understand the progress they are making toward their goals.[87] In our May 2010 report, we noted several efforts DOT initiated to strengthen its capacity to assess the impact of Recovery Act funds. For example, DOT is exploring opportunities to link databases that stored information about road smoothness and congestion, bridge structural sufficiency, and transit performance with financial data.

Our May report recommended that DOT assess the results of Recovery Act transportation investments and determine whether these investments produced long-term benefits. We further recommended that, in the near term, DOT determine the types of data and performance measures needed to conduct such an assessment and, as appropriate, identify specific authority DOT may need to collect and report on these measures. In its response, DOT noted that it expected to be able to report on Recovery Act outputs, such as the miles of road paved, bridges repaired, and transit vehicles purchased, but not on outcomes, such as reductions in travel time, nor did it commit to assessing whether transportation investments produced long-term benefits. DOT further explained that limitations in its data systems, coupled with the magnitude of Recovery Act funds relative to the overall annual federal investment in transportation, would make assessing the benefits of Recovery Act funds difficult. DOT indicated that, with these limitations in mind, it is examining its existing data availability and, as necessary, would seek additional data collection authority from Congress if it became apparent that such authority were needed. While we are encouraged that DOT plans to take some steps to assess its data needs, it has not committed to assessing the long-term benefits of Recovery Act investments in transportation infrastructure. We are therefore keeping our recommendation on this matter open.

---

[87]GAO, *Executive Guide: Effectively Implementing the Government Performance and Results Act*, GAO/GGD-96-118 (Washington, D.C.: June 1996).

DOT Plans to Report on State Progress in Meeting Maintenance-of-Effort Provisions

As we have previously reported, timely information on the progress states are making in meeting the Recovery Act maintenance-of-effort provisions could better inform policymakers' decisions on the usefulness and effectiveness of the maintenance-of-effort requirements and of including similar provisions in future legislation. The Recovery Act required governors to certify that their states will maintain the level of spending for the types of transportation projects funded by the Recovery Act that it planned to spend the day the Recovery Act was enacted. As part of this certification, the governor of each state was required to identify the amount of state funds planned to be spent from February 17, 2009, through September 30, 2010.[88] Timely information is also important to assessing the impact of Recovery Act funding and whether it achieves its intended effects of providing countercyclical assistance and increasing overall spending.

Our earlier reports have noted that DOT does not have current information on the progress states are making toward meeting their certified amounts. This is because the Recovery Act does not require states to report final expenditures until February 2011. As a result, DOT will not make a determination as to whether states have met their required program expenditures until some 6 months after the maintenance-of-effort provision time period expires on September 30, 2010. We have also reported that the challenges to implementing a maintenance-of-effort provision have been tremendous—as of mid-August 2010, for example, DOT had not yet fully accepted the certifications of three states.[89] As we have reported, these implementation challenges, coupled with the fiscal challenges states have faced, raise questions as to whether the maintenance-of-effort provision will achieve its intended purpose of preventing states from substituting federal funds for some of their planned spending on transportation programs. That said, DOT and FHWA have

---

[88]Recovery Act, div. A, title XII, § 1201(a). A state that does not meet its level of effort will be prohibited from participating in the redistribution of federal-aid highway obligation authority, scheduled to occur in August 2011.

[89]DOT officials indicated that Massachusetts and Minnesota agreed to correct errors in the amount identified for the states' transit programs, and the states agreed to provide this information to DOT by early September 2010. DOT was in discussion with Connecticut to determine whether there were errors to correct in the certification, and officials said this issue would also be resolved by early September.

invested a significant amount of time and work to ensure consistency across states on how compliance with the act is certified and reported. As a result, DOT is in an advantageous position to understand lessons learned—what worked, what did not, and what could be improved in the future.

Our March 2010 report recommended that DOT gather timely information on the progress states are making in meeting the maintenance-of-effort requirements.[90] Specifically, we recommended that DOT gather these data and report preliminary information to Congress within 60 days of the maintenance-of-effort period on (1) whether states met required program expenditures as outlined in their maintenance-of-effort certifications; (2) the reasons that states did not meet these certified levels, if applicable; and (3) lessons learned from the process. In response, DOT officials stated that DOT will encourage states to report preliminary data for the certified period ending September 30, 2010, and deliver a preliminary report to Congress within 60 days of the certified period. DOT officials said they have developed a timeline for obtaining information to produce this report and will issue guidance by October 1, 2010, requesting that states update actual aggregate expenditure data and provide the data to DOT by November 15, 2010. DOT officials said they will use this information to develop the report to Congress, and it will submit the report no later than November 30, 2010.

Publicly Available Information Continues to Overstate the Extent to Which Recovery Act Funds Were Directed to Economically Distressed Areas

Our previous reports have identified challenges DOT faced in implementing the Recovery Act requirement that states give priority to

---

[90]GAO, *Recovery Act: One Year Later, States' and Localities' Uses of Funds and Opportunities to Strengthen Accountability*, GAO-10-437 (Washington, D.C.: Mar. 3, 2010).

projects located in economically distressed areas.[91] In July 2009, we reported substantial variation in the extent to which states prioritized projects in economically distressed areas and how they identified these areas. Many states based their project selections on other factors and only later identified whether these projects were in economically distressed areas. We also found instances of states developing their own eligibility requirements for economically distressed areas using data or criteria not specified in the Public Works and Economic Development Act of 1965, as amended. In response to our recommendation, FHWA, in consultation with the Department of Commerce, issued guidance to the states in August 2009 that defined "priority," and directed states to give priority to projects that were located in an economically distressed area and could be completed within the 3-year time frame over other projects. In addition, FHWA's guidance set out criteria for states to use to identify economically distressed areas based on "special need."

Three states—Arizona, California, and Illinois—developed their own eligibility requirements or applied a special-need criterion that overstated the number of counties, and thus the amount of funds, directed to economically distressed areas. For example, California designated all counties as economically distressed, and we identified 219 projects with an estimated cost of $1.1 billion coded as being in economically distressed areas that should not have been so coded. In early February 2010, FHWA determined the documentation these states provided to justify these additional designations was not consistent with FHWA guidance.[92] In May 2010, we recommended that FHWA advise these states to correct the designations, and in July 2010, FHWA instructed its division offices to

---

[91]Specifically, the Recovery Act requires states to give priority to projects that can be completed within 3 years and to projects located in economically distressed areas. Economically distressed areas are defined by the Public Works and Economic Development Act of 1965, as amended. To qualify as an economically distressed area, an area must (1) have a per capita income of 80 percent or less of the national average; (2) have an unemployment rate that is, for the most recent 24-month period for which data are available, at least 1 percent greater than the national average unemployment rate; or (3) be an area that the Secretary of Commerce determines has experienced or is about to experience a "special need" arising from actual or threatened severe unemployment or economic adjustment problems resulting from severe short- or long-term changes in economic conditions.

[92]Each state used FHWA's special-need criterion that relates to severe job dislocation resulting from actual or threatened business closure or restructuring. These states were advised that in order to be consistent with the FHWA guidance, the states must have data that show a connection between demonstrated severe job losses and actual, identified firm closures and restructurings.

advise the states to revise their designations and to report these projects as being in noneconomically distressed areas.

In December 2009, DOT testified to the House Committee on Transportation and Infrastructure that 57 percent of projects were in economically distressed areas—including 99 percent and 100 percent of Recovery Act highway funding in California and Arizona, respectively. However, as we noted above, these data had not yet been corrected by DOT and therefore overstated the amount of funding, and this testimony is DOT's only public accounting of how states implemented this provision of the Recovery Act. Because FHWA's July guidance did not direct states other than Arizona, California, and Illinois to correct existing entries, we reviewed RADS data on projects in economically distressed areas. We found about 2,300 projects that did not appear to meet FHWA's guidance for classifying projects in economically distressed areas and thus appeared to contain errors that would result in an overstating of the funds directed to these areas. For instance, over 2,100 of these entries did not include an explanation justifying the designation of an area as economically distressed. In response to this information, DOT officials told us that they manually compared these entries with maps designating distressed area and other data sources. When we completed our review, FHWA officials said they were able to verify that most of these data were accurate; however, they did not provide documentation of the analysis to us. DOT stated it does not intend to correct this information because the Recovery Act does not contain a specific requirement that DOT report on the extent to which distressed areas prioritized and directed funds to economically distressed areas. However, without accurate publicly available information, it is difficult to determine the extent to which Recovery Act funds were directed to areas most severely impacted by the recession or to know the extent to which states prioritized these areas in selecting projects for funding.

Although Recovery Act Provisions Do Not All Contain Reporting Requirements, Additional Reporting Would Help Decision Makers and the Public Better Understand If Its Goals Were Met

The Recovery Act included a number of requirements and provisions designed to support the Act's goals of promoting economic recovery, creating jobs, and, in the case of transportation funds, making investments that contribute to long-term economic benefits. Although the Act included some reporting requirements to accompany these provisions, it did not specify such requirements in all cases. Noting the large amount of federal transportation funding provided in the Recovery Act, we have previously made recommendations that DOT take additional steps to go beyond the specific reporting requirements in the Act, and that DOT develop plans to assess the long-term benefits of Recovery Act funds on the transportation system. We have also made recommendations that DOT improve and correct the data it is collecting to better facilitate a public accounting of the use and impact of these funds. For instance, we have recommended that DOT report on the extent to which states met maintenance-of-effort requirements 60 days after the end of the certification period.

In his March 2009 memorandum to the heads of executive departments and agencies, the President emphasized the need for providing public transparency and accountability of these expenditures. We are making two new recommendations to DOT because of the value such information can offer policy decision makers and the public to better understand whether the use of Recovery Act funds met intended goals. We plan to continue to monitor these issues in our future work.

Recommendations

To ensure that Congress and the public have accurate information on the extent to which the goals of the Recovery Act are being met, we recommend that the Secretary of Transportation direct FHWA to take the following two actions:

- Develop additional rules and data checks in the Recovery Act Data System, so that these data will accurately identify contract milestones such as award dates and amounts, and provide guidance to states to revise existing contract data.

- Make publicly available—within 60 days after the September 30, 2010, obligation deadline—an accurate accounting and analysis of the extent to which states directed funds to economically distressed areas, including corrections to the data initially provided to Congress in December 2009.

DOE and Grant Recipients Are Working to Overcome Challenges in Spending, Monitoring, and Reporting Outcomes for New EECBG Program

The Energy Efficiency and Conservation Block Grant program (EECBG) is administered by the Office of Energy Efficiency and Renewable Energy within the Department of Energy (DOE). It was authorized in the Energy Independence and Security Act (EISA) of 2007[93] and funded for the first time by the Recovery Act. The EECBG program provides about $3.2 billion in grants to develop, promote, implement, and manage projects to improve energy efficiency and reduce energy use and fossil fuel emissions in local communities. Of this amount, approximately $2.8 billion has been allocated through formula grants to about 2,150 state, local, and tribal

---

[93]The Energy Independence and Security Act (EISA) of 2007 was signed into law on December 19, 2007. Pub.L. No. 110-140, 121 Stat. 1667.

governments (recipients) as of August 23, 2010.[94] Funding is allocated to state recipients based on their population and total energy consumption; to city and county recipients based on their resident and commuter populations; and to Native American tribes based on population and climatic conditions. Eligible applicants for formula EECBG grants include the 50 states; the District of Columbia (the District); five U.S. territories; cities or city equivalents, such as towns or villages with populations of at least 35,000; counties with populations of at least 200,000; and federally recognized Native American tribes. Each state-level recipient must use at least 60 percent of its allocation to provide subgrants to local government units that are not eligible for direct formula grants. In addition to these formula grants, the Recovery Act also includes approximately $400 million in EECBG funding to be awarded on a competitive basis. Competitive grants are designed to stimulate activities that can fundamentally and permanently transform energy markets and sustain themselves beyond the grant period. Our review focuses on the direct formula grants.

DOE Has Obligated Most Funds to Grant Recipients, Who Have Obligated about Half to Subrecipients; Overall Spending Rates Are at 11 Percent

The Recovery Act requires that DOE obligate $2.8 billion in formula EECBG funds by September 30, 2010. DOE has obligated most of the EECBG funds to recipients and has plans to obligate the remainder by the September 30 deadline. As of September 13, 2010, DOE has obligated to recipients more than 99 percent of this amount—$2.77 billion. Nearly all of the approximately 2,150 recipients nationwide—approximately 1,700 cities and counties, 56 states and territories, and 392 tribal communities—have received EECBG funding, with about 68 percent (approximately $1.9 billion) going to cities and counties, 28 percent (approximately $767 million) to states, territories, and the District, and 2 percent (approximately $55 million) to Native American tribes.[95] Steps are being taken to ensure that the remaining funds will be obligated to recipients by the September 30 deadline, and the DOE Inspector General has recently

---

[94]While about 2,350 recipients were authorized to receive EECBG formula funding, only about 2,150 EECBG formula grants were awarded to recipients. This is because about 100 Native American tribes consolidated their funds and were awarded EECBG funds as one group and because, as of July 1, 2010, 64 potential recipients (amounting to about $6.4 million) returned funds or didn't apply for grant funds. The remaining 36 recipients have not yet been allocated grant funds by DOE.

[95]Approximately 2 percent of the formula funding is for competitive grants to cities, counties, and tribes not eligible for direct formula funding.

reported[96] that there is nothing to indicate that DOE's plan to obligate the remaining Recovery Act funding by September 30 will not be effective.

DOE announced the opportunity for interested applicants to submit applications for EECBG formula funding on March 26, 2009. As part of the application process, interested states and local units of government were required to submit an Energy Efficiency and Conservation Strategy (EECS) that described their strategy for achieving the goals of the program. DOE reviewed recipients' EECS and had 120 days to approve or disapprove EECS strategies. DOE officials report that as of July 2010, most recipients have had their EECS plans approved and are now moving from the application to the execution phase. Also, as of July 2010, DOE officials report that EECBG grant recipients have obligated to subrecipients about half ($1.3 billion) of the $2.8 billion awarded to recipients through formula grants. While most recipients are moving to implement projects, recipients awarded larger grant amounts have obligated about twice as much as recipients awarded smaller grant amounts.[97] As of July 2010, the 291 recipients receiving EECBG grants above $2 million have obligated to subrecipients about half (approximately $1.1 billion) of the $1.9 billion awarded to them by DOE through formula grants. The remaining 1,860 or so smaller communities (communities with grants less than $2 million) have obligated only about one-quarter of their EECBG awards (approximately $0.2 billion) of the approximately $0.9 billion awarded to them by DOE through formula grants. To facilitate increased obligations, DOE has encouraged recipients to meet targets of obligating 90 percent or more of their funds by June 25, 2010.

Regarding spending, DOE reports that as of August 2010, about 18 months since the passage of the Recovery Act, recipients have spent about 11 percent (approximately $311 million) of the $2.8 billion authorized for formula funding for the program. Consistent with this, many recipients we visited had spent less than 8 percent of the amount awarded. While many recipients have spent only a small part of their funding, DOE is taking steps to accelerate spending. For example, DOE has encouraged recipients to meet a spending target of 20 percent by September 30, 2010. DOE officials believe this has had a positive impact on spending rates. In particular, DOE officials note that many recipients receiving less than

---

[96]DOE, *Special Report: Review of the Department of Energy's Plan for Obligating Remaining Recovery Act Contract and Grant Funding*, OAS-RA-10-15 (Aug. 4, 2010).

[97]GAO defines larger grant amounts as amounts greater than $2 million.

$250,000 met DOE's target of spending 20 percent as of June 30, 2010—3 months ahead of schedule. DOE officials also note that while spending rates are at 11 percent, much more of the funding is obligated and projects are in the process of being selected and started. They note that the actual costing of the funds for projects is one of the last steps in the process.

EECBG Funds Are to Be Used for a Variety of Energy-Efficient Projects; the Majority of Funds Are Slated for Energy-Efficiency Retrofits, Financial Incentive Programs, and Revolving Loan Funds

DOE placed restrictions on the selection of projects in line with EISA and the activities that funds are to be used for. DOE required that projects be selected from the 14 eligible activities identified in EISA. As of July 28, 2010, as shown in table 9, more than 60 percent of EECBG funds have been obligated for three purposes: energy-efficiency retrofits (35.3 percent), such as replacement of heating and cooling systems in fire stations and libraries in the District;[98] financial incentive programs, such as the rebate program in New Jersey that pays for energy-efficiency retrofits not already covered by existing incentives (15.6 percent); and building and facilities (11.1 percent), such as a geothermal system at a new corrections facility. In many of the communities we visited, energy-efficiency improvements were made to public buildings, but the types of projects selected for implementation in public buildings and facilities varied considerably. For example, projects included improvements to a waste treatment plant, occupancy sensor lighting at public schools, solar trash compactors to reduce the frequency of trash pickup, solar parking meters, and replacement of personal computer workstations with more energy-efficient virtual desktops that reduce both power consumption and environmental waste.

---

[98]To retrofit is to install new or modified parts or equipment not available or considered necessary at the time of manufacture in something previously manufactured or constructed or to adapt to a new purpose or need.

Table 9: EECBG Activity Budgets as of July 28, 2010

Activity	Proposed budget	Percentage of total grant allocation
Energy-efficiency and conservation strategy	$171,912,214	6.1
Technical consultant services	65,885,751	2.4
Residential and commercial buildings and audits	63,927,754	2.3
Financial incentive program	424,609,187	15.2
Energy-efficiency retrofits	958,917,290	34.2
Buildings and facilities	300,729,561	10.7
Transportation	105,925,582	3.8
Codes and inspections	19,292,035	0.7
Energy distribution	40,516,778	1.4
Material conservation program	30,114,903	1.1
Reduction/capture of methane/greenhouse gases	27,091,837	1.0
Lighting	168,743,145	6.0
On-site renewable technology	156,970,165	5.6
Other	157,000,296	5.6
Additional funds yet to be categorized by recipients	*22,343,300*	*0.8*
Competitive grant and administrative costs	*86,020,202*	*3.1*
Total grant allocation	**$2,800,000,000**	**100[a]**

Source: GAO analysis of DOE data.

[a]Percentages may not add due to rounding.

While not required, grant recipients were also encouraged to implement programs and projects that leveraged other public or private resources, enhanced workforce development, persisted beyond the funding period, and promoted energy market transformation, such as revolving loans and energy savings performance contracting.[99] Recipients that we visited indicated that their selection of projects was also based on a variety of additional criteria, including: communities' determination of energy savings; job creation; availability of staff and other resources; the extent to which communities could benefit after Recovery Act funds run out; the ease with which projects could be easily implemented; the potential for return on savings; and populations to be served. For example, the District chose to focus on target populations that they had been unable to serve,

---

[99]In addition, local recipients may use up to 20 percent of their funds, or $250,000, whichever is greater, to establish a Revolving Loan Fund.

such as nonprofits and small businesses. Kent County, Michigan also considered the availability of county staff to complete the project. Several recipients have selected projects that leverage other state energy efficiency programs. For example, in Arizona, EECBG funds were used to take advantage of a program that encourages commercial and government customers to implement energy efficiency projects for which a public utility will pay up to 30 percent of the cost. In addition, a few of the recipients we visited had developed a revolving loan fund to provide low-interest loans for energy-efficient improvements in businesses and commercial buildings and facilities.

Unclear Guidance Has Hampered Project Implementation; DOE Is Taking Steps to Provide Greater Assistance

While many recipients we visited reported that technical assistance, especially that provided by DOE project officers, was helpful, timely, and sufficient, some recipients and DOE project officers we interviewed reported that project implementation guidance, especially early in the process, was unclear and overwhelming and that such guidance has contributed to the delay of project implementation. In particular, several recipients we visited indicated that DOE guidance regarding timeline requirements, drawing down funds, and Buy American requirements was at times unclear, duplicative, and ever-changing. DOE is working to provide greater assistance to recipients that DOE officials believe will increase responsiveness and clarify guidance. In particular, DOE is adding staff in order to reduce the workload of project officers and monitors to give them more time to assist recipients. DOE also recently issued guidance that reduces reporting requirements, reduces workloads, and streamlines communication with recipients.

Regarding timeline requirements, grant recipients reported that DOE's guidance on the timeline for obligating, spending, and drawing down EECBG funds has been confusing. For example, DOE's Funding Opportunity Announcement, as well as its Program Notice 10-011 for the EECBG program, states that EECBG recipients are to obligate all funds within 18 months of the effective date of their award and expend all funds within 36 months of the effective date of their award.[100] Most recipients had been awarded funding in the fall of 2009, and several of the recipients we visited believed they were on track to obligate funds within 18 months

---

[100]DOE, *Funding Opportunity Announcement DE-FOA-0000013 for the Energy Efficiency and Conservation Block Grant Program – Formula Grants* (Mar. 26, 2009). Also in DOE, *Energy Efficiency and Conservation Block Grant Program Notice 10-011* (Apr. 21, 2010).

of the effective date of their award (by the spring of 2011).[101] However, in April 2010, DOE set internal milestones designed to help recipients ensure that they are on track to meeting their obligation and expenditure deadlines. Specifically, DOE requested that recipients have 90 percent of their funds under contract and obligated by June 25, 2010, and to spend a minimum of 20 percent of their funds by September 30, 2010. While DOE reports that some recipients found the guidance useful and that the new guidance was helpful in getting many recipients to obligate funds quickly, several recipients we visited said they were confused by this new guidance. These recipients expressed concern that because of the milestones, they had to obligate funds sooner than expected—instead of having 18 months to obligate funds, they had to have funds obligated in half the time—approximately 9 months after funds had been awarded. In addition, National Association of State Energy Officials (NASEO) representatives said that DOE had not made clear to recipients that the revised timelines were "milestones" and not deadlines and that several recipients had the impression that funds could be taken away if recipients did not meet the revised spending targets.

Regarding requirements on drawing down funds, while DOE reports that many recipients found information on drawing down funds helpful, a few recipients we visited were confused about when they needed to draw down funds to their accounts.[102] These recipients believed that based on DOE guidance, they should draw down their entire award soon after it was awarded. For example, Colorado Springs, Colorado, officials reported that they drew down the entire $3.7 million award as of March 2010 based on their understanding of the Funding Opportunity Announcement, even though they were not yet ready to spend it. In April, a Colorado Springs official realized the mistake, and the city paid back $3.1 million in mid-May 2010. However, in Jackson County, Michigan, local officials also mistakenly drew down their award and told us that when they tried to return the money, DOE required them to make interest payments on the amount. DOE issued guidance on June 23, 2010, in response to recipient questions on drawing down funds.

---

[101]DOE defines the effective date of the award as the date that the DOE contracting officer signed the award document.

[102]Drawing down is the process in which recipients request and receive authorized federal funds for projects under the terms of the grant.

Regarding Buy American requirements, recipients report that guidance on the Buy American requirement was difficult to understand and ever-changing. The Buy American requirement of the act generally requires that grant recipients use iron, steel, and manufactured goods produced in the United States on all Recovery Act-funded projects. However, some recipients found that it was unclear how to comply with the Buy American requirements in a reasonable way and that the guidance was lacking or difficult to understand. For example, Colorado Springs officials said that DOE did not have a list of eligible vendors and that trying to ensure compliance with the Buy American requirement delayed their light emitting diode (LED) street lighting-replacement projects by at least 4 months.[103] For Berks County, Pennsylvania, officials, it was difficult to determine the source of some components of a product and therefore whether the product could be used. NASEO representatives said that DOE's guidance did not provide sufficient detail to enable officials to determine the types of brands or goods they could purchase and that recipients did not have the expertise to trace the supply chain of manufactured goods to determine origin. In recent months, DOE has made numerous attempts to help recipients understand Buy American requirements, including guidance e-mailed to all recipients in May, a webinar in June, and subsequent notice to recipients regarding the guidance. DOE officials did note that they were concerned about providing lists of vendors because that might be viewed as an endorsement of particular vendors at the potential exclusion of other eligible vendors. DOE officials said that DOE cannot recommend specific products, in part, due to the large number of eligible products and because of the potential ethical and liability concerns associated with a federal agency recommending specific manufacturers.

While many recipients have not had problems understanding program requirements and have successfully navigated requirements through training and technical assistance provided by project officers, DOE is working to give project officers the tools to better assist recipients in navigating DOE guidance. In particular, since March and April 2010, DOE has added staff in order to reduce the workload of project officers and monitors, which DOE officials believe has increased its responsiveness to recipients in clarifying guidance. In addition, as of July 2010, DOE is

---

[103] In a June 25, 2010 notice, DOE indicated that it expected to get a list from the National Electrical Manufacturers Association of domestic producers that can meet the Buy American criteria; however, as of August 16, 2010, this information was not yet available.

providing project officers with the Automated Standard Application for Payment (ASAP) reports, so that they can monitor the drawdown of funds. DOE has also recently standardized e-mail distribution lists and provided more frequent communication to recipients.

DOE and States Are Beginning to Monitor Grants, as Many Localities Rely on Existing Controls

DOE monitors grant recipients primarily through its project officers and monitors. DOE project officers and monitors work directly with recipients to provide guidance and evaluate performance. They also gather and analyze information about project planning, implementation, and outcomes to help ensure data quality and to ensure that statutory requirements are met. There are three levels of review: desktop, on-site, and work-site reviews. During desktop monitoring, monitors examine recipients' reports to assess progress and determine compliance with federal rules and regulations, goals, and objectives of the grants and the reporting and tracking of resources expended by the recipient and its subrecipients. During on-site monitoring, monitors review deficiencies identified through routine monitoring and how the recipient is resolving the outstanding quality and operational issues. On-site monitoring may also include interviews with contractors to determine whether follow-up protocols were conducted and deficiencies were corrected. During work-site monitoring, monitors review the project, facility, or building being completed. One of the project officers' key functions is to conduct both on-site and desktop monitoring. DOE monitoring is conducted at minimum frequencies (see table 10), depending on the funding received by the recipient, and can be increased if project officers have sufficient cause, resources, time, and approval of management. In these reviews, project officers evaluate both financial and project status by evaluating financial records, activities, budgets, and spending plans to ensure sufficient progress is being made against planned activities. The monitoring questions were updated on July 30, 2010, downsizing the number of questions asked from over 100 to about 30 questions in on-site reviews and about 6 multi-part questions in quarterly reviews. Now, the desktop monitoring quarterly checklist consists of financial questions such as "For each activity, does the expenditure match, within reason, the amount of work completed?" and programmatic questions such as "For each activity, is the grantee on track to meet performance goals?" DOE is also developing guidance that includes best practices for how states should monitor their subrecipients.

Table 10: DOE Requirements for Frequency of Monitoring

Type of monitoring	Localities receiving greater than $2 million	Localities receiving $1 million to $2 million	Localities receiving $250,000 to $1 million	Localities receiving less than $250,000
Desktop reviews	Monthly	Quarterly	Quarterly	Quarterly
On-site reviews	1-2 per year	1 in the life of the grant	1 in the life of the grant for 25% of the grants	1 in the life of the grant for 10% of the grants
Work-site reviews	As needed	As needed	As needed	As needed

Source: DOE.

As of July 28, 2010, DOE has conducted 3,985 desktop reviews of the EECBG program, and about 170 on-site reviews. Through its monitoring, DOE has found that smaller recipients have been more likely to fail to complete quarterly programmatic and financial reporting to DOE. While 97 percent of larger recipients (recipients with grants greater than $2 million) have completed required quarterly reports due April 30, only 79 percent of recipients receiving less than $250,000 completed quarterly reports.

While DOE monitors its grant recipients (as well as conducts work-site reviews of subrecipients as needed), grant recipients[104] are expected to monitor their subrecipients.[105] While DOE does not expect grant recipients to have a formal monitoring plan, DOE does require that state recipients "develop a sub-granting process...that prevents fraudulent spending"[106] DOE is also developing guidance that includes best practices for how states should monitor their subrecipients. Several of the states we visited do have a formal plan in place for monitoring their subrecipients. A few of the states we visited have begun monitoring their subrecipients. For example, Colorado reviews monthly reports prepared by subrecipients, Michigan project managers review detailed expenditure and employment data submitted by subrecipients on a quarterly basis, and Massachusetts is beginning to monitor subrecipients through regular interactions with subrecipients.

---

[104]Grant recipients may include states, cities, counties, and Native American tribes.

[105]Subrecipients: For states, this term defines nonentitled (to direct federal funding) cities and counties, and for cities and counties, the term typically defines subcontractors and vendors.

[106]In addition, DOE officials told us that DOE is developing guidance that includes best practices on how states should monitor their subrecipients.

DOE also expects localities to have a system for monitoring to ensure that subrecipients comply with EECBG requirements. However, for localities that received direct funding, and as we also found in our May 2010 report on DOE's Weatherization Assistance Program, DOE provides localities with discretion in developing and implementing internal controls, and as a result, several localities we visited did not have a formal monitoring plan in place for monitoring subrecipients or work performed.[107] Many of the localities we visited have developed a system for monitoring, which may include monitoring procedures such as evaluation of the reasonableness of costs, monitoring of building improvements and post-improvement audits, checking payroll for compliance with Davis-Bacon requirements, checking the validity of expenses, and announced and unannounced site visits. However, despite guidance on how to report jobs, it is unclear if all localities' systems for monitoring include measures to ensure the reliability of reported data. For example, in one locality, an official reported that there were no data quality steps to ensure the reliability of the total job count. Another recipient said that it requested greater clarification on what was expected from DOE regarding internal controls but did not get more than a general answer about providing good accountability for the use of funds.

Recipients Face Challenges as They Begin to Report Outcomes While DOE Works to Provide Guidance

EECBG recipients are required to report on outcomes quarterly to DOE on three categories of activity and results metrics. The categories are jobs created or retained; standard programmatic metrics, such as obligations, outlays, and metrics associated with the EECBG activity undertaken;[108] and other critical metrics, such as energy savings and energy cost savings. Recipients report to DOE through its Performance and Accountability for Grants in Energy system (PAGE). In addition, recipients of grants greater than $2 million must report to DOE monthly on funds spent and funds obligated, amount of relevant activity completed, and additional information as required per activity. Several recipients we visited were reporting programmatic metrics such as obligations, expenditures, and jobs created. In addition, several recipients we visited were just beginning to implement projects. However, DOE officials have told us that they are

---

[107]GAO, *Recovery Act: States' and Localities' Uses of Funds and Actions Needed to Address Implementation Challenges and Bolster Accountability*, GAO-10-604 (Washington, D.C.: May 26, 2010).

[108]Standard programmatic metrics are categorized by EECBG activity. For example, a recipient undertaking a building retrofit must report on five metrics—outlay of Recovery Act funding, outlay of non-Recovery Act funding, obligations, number of buildings retrofitted (by sector), and square footage of buildings retrofitted (by sector).

not required to report until the completion of their projects. As a result, several recipients do not yet have data to report for critical outcome metrics such as energy savings and emissions reductions.

Some recipients we visited experienced challenges reporting outcomes using these metrics. For example, in one locality, officials said that they planned to estimate jobs because they do not have hourly contracts. Similarly, in another locality, officials were not aware of how to calculate full-time equivalents (FTE) per OMB guidance. In addition, because they experienced challenges in measuring impact metrics, recipients in Georgia have a variety of methods for calculating a metric value. For example, officials from Columbus, Georgia, stated that energy savings from upgrades to traffic lights will be estimated by making assumptions on the amount of energy used by the original lights compared to improved traffic lights. A Warner Robins, Georgia, official explained the city intends to report project impacts by comparing past monthly utility bills for the water treatment plant to new monthly utility bills. To measure the impact of energy efficiency improvements, Cobb County, Georgia, plans a mixed approach. According to officials, the county will take field measurements of the performance of old equipment prior to removal and replacement equipment as well as use energy models or engineering estimates, including estimates provided by the county's energy audit consultant. Cobb County also intends to use the new energy software procured through the EECBG grant to benchmark and track energy use, cost, and savings and revise calculations based on observed energy usage for each facility. To help ensure consistency, Georgia has provided guidance from DOE to its subrecipients detailing instructions on estimating and reporting energy savings.

In addition, some recipients experienced challenges in the process for reporting metrics, especially due to DOE's reporting system, PAGE. DOE provides resources to assist recipients in navigating the PAGE reporting system on a Web site and offers assistance to recipients via a helpdesk. However, several recipients described the reporting process as overwhelming or frustrating and that reporting was time consuming and required extensive resources. One DOE project official said he would like to see the reporting process streamlined because it is too complicated for recipients. An official from one EECBG locality in California said that if he had known about the extent of the reporting burden, he may not have applied for the grant. In particular, some recipients said the PAGE reporting system was not user-friendly, and others were confused about what to input into the PAGE system. Similarly, one DOE project officer said that it seems that every time recipients log in, there is a new structure or a new report that is required to be filled out. Other grant recipients said that using OMB's federalreporting.gov and DOE's PAGE system is difficult because the systems ask for information to be reported in different ways. In addition, some officials have reported challenges in understanding for how many quarters they are required to report some metrics, especially energy saved once a project has been implemented.

Adding to recipients' frustration about the reporting process has been the volume of contact from various DOE offices about reporting requirements or changes in reporting requirements. For example, one DOE project officer that we spoke with said that grant recipients have expressed frustration at having received so much e-mail about guidance or changes to guidance received from different DOE offices. In addition, in Redding, California, officials initially expressed frustration that questions about reporting guidance required calls to several DOE staff to find the right person to answer their questions. Kent County, Michigan, officials said that reporting has been challenging because of the multiple guidance released and because DOE's PAGE system was not user-friendly.

DOE is beginning to take steps to deal with the amount of guidance and requirements being provided to recipients. DOE plans to issue guidance in August 2010 to assist recipients in navigating the PAGE system, how to correctly categorize metrics and how to interpret and understand financial reporting requirements. In addition, DOE expects to issue formal guidance for the reporting period ending August 30, 2010, in which DOE will no longer require recipients with formula awards greater than $2 million to report obligations and performance metrics on a monthly basis. In addition, all recipients will no longer report hours worked through nonfederal funds or outlays of nonfederal funds on a quarterly basis. DOE estimates that these changes will increase administrative reporting efficiency by approximately 40 percent across the program. In addition, in June 2010, DOE began an effort called "One Voice" that is intended to improve and streamline communication with recipients. This effort will entail the circulation of a weekly newsletter with announcements regarding guidance, training, and events and will also include an effort to streamline communication via e-mail. DOE is also working on developing specific requirements for closing out EECBG grants that should clarify when recipients can stop reporting, and a working group within DOE plans to clarify the energy metrics reporting guidance.

Recipients of State Energy Program Funds Are Beginning to Obligate Funds, Monitor, and Report on Project Outcomes

The Recovery Act appropriated $3.1 billion to the State Energy Program (SEP), which is to be administered by the Department of Energy (DOE) and spent over a 3-year period by the states, U.S. territories, and the District of Columbia (the District) for 56 recipients.[109] The SEP provides funds through formula grants to achieve national energy goals such as increasing energy efficiency and decreasing energy costs. Created in 1996, the SEP has typically received less than $50 million per year. As such, the Recovery Act provided a substantial increase in funding for this program.

Recipients Are Making Progress Obligating Recovery Act Funds

Recipients are making progress obligating SEP funds, according to August 30, 2010, data from DOE. As of August 30, 27 states, territories, and the District of Columbia reported obligating at least 80 percent of their funds, meeting a departmental goal, with another 24 states and territories reporting obligating between 50 percent and 80 percent of their funds. Some states and territories continued to lag in obligating funds—5 states and territories reported obligating less than 50 percent of their funds.

Currently, a limited amount of national data is available on planned or actual state spending trends. DOE officials noted that they would not have final aggregate national spending data until the funds are fully obligated by recipients in late 2010. Until that time, funding may still shift among spending categories. The data provide information on different spending categories that have been recommended by DOE to recipients. The most recent data available in August 2010 indicated that the funds were directed to the following:

- buildings (50 percent)—programs such as school and government improvements, energy-efficiency building code adoption and training, and revolving loan programs.

- electric power and renewable energy (30 percent)—examples include wind turbine deployment, ground source heat pumps, and solar generation.

- industry (8 percent)—programs such as those for energy audits, waste reduction management, water conservation, and manufacturing energy efficiencies.

---

[109]Along with the states, and the District, the U.S. territories American Samoa, Guam, Northern Marianas, Puerto Rico, and the Virgin Islands also received funds.

- policy, planning, and energy security (4 percent), which includes programs such as developing state energy strategic plans, energy policy development, and legislative initiatives.

- transportation (4 percent), which includes programs related to mass transit use, bike to work, telecommuting, and street light replacement.

- energy education (3 percent)—specific programs include those such as curricula development and K-12 education, training workshops, and technical and college course development.[110]

Recipients Are Targeting Recovery Act Funds on a Variety of Different Projects

Nationally, as of August 25, 2010, approximately 75 percent ($2.31 billion) of funds have been obligated by recipients and 10.8 percent ($332 million) have been spent, out of the total $3.07 billion in SEP funds available for grants. Individually, state recipients have reported targeting funds to meet Recovery Act goals such as creating or retaining jobs while also generating-long term benefits such as energy and cost savings. Recipients have prioritized their spending priorities differently:

- California allocated the largest portion of its $226 million in total funds—$110 million—to improve various types of facilities, including residential, municipal, and commercial buildings.

- New York allocated the largest portion of its $123 million in funds—$74 million—for energy conservation projects: energy efficiency, renewable energy, and clean fleets.

- Pennsylvania targeted the largest share of its $99.7 million in funds—$22.8 million—to help leverage private investments from wind energy developers and manufacturers to develop projects through a state wind initiative.

Recipients Are Uncertain of DOE Funding Milestones and Deadlines

Though recipients are making progress meeting DOE funding goals, state energy officials noted uncertainty with meeting changing DOE obligation timetables. For example, in the initial funding announcement sent by DOE on April 24, 2009, DOE stated that funds must be obligated by recipients within 18 months of the award of the grant or face potential cancellation by DOE and spent within 36 months. However, the same guidance also indicates that 100 percent of funds must be obligated by September 30, 2010, to meet departmental and congressional goals. State energy officials noted that DOE later provided an updated correspondence on April 21,

---

[110]Totals do not sum to 100 percent due to rounding.

2010, informing states that they were encouraged to obligate 80 percent of their funds by June 30, 2010, and spend 20 percent by September 30, 2010. DOE officials stated that the June 30 date was meant to help keep states on track to meet the September 30 goal. In many cases, however, states interpreted these dates as new deadlines and were concerned that they would lose access to funds partly because they had experienced pressure from both the administration and the department to meet these new funding milestones. DOE officials stated that they would be unable to deobligate the funds from states if the funding milestones were not met but also stated that they did not know whether funds could be reappropriated if states are unable to obligate those funds by September 30, 2010, as policy guidance has not been provided by the administration and Congress. We have previously reported that DOE has provided unclear funding deadlines for the Recovery Act weatherization program, creating confusion among state recipients trying to meet DOE Recovery Act deadlines.[111]

Lack of Guidance and Other Obstacles Hampered Obligating and Spending Funds

State energy officials told us that delays by DOE in providing guidance hampered early obligating and spending on Recovery Act projects. For example, both Iowa and New York state energy officials noted that they waited for DOE to provide guidance before moving forward on projects. Additionally, other state energy officials we spoke with through the National Association of State Energy Officials (NASEO) stated that while DOE guidance has significantly improved, it was not always timely or complete for issues such as the Recovery Act's Buy American and Davis-Bacon requirements. For example, similarly to the problems noted by EECBG funding recipients, several state energy officials said that while DOE provided broad guidance for meeting Buy American requirements, this guidance did not provide sufficient detail that would enable officials to determine the types of brands or types of goods they could or could not purchase. DOE officials stated that DOE is not capable of recommending specific products requested by recipients partly because of the large number of products requested. Further, DOE officials stated that there were potential ethical and liability concerns associated with a federal agency recommending specific manufacturers.

While the state officials stated that they did ask DOE for further advice, the response was not always timely. As an example, several state energy officials described one Recovery Act project that was held up several

---

[111]GAO-10-604.

weeks in order to determine if energy-efficient lights purchased for the project met Buy American requirements. States further encountered challenges with meeting National Environmental Policy Act (NEPA) and National Historic Preservation Act policies. DOE officials acknowledged that NEPA requirements had added significant time to the process but stated that progress had been made through the use of categorical exclusions for projects.[112] As of August 23, 2010, 87 percent ($2.65 billion) of all SEP Recovery Act-funded projects have been granted categorical exclusions, and 75 percent ($2.31 billion) of funds have been obligated to subrecipients for specific activities. Pennsylvania officials noted that National Historic Preservation Act requirements had slowed some projects but that the situation has improved through an agreement set up between DOE and the state historic preservation offices. While DOE officials have acknowledged they initially lacked the infrastructure necessary for rapid implementation of a SEP, they noted that DOE has made significant improvements in the level of guidance provided to recipients. For example, DOE has developed a Web site to provide information and guidance for recipients to comply with the Buy American requirements.[113] DOE officials further stated that in addition to their guidance, states can also contact their DOE project officer for assistance on meeting Recovery Act and program requirements and deadlines. Overall, state energy officials spoke positively about their project officers, though DOE has only recently filled many of these positions.

Several state energy officials also noted that other obstacles such as the lack of energy management staff has made it more difficult to administer SEP projects. Specifically, District officials stated it was difficult to hire highly qualified people because potential staff did not want to leave a current permanent position for a temporary Recovery Act position that might only last 2 years. Similarly, Iowa officials noted that their efforts were hindered by the loss of two key staff in 2010 and that they did not want to hire staff for a limited duration. Additionally, California's state auditor reported in December 2009 that the state was not prepared to administer Recovery Act funds for the SEP and listed insufficient staffing as one cause for the lack of preparedness. The report also indicated that

---

[112]Categorical exclusions are provided to types (or classes) of actions that normally do not have the potential to cause significant environmental impacts and, thus, are categorically excluded from the need to prepare an environmental assessment or environmental impact statement.

[113]See http://www1.eere.energy.gov/recovery/buy_american_provision.html.

the lack of preparedness raised the potential for misuse of Recovery Act funds.[114] California officials stated that following the state auditor's report, they have since taken actions to address inadequate staffing through the hiring of additional contractors.

Tracking of Recovery Act Spending for SEP Can Take Place Significantly after the Funds Have Been Obligated

Both state recipients and DOE reported that the final reporting of spending of state energy funds can take place significantly after the funds have been obligated and work has begun. For example, District officials told us that school improvements were scheduled for late June, but the funds would not be reported as spent until significantly later because the contractor would not be paid until the work was completed. District officials also noted there would also be an additional delay in reporting the final outlay because the work was being conducted though a sister agency. Pennsylvania officials also reported delays between the time work was performed and the final spending was reported. State officials told us that they reimburse SEP subrecipients on a cost reimbursement system, after work is completed and invoices and proof of payment have been submitted, reviewed, and approved. District and Pennsylvania officials both said that reimbursing costs only after work is completed helps to ensure that the funds are spent appropriately. DOE officials stated that they have tried to increase the speed at which invoices have been paid to better demonstrate the timely use of Recovery Act funds. For example, through program guidance, DOE has encouraged states to pay contractors after specific work milestones have been achieved rather than after the project has been completed.

DOE Is Beginning to Monitor Recovery Act Recipient Spending

DOE officials stated that they are currently on track to meet their monitoring goals. The SEP Recovery Act Monitoring Plan developed by DOE calls for each recipient to be visited twice a year. DOE officials stated that the plan provides guidance for various classes of enhanced monitoring and visitation, but leaves it to the discretion of the DOE field office to plan these trips. DOE state project officers give priority, on a case by case basis, to recipients facing special challenges. The frequency of monitoring may be increased if prior monitoring reports uncovered significant deficiencies in how a recipient is administering and managing its program. Visits to recipients with low obligation or expenditure rates are focused on providing technical assistance to help increase the rates.

---

[114]California State Auditor, Bureau of State Audits, *California Energy Resources Conservation and Development Commission: It Is Not Fully Prepared to Award and Monitor Millions in Recovery Act Funds and Lacks Controls to Prevent Their Misuse,* Letter Report 2009-119.1 (Sacramento, Calif., Dec. 1, 2009).

Overall, DOE officials stated that on-site monitoring will increase as payments grow larger.

DOE also conducts on-site monitoring visits at the subrecipient—local agency—level. DOE's target is to conduct on-site monitoring of about 10 percent of all subrecipients nationwide. However, if the risks to the particular state are higher, then the state would be given closer attention by DOE staff for potential assistance. While DOE does conduct some on-site monitoring of subrecipients, the officials clarified that the main monitoring relationship is between the state recipient, the state energy official, and the DOE project officer. DOE officials stated that they view state recipient monitoring as DOE's main responsibility.

DOE reported that it is on track to meet its monitoring goals:

- As of late June 2010, DOE staffed a total of 29 project officers to 56 recipients, exceeding its goals of one officer per two recipients. Though meeting their goal, DOE officials noted that 12 of these officers had been hired in the past 6 weeks.

- By the end of September 2010, DOE anticipates that all 56 recipients will have received the first of their required annual site visits, with the second follow-up site visit to be performed by the end of the calendar year. In addition to on-site monitoring of the states, project officers are also required to visit between 5 percent and 10 percent of all subrecipients each year.

- To date, DOE has not determined any projects that are "at variance," indicating a high risk for funding misuse.

DOE officials noted that the primary monitoring challenge facing project officers and state recipients during desktop and on-site visits is gathering the quantity of information and other process indicators needed for compliance certification by the project officer. DOE officials stated that assistance from the field offices, the technical assistance provider network, and best practices from the state's own NASEO peer organization are helping to address this situation to assist states in developing effective documentation in a timely manner.

Recipient Monitoring Practices Vary, and Some Recipients Are Just Starting Recovery Act Projects

Planned state recipient monitoring practices vary, and some recipients are just beginning their monitoring activities because they are just starting projects. For example, District officials plan to monitor projects via video and desk monitoring but noted that they have not yet started monitoring in the field. Planned monitoring will focus on ensuring that the work being done is consistent with the agreed-upon scope of work. Additionally, District officials have developed monitoring procedures that will include monitoring checklists of programmatic and financial questions, desktop monitoring, and financial monitoring by the District SEP/Recovery Act financial Officer. Pennsylvania has also developed monitoring procedures; project advisers from state regional offices are assigned to each SEP project and, using an inspection form, conduct initial and final inspections of projects and are encouraged to perform other inspections as needed. Project advisers also communicate on a weekly basis with SEP recipients and update project status in the agency's reporting system.

Some state recipients in our review are also using independent contractors to aid in grant monitoring at varying levels. For example, Colorado, California, and New York all reported hiring outside contractors to supplement their monitoring activities. Colorado hired an outside firm to manage its rebate program for appliances, energy-efficient measures, and renewable-energy systems, citing a need for expertise to handle the large growth in the program due to the addition of Recovery Act funds. Additionally, Colorado also recently issued a Request for Proposal for measurement and verification activities for its grant funds. Due to the significant increase in the size of Colorado energy programs, Colorado officials determined that oversight by state program managers alone is no longer sufficient. California officials set aside $6 million of its $226 million grant to hire contractors to provide, among other things, monitoring, verification, and audit support.

Though still in their early stages of oversight, some state energy officials have noted monitoring challenges. For example, Arizona officials noted that some rural grant recipients were more challenging to monitor due to their remote location. Additionally, Colorado officials told us that detecting fraud in rebate programs is difficult and that while the contractor administering the program has procedures in place to detect fraudulent rebate claims, it is not possible to ensure that 100 percent of the claims will be legitimate. Colorado officials further noted that there was not a clear standard for how to monitor certain programs such as rebate programs. DOE officials have acknowledged that grant programs such as revolving loan programs can require special skill sets to monitor and reported that they are taking steps to provide recipients with technical resources by early September 2010.

DOE and Recipients Have Reported Challenges in Meeting Recovery Act Outcome Reporting Requirements

DOE officials stated that recipients have experienced challenges with meeting Recovery Act reporting requirements. Similar to EECBG, DOE requires monthly and quarterly reporting by SEP recipients to DOE. DOE officials stated that many state recipients have as many as 17 different Recovery Act programs and must coordinate with many different state agencies to fulfill their reporting requirements. In turn, state agencies must also coordinate with local agencies. The officials said that they faced the problem of balancing state and DOE needs with collecting information; asking states to collect too much information would be overly burdensome, while collecting insufficient information would not allow states or DOE to track long-term outcomes. To help decrease the administrative burden of reporting, DOE decreased both its monthly and quarterly reporting requirements effective for the August 30, 2010, reporting deadline. The changes will decrease the amount of job, performance, and funding information reporting required and will help states focus on expending Recovery Act funds.

Both DOE and state energy officials have noted that reporting on outcome measures has been limited because SEP Recovery Act projects are in their early stages. For example, DOE officials stated that SEP recipients first had to report quarterly beginning in January 2010 but that the early reports by recipients did not include many critical metrics, such as total energy saved and dollars savings. DOE officials further stated that because outcomes such as total energy cost savings take time to achieve, and because the state energy offices were still in the initiation phases earlier in 2010, there are few outcomes to report. State officials have also noted that outcome data are currently limited due to the early stage of SEP Recovery Act projects. For example, District energy officials noted that they won't have data on calculating energy savings until projects are complete. Specifically, the District plans to report on energy savings and greenhouse gas emissions by calculating the building square footage, pre- and post-installation utility bills, as well as the energy-savings measures installed and the dollars spent. On-site monitoring will be an important part of the verification process.

State energy officials have indicated difficulties with reporting information into DOE's primary reporting system, PAGE. For example, Iowa noted that PAGE was not compatible with their existing grant management system or other federal reporting systems, which meant that data had to be input twice. DOE's Inspector General also described significant issues with

PAGE in a recent report.[115] Along with other concerns, the report indicated that DOE officials "did not seek input from grant recipients—the system's external users—related to the design of PAGE due to the limited time before the system had to be operational." To assist states with reporting, a NASEO official stated that DOE has asked NASEO to work with each recipient to complete the submissions through PAGE. Additionally, DOE officials stated that the contractor that developed PAGE is providing additional assistance and feedback to the recipients on data entry issues.

DOE's Weatherization Assistance Program

The Recovery Act appropriated $5 billion for the Weatherization Assistance Program, which the Department of Energy (DOE) is distributing to each of the states, the District of Columbia (District), all five territories, and two Indian tribes. According to DOE, during the past 33 years, weatherization has helped more than 6.4 million low-income families by making long-term energy-efficiency improvements to their homes such as installing insulation; sealing leaks; and modernizing heating equipment, air circulation fans, and air conditioning equipment. These improvements enable families to reduce energy bills, allowing them to spend their money on more pressing needs. The Recovery Act appropriation represents a significant increase for a program that has received about $225 million per year in recent years.

During 2009, DOE obligated about $4.73 billion of the Recovery Act's weatherization funding to the states, territories, and tribes, while retaining about 5 percent of funds to cover the department's expenses. Initially, DOE provided each recipient with the first 10 percent of its allocated funds, which could be used for start-up activities such as hiring and training staff, purchasing needed equipment, and performing energy audits of homes, among other things.[116] Before recipients could receive the next 40 percent of their funds, DOE required each to submit a weatherization

---

[115]U.S. Department of Energy, Office of Inspector General, *Management Controls over the Development and Implementation of the Office of Energy Efficiency and Renewable Energy's Performance and Accountability for Grants in Energy System*, OAS-RA-10-14 (July 22, 2010).

[116]During an energy audit, auditors visually inspect the building shell and mechanical systems; conduct diagnostic, health, and safety tests; and record the location, condition, and dimensions of walls, ceilings, floors, windows, doors, and mechanical systems. According to DOE, before work is conducted, auditors should use this information to select cost-effective measures that would make the unit more energy-efficient and prepare work orders to ensure that appropriate measures are installed. After weatherization work is completed, another energy audit and final inspection should be conducted.

plan outlining how it would use its Recovery Act weatherization funds. These plans identified the number of homes to be weatherized and included strategies for monitoring and measuring performance. By the end of 2009, DOE had approved the weatherization plans of all 58 recipients and had provided all recipients with half of their weatherization funds under the Recovery Act.[117] According to DOE officials, as of June 30, 2010, about 166,000 homes have been weatherized nationwide, or about 29 percent of the approximately 570,000 homes currently planned for weatherization. To release the remaining 50 percent of funds, DOE requires that recipients complete weatherizing 30 percent of the homes identified in their weatherization plans and meet other requirements— namely, fulfilling the monitoring and inspection protocols established in its weatherization plan; monitoring each of its local agencies at least once each year to determine compliance with administrative, fiscal, and state policies and guidelines; ensuring that local quality controls are in place; inspecting at least 5 percent of completed units during the course of the respective year; and submitting timely and accurate progress reports to DOE, and monitoring reviews, to confirm acceptable performance. Recovery Act funds are available for obligation by DOE until September 30, 2010, and DOE has indicated that the recipients are to spend their Recovery Act weatherization funds by March 31, 2012.

Recipients' Access to Recovery Act Funding for Weatherization Varies Due to Uneven Progress in Meeting DOE's Requirements

Recipients' ability to access all of their Recovery Act weatherization funding by meeting DOE's requirements varies considerably. DOE records indicate that as of June 30, 2010, 29 states had weatherized at least 30 percent of their total planned units. As of August 2010, DOE reported it had released the remaining 50 percent of funds to 22 states that had met the other requirements.[118] Of the 7 states and the District in our review for the Recovery Act weatherization program, two states, Iowa and Arizona, have been granted access to their remaining 50 percent.[119] In Iowa, DOE

---

[117]June 30, 2010, is the most recent quarter for which the states are required to report data under the Recovery Act. The 58 recipients include all of the states, the District, all five territories, and two Indian tribes.

[118]Based on June production totals, DOE released the remaining 50 percent of funds to 19 states: Arizona, Colorado, Idaho, Illinois, Indiana, Iowa, Maine, Minnesota, Mississippi, Montana, New Hampshire, New Mexico, Nevada, Ohio, Oregon, Tennessee, Vermont, Washington, and Wisconsin. Based on July production totals, DOE released the remaining 50 percent of funds to the following three states: Kentucky, North Dakota, and Wyoming.

[119]Our discussion on weatherization is limited to the following 7 states and the District of Columbia that are the focus of this report: Arizona, California, Florida, Georgia, Iowa, New York, and Pennsylvania.

released about $40.4 million after the state reported its completion of weatherizing 2,179 homes—more than 30 percent of its target of 7,196 homes. Similarly, in Arizona, officials reported the state had weatherized 1,930 homes, about 30 percent of its 6,414 total estimated homes, and gained access to the remaining $28.5 million.

Additionally, other states, such as California and Florida, are close to meeting their 30 percent production targets. Despite a delayed start in spending Recovery Act funds, California reported weatherizing 8,679 homes out of its total estimated production target of 43,150 units as of June 30, 2010. Similarly, Florida officials reported a total of 3,878 single-family residences had been weatherized, or about 20 percent of the total 19,090.[120] Furthermore, both California and Florida officials report they are on track to weatherize 30 percent of their total estimated units by September 30, 2010.

Some recipients that we found to be behind schedule in our May 2010 report, such as the District and Georgia, have since increased their weatherization of units; however, these recipients still have not met production goals requested by DOE.[121] For example, as of March 31, 2010, we found service providers in the District and Georgia had weatherized about 14 percent and 11 percent of homes identified in their state weatherization plans, respectively. By the end of June 2010, although both recipients' production targets were still below DOE's approved goal of 30 percent, the District and Georgia reported they have increased their production to about 25 percent and about 22 percent, respectively.

Some Recipients Still Face Challenges with Implementing Internal Controls to Ensure Program Compliance

Some recipients are still challenged with establishing controls to ensure compliance with weatherization program and Recovery Act requirements. DOE has issued guidance requiring recipients of Recovery Act weatherization funds to implement a number of internal controls to mitigate the risk of fraud, waste, and abuse. In our May 2010 report, we recommended that DOE should develop best practices for key internal controls that should be present at the local weatherization agency level to ensure compliance with key program requirements.[122] DOE provides

---

[120]As of June 30, 2010, the agency responsible for administering the Recovery Act weatherization program had not yet approved weatherization of multifamily residences, but it reported having received proposals.

[121]See GAO-10-604.

[122]See GAO-10-604.

recipients with the discretion to develop and implement these internal controls in accordance with each state's weatherization plan. Local agencies use various methods to prevent fraudulent or wasteful use of Recovery Act funds, such as conducting risk assessments.

Since our last report, we have identified challenges in the implementation of internal controls for some local weatherization agencies. For example, in the District, we conducted client file reviews and found that while some weatherization project data were not present in the physical files, much, but not all, of this data was in an online software system used to manage weatherization projects. While the online system appeared to be a useful tool in managing weatherization projects, it has not yet been fully implemented and does not contain all of the data necessary to track individual weatherization projects from start to finish. As a result, at the time of our review, neither the physical files nor the online weatherization management system presented a complete record of weatherization projects. District officials reported that they conducted inspections of local weatherization agencies in early July 2010—roughly 2 weeks after our review—and found that all agencies they reviewed had copies of all required documentation in the physical files. Additionally, District officials reported they are continuing to fully implement the online reporting system and address issues associated with incomplete data. In Florida, the state agency responsible for administering the program had instituted various management controls over the program, but our review of two local weatherization agencies revealed internal control gaps and compliance issues similar to those identified in our May 2010 report.[123] For example, weatherization work done was often not consistent with the recommendations of home energy audits and no reasons were given for the differences; in some instances, work was charged to the program but not done or lacked quality; several potential health and safety issues were not addressed; and contractors' prices were not being compared to local market rates, as required by the state weatherization agency. State officials have acknowledged these problems and have taken steps to address the problems, including changing procedures and guidelines and instructing contract field monitors to be more attentive to these issues. The two local weatherization agencies we reviewed also agreed to take corrective actions.

[123]See GAO-10-604.

Most States We Reviewed Have Varying Levels of Monitoring Procedures

Most of the states we reviewed have oversight procedures in place to monitor local agencies; however, the level of monitoring varies considerably. DOE requires state weatherization agencies to conduct on-site monitoring of all weatherization service providers to inspect the management of funds and the production of weatherized homes at least once a year. These monitoring visits consist of a financial review of the service provider's records pertaining to salaries, materials, equipment, and indirect costs; program reviews of the service provider's records, contracts, and client files; and a production review, consisting of the inspection of weatherized homes by the state agencies and by the service provider. In our May 2010 report, we recommended that DOE set time frames for development and implementation of state monitoring programs; DOE generally agreed with this recommendation and indicated it will take steps to address this issue.

We found in the states we reviewed that levels of monitoring varied considerably. Some state monitoring plans are fully implemented. For example, in Arizona, state officials reported program monitors conduct file reviews of all completed units each month using a statewide database. Also, program monitors visit each of the 10 service providers at least once a month, exceeding DOE's requirement of yearly visits to local service providers. Iowa officials reported inspecting at least 5 percent of the weatherized homes for each local agency and providing monitoring at 15 of 18 local agencies.

In contrast, monitoring procedures in other states have either just been fully implemented or are still facing challenges. We identified some issues in our May 2010 report related to weatherization monitoring in Georgia. Some monitoring positions remained vacant, and oversight of the providers had been slow to start.[124] However, state officials at the agency responsible for the weatherization assistance program have since taken steps to address these issues. Specifically, they told us that their contractor had filled all monitoring positions, and all 22 of its providers have received monitoring visits. Additionally, Pennsylvania officials are still facing challenges. For example, state officials reported weatherization program monitors are not in compliance with some Recovery Act monitoring procedures, and they are not getting about half of their monitoring reports back to the agencies within 30 days of the site visit. DOE reported the need for Pennsylvania's department responsible for

---

[124]See GAO-10-604.

administering the program to improve the financial management system to better track actual costs for each unit weatherized on a service provider basis. State officials reported they are working on corrective actions to address these concerns by August 2010.

Finally, some recipients, such as California and the District, were delayed in spending Recovery Act weatherization funds and have just begun to implement monitoring efforts. For example, in California, program officials recently began on-site monitoring of Recovery Act activity in June 2010, and by July 31, they visited seven of the 38 service providers. Additionally, program officials also conduct quarterly performance visits as needed for providers with production deficiencies, monthly Recovery Act expenditure and performance analyses, fiscal monitoring, on-site monitoring of whistleblower complaints and high-risk agencies, and Davis-Bacon on-site reviews to ensure employees are paid appropriately and paperwork is in compliance. Similarly, District officials reported a number of monitoring procedures are in place, such as annual monitoring reviews of local weatherization agencies and site inspections of at least 10 percent of weatherized units. District officials told us that, as of July 15, 2010, their program managers had conducted monitoring visits of all seven local weatherization agencies, and program auditors had begun conducting site inspections for the quality assurance of work completed by contractors.

Some States Are Measuring Long-Term Energy Savings Resulting from the Recovery Act Weatherization Funds, While Others Are Still in Development

With respect to energy cost savings, some states are actively measuring energy savings, while others are beginning to develop methods to do so. As with EECBG and SEP, weatherization recipients are required to report on different program metrics, both monthly and quarterly. A long-term goal of the weatherization program is to increase energy efficiency through cost-effective weatherization work, and DOE relies on its recipients to ensure compliance with this cost-effectiveness requirement. For example, in Arizona, the agency responsible for administering the weatherization program calculates the estimated kilowatt hour usage reduction and utility costs savings resulting from weatherization work performed on homes. As of June 2010, officials estimated that Recovery Act weatherization services have resulted in approximately $267,000 in savings for the residents in the 1,930 homes weatherized. Florida officials reported contracting with the University of Florida to conduct a study of overall energy savings utilizing consumption data obtained from clients' utility bills. Alternatively, District officials are still developing a methodology to capture energy savings for weatherized homes. In July 2010, Georgia officials stated it had begun using a Web-based reporting tool to track real-time information on energy savings. In addition, program monitors will track and compare energy costs after weatherization work has been completed for 3, 6, and 12 months. While California estimated annual energy savings of about $1.5 million resulting from Recovery Act funds, state officials currently do not anticipate attempting to calculate actual energy savings and noted that they would like more guidance from DOE on its effort to study energy savings.

DOE Generally Agreed with the Recommendations Issued in Our May 2010 Report and Has Taken Some Steps toward Implementation

In our May 2010 report, we provided eight recommendations and raised concerns about whether program requirements were being met.[125] DOE generally agreed with all of our recommendations and has begun to take several steps in response. For example, DOE reported that it has drafted national workload standards to address our concerns regarding training, certification, and accreditation. DOE plans to issue these standards to recipients in October 2010. DOE is still in the process of considering our recommendations and will provide additional information on how they plan to fully implement our recommendations at a later date.

Housing Agencies Have Been Using Recovery Act Funds for a Variety of Projects, and HUD's Initial Monitoring Efforts Have Identified Problems with Obligations for Some Projects

Competitive Grants for Public Housing Capital Fund Have Supported a Variety of Projects

The Recovery Act requires the U.S. Department of Housing and Urban Development (HUD) to distribute nearly $1 billion to public housing agencies based on competition for priority investments, including investments that leverage private sector funding or financing for renovations and energy conservation retrofitting. In September 2009, HUD awarded 396 competitive grants in the amount of $995 million to 212 public housing agencies. (Subsequently, three housing agencies returned competitive grants totaling approximately $14 million to HUD). The Recovery Act required housing agencies that received competitive grants to obligate 100 percent of their competitive grant funds within 1 year of the date when competitive funds became available to agencies for obligation, which means they have until September 2010 to obligate 100

---

[125]See GAO-10-604.

percent of their funds.[126] As of August 7, 2010, 179 housing agencies reported obligations totaling about $460.1 million for 340 grants. This reflects about 46.3 percent of the total Public Housing Capital Fund competitive funds allocated to them (see fig. 24). In addition, there were 57 grants (14 percent) located at 39 housing agencies for which no competitive funds had been obligated. Further, another 102 grants (26 percent) had less than 20 percent of their funds obligated. As the September 2010 obligation deadline approaches, HUD officials said they are working to ensure that housing agencies meet the deadline, but expect that some housing agencies may not. HUD will recapture any funds not obligated by the deadline and return them to the Department of the Treasury. One hundred forty-four housing agencies had also drawn down funds to pay for project expenses already incurred. As of August 7, 2010, these 144 public housing agencies had drawn down about $93.5 million, or about 9.4 percent of the total allocated to them. The Recovery Act required housing agencies to expend 60 percent of obligated funds within 2 years and expend 100 percent of Recovery Act funds within 3 years of the initial date when funds were provided to agencies for obligation.

[126]HUD awarded the competitive grants to housing agencies at varying dates in the month of September 2009. As a result, the 1-year deadlines for obligating these funds vary by category of competitive grant. The deadlines include September 8, 2010, September 22, 2010, September 23, 2010, and September 27, 2010.

Figure 24: Percentage of Public Housing Capital Fund Competitive Grants Allocated by HUD That Have Been Obligated and Drawn Down Nationwide as of August 7, 2010

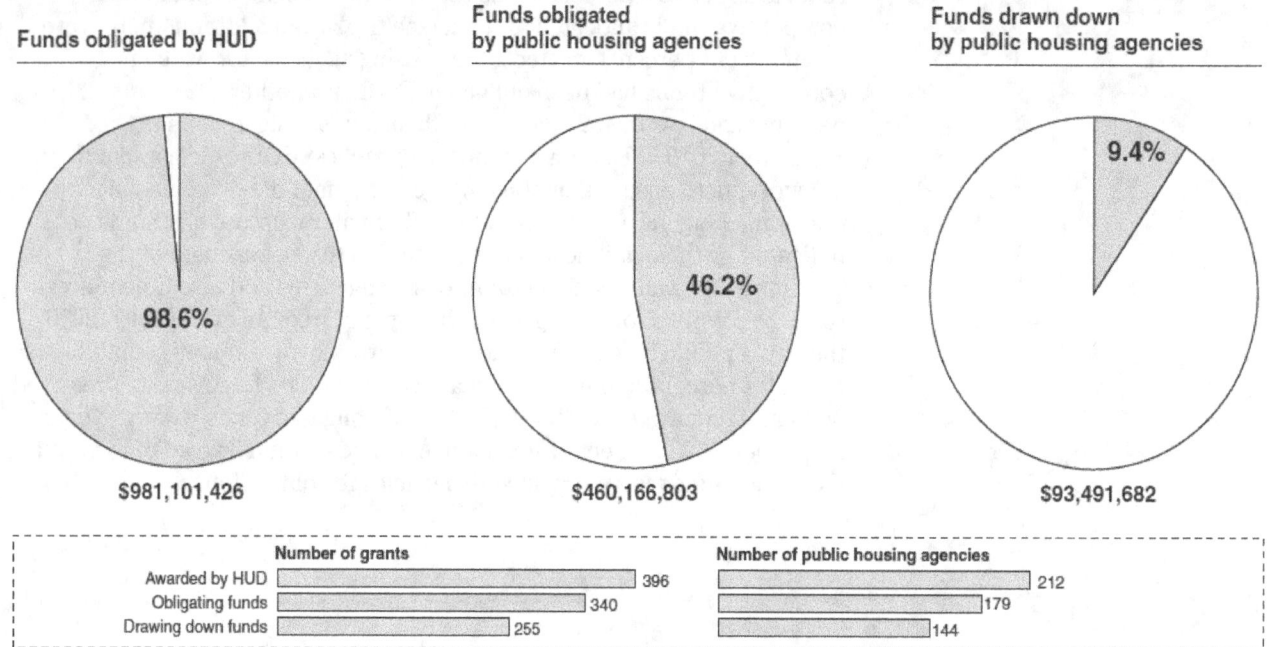

Funds obligated by HUD

98.6%

$981,101,426

Funds obligated by public housing agencies

46.2%

$460,166,803

Funds drawn down by public housing agencies

9.4%

$93,491,682

	Number of grants		Number of public housing agencies
Awarded by HUD	396		212
Obligating funds	340		179
Drawing down funds	255		144

Source: GAO analysis of data from HUD's Electronic Line of Credit Control System.

More specifically, housing agencies have been using their competitive grants for the creation of energy-efficient communities, gap financing for projects stalled because of financing issues, public housing transformation, and improvements addressing the needs of the elderly or persons with disabilities:

- For the creation of energy-efficient communities, HUD awarded 36 grants totaling $299.7 million for substantial rehabilitation or new construction and 226 grants totaling $305.8 million for moderate rehabilitation. For example, in New Jersey funds are to be used to incorporate green features in two new buildings with public housing units. Some of the energy-efficient features of the project include water conserving fixtures, Energy Star lighting packages in all interior units, and Energy Star or high-efficiency commercial grade fixtures in all common areas, as well as daylight sensors or timers on all outdoor lighting. In Massachusetts, funds are to be used to reduce the annual energy and water costs of more than $4,000 per unit in a physically distressed site. The project will redevelop a portion of the site into innovative, high-efficiency affordable housing for current residents with the new construction of 96 affordable rental units and a community center.

- For gap financing for projects that were stalled due to financing issues, HUD awarded 38 grants totaling $198.8 million.[127] For example, in Pennsylvania, $10 million in funds are to be used to construct 50 units of a 101-unit development that will be a mixture of walk-up and duplex apartments and three-scattered site buildings replacing a high-rise building demolished in 2008.

- For public housing transformation, HUD awarded 15 grants totaling $95.9 million to revitalize distressed or obsolete public housing projects. For example, in Illinois, funds are to be used on a multiphase, mixed-finance project that will build public housing, rental, and for-sale apartments and houses on housing agency land and vacant city lots.

- For improvements addressing the needs of the elderly or persons with disabilities, HUD awarded 81 grants totaling $94.8 million. For example, in Texas, funds are to be used to complete work on common areas to make them accessible and ADA-compliant, upgrade and improve space used for supportive services, and add energy-efficient lighting, heating, ventilating, and air conditioning in properties housing the elderly. In California, funds are to be used to provide upgrades to nine dwelling units for accessibility improvements for the elderly and disabled, as well as improvements to common spaces used for supportive services targeted to those residents.

As discussed above, HUD officials expect that some housing agencies may not meet the September 2010 competitive grant obligation deadline. They noted that among all the competitive grant projects nationwide, the 75 grants supported by mixed-financing have been at greatest risk of missing the obligation deadline. HUD's Office of Urban Revitalization has assigned a grant manager to each of the mixed-finance competitive grant projects to track and monitor their progress. Officials with 5 of the 10 housing agencies we visited that had received competitive grants told us they were experiencing challenges related to mixed-financing of their projects, but they still anticipated meeting the deadline. Because funding for these projects comes from multiple sources, if one financing party is not able to

---

[127]Gap financing is the process of providing funding to housing agencies for projects that are ready to proceed but are stalled due to the inability of the housing agency to obtain anticipated private funding for the projects.

finalize its part of the contract by the obligation deadline, the housing agency will not be able to close on the contract. As a result, the housing agency would not be able to obligate its competitive grant funds on time and the funds would be recaptured. For example, one housing agency is relying on a 4 percent low-income housing tax credit to pay for about $10 million of the $40 million cost for the first phase of its project. The 4 percent tax credit was contingent on the state selling tax-exempt bonds, and according to HUD field office officials, the state's difficulty doing so had prevented the housing agency from securing the tax credit. State officials told us they notified the project developer on August 5, 2010, that the tax-exempt bonds, which will generate the tax credits, had been approved, which would allow the housing agency to submit its final paperwork to HUD by September 18, 2010.

Additionally, HUD field staff have taken several steps to assist public housing agencies in obligating Recovery Act competitive grant funds by the September 2010 deadline. HUD field officials told us that they have been communicating regularly with housing agencies via e-mail and telephone to address their questions, provide technical assistance, and monitor their progress. For example, field staff in one field office in Texas use weekly conference calls to communicate with all of the housing agencies in their jurisdiction and answer their questions about obligation-related issues for competitive grants. The officials also told us they have dedicated three staff to work with the five public housing agencies under their jurisdiction that received 14 competitive grants. HUD field staff in Illinois have contacted each competitive grant recipient in their region on a weekly basis and use an internal tracking sheet to monitor progress. HUD officials in Massachusetts have provided additional oversight to smaller housing agencies to help them better understand federal procurement policies. Based in part on these efforts, HUD field staff believed that housing agencies in Massachusetts would meet the September 2010 obligation deadline.

As we note in our May 2010 Recovery Act report, HUD plans to redistribute $17.16 million of competitive and formula grant funds that were rejected or returned by housing agencies by awarding a new set of competitive grants.[128] HUD plans to redistribute these funds to qualified housing agencies that previously applied for competitive grants but did not receive them because HUD had obligated all of the nearly $1 billion allocated to the program. Given HUD's emphasis on green, energy-efficient housing, HUD will limit the redistribution of funds to those applications for energy retrofit projects. Prior to funding any of the remaining applications, HUD planned to verify that potential recipients still would be able to complete the work outlined in their original applications and that they currently are in compliance with Recovery Act requirements. Of the 23 public housing agencies that HUD has contacted and verified their eligibility to receive additional competitive grant funds, 22 agencies accepted the additional funds. According to HUD officials, they may be able to redistribute these funds by the end of fiscal year 2010. According to HUD officials, once the housing agencies receive the redistributed funds, housing agencies must obligate 100 percent of the funds within 1 year, expend 60 percent within 2 years, and expend 100 percent within 3 years.

Public Housing Capital Fund Formula Grants Have Also Supported a Variety of Projects

The Recovery Act required HUD to allocate $3 billion through the Public Housing Capital Fund to public housing agencies using the same formula for amounts made available in fiscal year 2008. HUD allocated Capital Fund formula dollars to 3,134 public housing agencies shortly after passage of the Recovery Act and, after entering into agreements with housing agencies, obligated these funds on March 18, 2009. As we previously reported, all housing agencies met the March 17, 2010, obligation deadline for formula grants by either obligating all of their funds or rejecting or returning a portion of the funds.[129] The Recovery Act also required that public housing agencies expend 60 percent of their formula funds within 2 years from when the funds became available and expend 100 percent of their formula grant funds within 3 years from when the funds became available. Housing agencies have been making progress in drawing down funds in accordance with these deadlines. According to HUD data, as of August 7, 2010, 3,075 housing agencies had drawn down funds totaling more than $1.6 billion from HUD, or about 55 percent of the

---

[128]According to HUD officials, funds that are recaptured from housing agencies after passage of the Dodd-Frank Act will have to be returned to the Department of the Treasury (because of congressional concerns about debt reduction, the Dodd-Frank Act required unobligated Recovery Act funds to be returned to the Treasury). However, because the initial $17.16 million in returned formula and competitive grant funds was returned to HUD before passage of the act, HUD is still able to redistribute them to other housing agencies.

[129]According to HUD officials, 21 housing agencies refused to accept or returned to HUD approximately $3.26 million in Recovery Act formula grant funds.

total allocated to the housing agencies, to pay for project expenses already incurred (see fig. 25).

Figure 25: Percentage of Public Housing Capital Fund Formula Grants Allocated by HUD That Have Been Obligated and Drawn Down Nationwide as of August 7, 2010

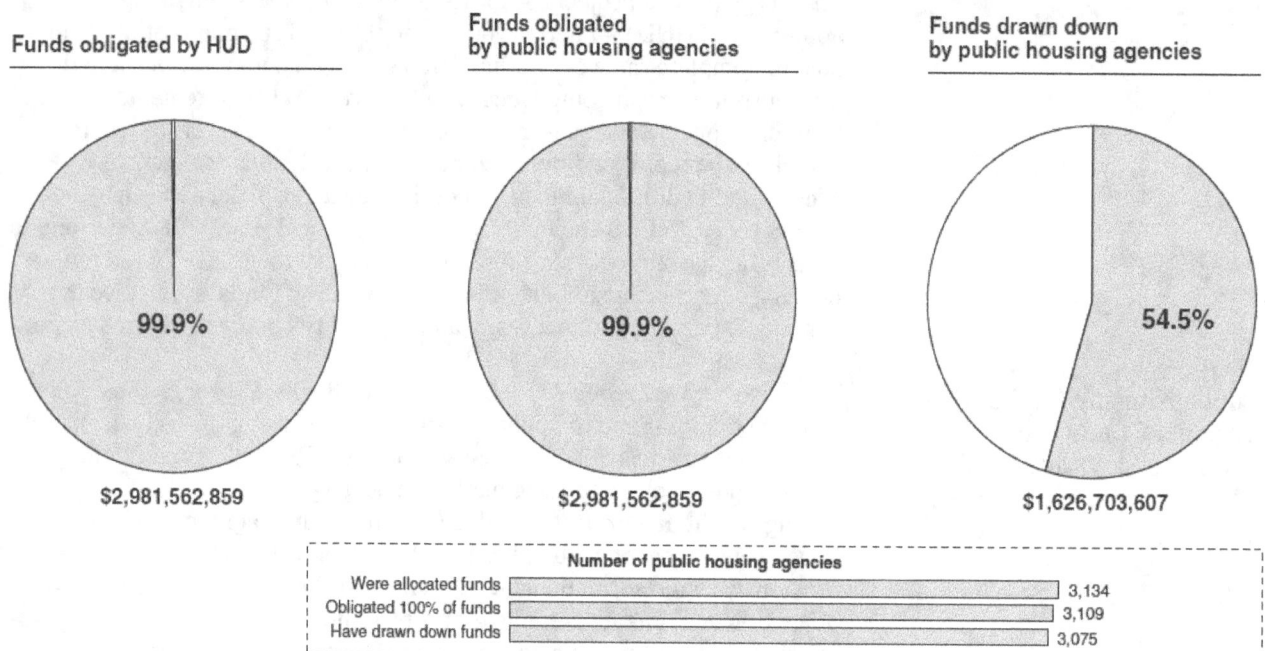

Funds obligated by HUD

99.9%

$2,981,562,859

Funds obligated by public housing agencies

99.9%

$2,981,562,859

Funds drawn down by public housing agencies

54.5%

$1,626,703,607

Number of public housing agencies

Were allocated funds	3,134
Obligated 100% of funds	3,109
Have drawn down funds	3,075

Source: GAO analysis of data from HUD's Electronic Line of Credit Control System.

Public housing agency officials said they have been using these funds to support a variety of improvement projects at public housing sites, including performing roofing and gutter work, replacing windows and doors, rehabilitating unit interiors, and replacing heating, cooling, and hot water systems. For example, a housing agency in California used formula funds to rehabilitate vacant units at two sites quickly to make them available for lease to prospective low-income tenants. Work at both sites included repairing damaged walls, ceilings, and floors; removing old plumbing fixtures; replacing tile and appliances; and painting the interiors of units (see fig. 26).

Figure 26: Before and After Photographs of the Alice Griffith Project in San Francisco, California

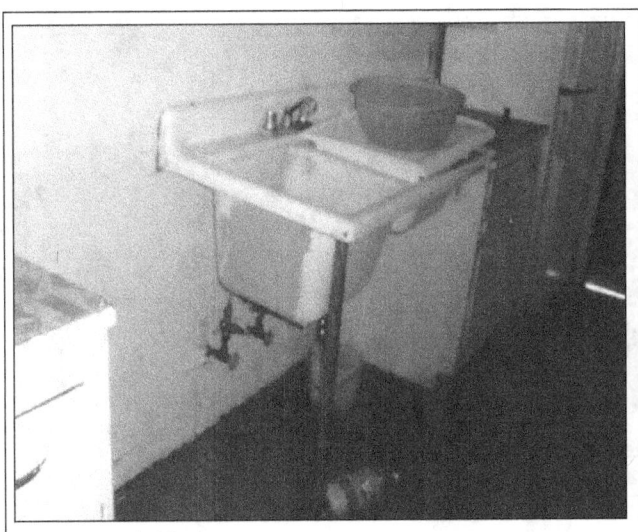

Sink prior to rehabilitation

Sink after rehabilitation

Source: San Francisco Housing Authority.

In Pennsylvania, a housing agency is using formula funds to rehabilitate 23 row houses on the last remaining blighted block adjacent to a large redevelopment the housing agency had already completed. Combined with the previous redevelopment, once this project is complete, there will be more than 700 total units in an approximate four square block area. Work on the last block of the development began in March 2010 (see fig. 27). According to housing agency officials, this redevelopment project not only has provided additional public housing units, but also has increased property values for row homes in the area from $40,000 or $50,000 to asking prices of up to $125,000.

Figure 27: Public Housing Rehabilitation Using Recovery Act Capital Fund Competitive Grant in Philadelphia, Pennsylvania

Public housing units under rehabilitation

Public housing units previously rehabilitated

Source: GAO.

Results of HUD's Initial Second Year of Monitoring Efforts Have Identified Few Problems with Housing Agencies' Obligations of Funds

HUD has employed multiple monitoring efforts for Recovery Act funds and has found that only a few housing agencies had deficiencies relating to their obligations. For the second year of implementation, HUD's strategy for monitoring Recovery Act formula and competitive grant funds includes a combination of remote and on-site reviews of housing agencies' administration of Recovery Act requirements, the same approach it used for monitoring housing agencies during the first year of the Recovery Act. Specifically for the formula grant funds, HUD developed a four-tier monitoring approach that includes

- quick-look reviews of all Recovery Act formula grant obligation documents generated from February 26, 2010, to March 17, 2010, by 543 housing agencies that had obligated less than 90 percent of formula grant funds as of February 26, 2010. HUD completed the quick-look reviews in July 2010;[130]

---

[130]HUD was concerned that housing agencies may not have followed proper procedures or may have directed funds to ineligible uses in the rush to meet the March 17, 2010, formula grant obligation deadline. HUD officials decided to review the obligation documents of those housing agencies that obligated the majority of their funds just prior to the deadline. These quick-look reviews were conducted by HUD field staff using a checklist that included questions such as whether necessary approvals were in place for work items and whether obligations correspond to work items in the housing agency's approved annual plan.

- on-site and remote reviews. Housing agencies currently designated as troubled will have a minimum of one on-site review. Housing agencies that are nontroubled may be subject to additional remote or on-site reviews depending upon factors including having open audit findings, failing to expend funds in prior years, and having procurement-related deficiencies such as not revising procurement policies to reflect Recovery Act requirements. HUD anticipates that about 25 percent of grant recipients will be subject to these reviews, which the agency plans to complete by February 2011;
- quality assurance and quality control reviews by HUD's Office of Field Operations, which HUD plans to conduct between December 2010 and March 2011; and
- independent reviews (performed by an outside contractor) of housing agencies that HUD identified as being the top 100 to 125 funded agencies with the largest formula grant award amount. The independent reviews are to be completed by June 2011.

According to HUD officials, as a result of its quick-look reviews of 543 housing agencies, HUD staff identified 26 housing agencies that were potentially deficient in meeting HUD requirements for obligating formula grant funds and required further review. For example, some housing agencies signed contracts to obligate funds after the March 17, 2010, deadline. HUD staff also determined that some housing agencies obligated funds for products and services that were not approved for Recovery Act use, such as paying the local police department to provide security services. In addition, HUD staff identified 24 housing agencies with minor deficiencies that did not warrant further review. Finally, there were 22 housing agencies that did not submit final documentation requested by HUD staff for the quick-look reviews. HUD plans to conduct on-site reviews of those housing agencies if they do not submit the requested documentation.

HUD created a panel comprised of officials from its Office of Field Operations, Office of Capital Improvements, and Office of General Counsel to examine in greater detail those 26 housing agencies with potential deficiencies identified via the quick-look reviews, as well as potential deficiencies identified by other means. Of the 26 housing agencies, the panel determined that deficiencies at 8 housing agencies were significant and necessitated a recapture of funds. As of August 27, 2010, the panel reviews identified approximately $1 million in Recovery Act funds that necessitated recapture. HUD is in the process of recapturing these funds and will return them to the Department of the Treasury. HUD plans to continue conducting panel reviews and will recapture Recovery Act funds from any housing agency found to have deficiencies.

HUD adopted a similar multireview approach for its second-year monitoring of Recovery Act competitive grant funds. HUD has been conducting remote reviews of all 393 competitive grants and had planned to complete them by August 20, 2010. As of August 23, 2010, HUD field staff reported having completed 371 remote reviews of competitive grants. HUD officials are in the process of analyzing the results of these reviews. While HUD officials have not completed their reviews, as of August 27, 2010, the agency may recapture approximately $12 million in competitive grant funds based on remote review findings and other means. For example, after reviewing one project's proposed building site, HUD staff found that the project would be located in an industrial space next to a railroad track with little access to roadways, raising both transportation and environmental concerns. HUD also plans to conduct quality assurance and quality control reviews for a random sample of 20 to 25 percent of the remote reviews, which HUD plans to complete by September 2010. In October and November 2010, HUD also plans to review obligations made by housing agencies that had not fully obligated their grant funds within 2 weeks of the September 2010 deadline. Finally, from January to March 17, 2011, HUD plans to conduct on-site reviews of all eight housing agencies that received competitive grant funds and were designated as troubled as of September 30, 2009. Given that less than half of the competitive grant funds have been obligated to date, we believe that it is important for HUD to continue to closely monitor progress in meeting the obligation deadline. In addition, because HUD identified some deficiencies among those housing agencies that obligated their formula grant funds near the deadline, we believe it will be important for HUD also to review those competitive grant obligations made by housing agencies just prior to the deadline.

As part of its second-year strategy, HUD developed a management plan for the administration of Recovery Act funds, including the need for an additional 11 FTEs to carry out Recovery Act responsibilities. This was in response to our March 2010 recommendation that HUD develop such a plan to address its resource needs for both the Recovery Act funds and the existing Capital Fund program.[131] Similarly, HUD's Office of Public and

---

[131]GAO, *Recovery Act: One Year Later, States' and Localities' Uses of Funds and Opportunities to Strengthen Accountability*, GAO-10-437 (Washington, D.C.: Mar. 3, 2010).

Indian Housing also agreed to develop a management plan addressing the activities and resources needed to administer its existing Capital Fund program. In July 2010, HUD provided us with its management plan for the Public Housing Capital Fund program. The plan summarized the key activities HUD undertakes to monitor and facilitate the use of these funds by program area, including rule and policy development, planning, program awards, program management, technical assistance, and reporting. The plan also included the specific activities, tasks, and resources used for each of these existing program areas, identifying approximately 91 existing FTEs in its headquarters and field offices to support these activities. According to HUD's management plan, HUD's current staffing level is sufficient to manage its existing Capital Fund program, but the agency could more efficiently utilize its current resources. As a result, HUD plans to realign current staff to focus on its core missions, including Recovery Act responsibilities.

HUD's management plan for its existing Capital Fund program states that HUD currently has the staff and resources required to effectively implement its core programs. However, officials in two HUD field offices we visited stated that they revised their oversight strategies for their regular programs to accommodate Recovery Act work. For example, officials in one HUD field office told us that most of the field office's resources have been devoted to the Recovery Act and, as a result, staff have done less on-site monitoring of non-Recovery Act grant recipients. However, the officials noted that their staff still have been conducting remote monitoring of all recipients, although staff have not conducted any asset management reviews of grant recipients this year.[132] At another HUD field office, an official told us that since the Recovery Act was passed, Recovery Act work has been a top priority for HUD nationwide. He noted that other housing work, especially conducting on-site reviews, has been deferred to meet Recovery Act requirements. According to HUD headquarters officials, as a consequence of field office monitoring of Recovery Act requirements, field staff conducted reviews (on-site or remote) of every housing agency in the country, something they would not have accomplished in the course of their routine monitoring activities. HUD officials also stated that field staff were able to strengthen housing agency officials' knowledge of contract administration and forge stronger

---

[132]Asset management reviews examine how the asset is being managed in areas including whether the housing agencies are renting to the types of tenants specified by the terms of HUD funding, or whether the asset is being maintained in accordance with HUD safety standards.

relationships with a greater number of housing agencies as a result of their Recovery Act oversight.

HUD Has Taken Additional Action to Improve Quality of Recipient Reported Data

HUD officials told us they have been using the same quality review procedures for the fourth recipient reporting period as they did for the third reporting period. However, HUD also issued additional guidance to recipients to help them more accurately report job-related data. Although HUD does not play a direct role in compiling the recipient data, officials noted they continued to support recipients' report preparation by providing technical assistance, including issuing guidance, conducting conference calls, manning a call center, and transmitting regular e-mail correspondence. Officials also told us that their data quality reviews of recipient reports continued to include automated data checks to flag values in specific fields that were incorrect or that fell outside of parameters that HUD had defined as reasonable and to generate comments notifying housing agencies of the potential errors. HUD officials told us that they also have been using the same processes from the third reporting period for checking for and addressing errors in job-count totals for the fourth reporting period. The officials noted that their on-time reporting rate for the fourth reporting period was high and their error rate continues to decline with each reporting cycle. We are in the process of assessing the transparency of information reported in Recovery.gov for three HUD Recovery Act programs, including formula grants awarded through the Public Housing Capital Fund program.

As we reported in May 2010, officials with two housing agencies reported using an out-of-date version of HUD's jobs-counting calculator for the third round reporting period. To ensure that housing agencies use the correct jobs calculation, we recommended that HUD clearly emphasize to housing agencies that they discontinue use of the outdated jobs calculator provided by HUD in the first round of recipient reporting. In response to our recommendation, HUD sent an e-mail to housing agencies on June 30, 2010, that explicitly instructed them not to use the outdated jobs-counting calculator, as it was not correctly computing the FTE calculation per updated OMB guidance. This e-mail also included a link to HUD's new online jobs-counting calculator and instructed housing agencies to use this calculator for the July, and all future, reporting periods.

OMB's December 2009 guidance states that to the maximum extent practicable, job information should be collected from all subrecipients and vendors in order to generate the most comprehensive and complete job impact numbers available. As we reported in May 2010, for the third reporting period, at least one housing agency did not report job information for subcontractors even when the subcontractors were providing essential goods and services for Recovery Act-funded projects. We recommended that HUD issue guidance to housing agencies that explains when the prime recipient should report FTEs attributable to subcontractors. In response to our recommendation, HUD notified housing agencies in a June 30, 2010, e-mail that it had developed additional guidance for housing agencies to use when determining whether prime recipients should report FTEs for subcontractors and provided a link to the guidance on its Web site. The guidance noted that housing agencies should include Recovery Act-funded hours that contractors and subcontractors worked as part of their FTE calculation.

HUD and Treasury Continue Making Progress Outlaying TCAP and Section 1602 Program Funds, but Opportunities Exist to Improve Plans for Oversight and Meeting Challenging Project Spending Deadlines

The Recovery Act established two funding programs that provide capital investments to Low-Income Housing Tax Credit (LIHTC) projects: (1) the Tax Credit Assistance Program (TCAP) administered by HUD and (2) the Grants to States for Low-Income Housing Projects in Lieu of Low-Income Housing Credits Program under Section 1602 of the Recovery Act (Section 1602 Program) administered by the Department of the Treasury (Treasury).[133] Before the credit market was disrupted in 2008, the LIHTC program provided substantial financing in the form of third-party investor equity for affordable rental housing units.[134] As the demand for tax credits declined, so did the prices third-party investors were willing to pay for them, which created funding gaps in projects that had received tax credit allocations in 2007 and 2008. TCAP and the Section 1602 Program were designed to fill financing gaps in planned tax credit projects and jumpstart stalled projects.

[133]State housing finance agencies award LIHTCs to owners of qualified rental properties who reserve all or a portion of their units for occupancy for low-income tenants. Once awarded LIHTCs, project owners typically attempt to obtain funding for their projects by attracting third-party investors that contribute equity to the projects. These investors can then claim the tax credits for 10 years if the property continues to comply with program requirements. This arrangement of providing LIHTCs in return for an equity investment is generally referred to as "selling" the tax credits. Some project owners sell the LIHTCs to an investor that will invest directly in the LIHTC project while others use a syndicator, which assembles a group of investors and pools funds that are then invested in the LIHTC project. For purposes of this report we refer to direct investors and syndicators generally as "third-party investors" or "investors."

[134]Because many of the affordable housing tax credit projects generate small amounts of cash flow from rental income, they rely on LIHTC together with other forms of subsidies like the HOME Investment Partnerships Program, Community Development Block Grants, and state funds to develop, rehabilitate, and adequately maintain projects.

For TCAP, the Recovery Act requires HUD to obligate $2.25 billion to 52 housing finance agencies (HFA) for gap financing of LIHTC projects that included some LIHTCs.[135] HFAs had to give priority to projects that were "shovel ready" and expected to be completed by February 2012. HFAs and project owners face three milestones for committing and disbursing TCAP funds.[136]

- HFAs had to commit 75 percent of their TCAP awards by February 16, 2010. According to HUD officials, all HFAs met the February 16, 2010, deadline except for South Carolina because it did not have enough affordable housing projects that needed TCAP assistance.

- The Recovery Act requires that HFAs disburse 75 percent of the TCAP awards by February 16, 2011.

- The Recovery Act requires that project owners spend all of their TCAP funds by February 2012.

As of the end of July 2010, HUD had outlayed 32.6 percent (about $733 million) of the TCAP funds, up from 16.5 percent as of April 30, 2010, that we reported in May (see fig. 28).

---

[135]HUD obligated funds to the 50 states, the District of Columbia, and Puerto Rico. The Recovery Act directed HUD to distribute TCAP funds in accordance with the fiscal year 2008 HOME Investment Partnerships Program (HOME) formula allocations to state participating jurisdictions, thereby limiting the funds to states as defined by the HOME requirements (HOME formula). Guam and the U.S. Virgin Islands are defined as "insular areas" under HOME, rather than as "states," and therefore, did not receive TCAP funds.

[136]This report uses the terms obligation and outlays when discussing funds that HUD and Treasury provide to HFAs. By obligation, we mean that the respective federal agencies have entered into agreements with HFAs for a specified amount of funds. By outlays, we mean that the federal agencies have released funds to an HFA. We use the terms commitments and disbursements to discuss funds provided by HFAs to projects. By commitments, we mean the HFA has entered into an agreement to provide funds to a project owner. By disbursement, we mean that the HFAs have released funds to project owners.

Figure 28: HUD Outlays of TCAP Funds, as a Percentage of Total Recovery Act Obligations as of April 30 and July 31, 2010

April 30, 2010

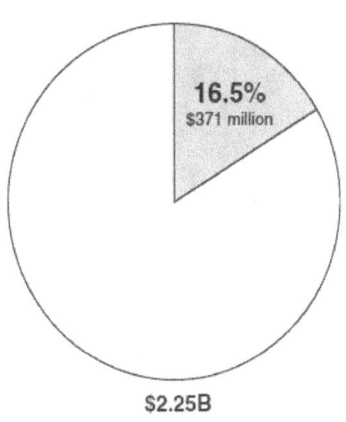

$2.25B

July 31, 2010

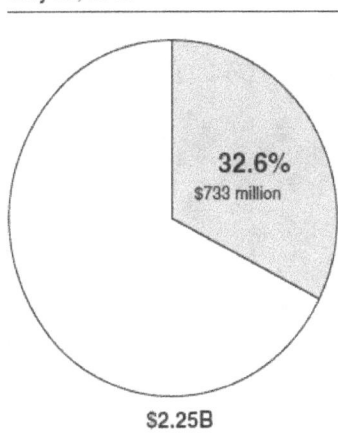

$2.25B

Source: GAO analysis of HUD data.

Although HUD originally made obligations of $2.25 billion to HFAs, HUD officials told us that they have taken back TCAP funds from HFAs that either did not commit 75 percent of funds by February 2010, did not have enough demand for the funds, or both. South Carolina—which did not meet the February deadline and did not have enough demand—returned $13 million of its original $25.4 million TCAP allocation. Alabama, which did meet the deadline, returned $3 million of its original $32 million allocation because it did not have enough demand for TCAP funds and would not be able to use all the funds. (We further discuss why some HFAs were challenged to meet deadlines for TCAP and the Section 1602 Program later in this section.) HUD officials told us that they plan to reallocate the $16 million through a competitive process and develop criteria to be issued in a HUD notice this fall. HUD officials said they expect only HFAs that have demonstrated program progress to be eligible for consideration since the existing TCAP deadlines for disbursing 75 percent of funds by February 2011 still would apply. HUD officials told us that they heard informally from about 20 HFAs interested in receiving additional TCAP funds.

For the Section 1602 Program, Treasury had obligated $5.5 billion and outlayed about 25.5 percent ($1.4 billion) as of July 31, 2010, up from the 13.6 percent outlayed as of April 30, 2010 (see fig. 29).

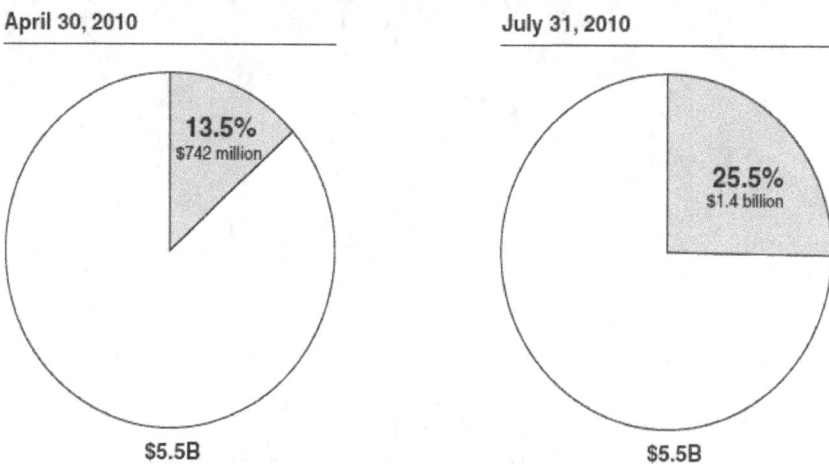

Figure 29: Treasury Outlays of Section 1602 Program Funds as a Percentage of Total Recovery Act Obligations as of April 30 and July 31, 2010

April 30, 2010

13.5%
$742 million

$5.5B

July 31, 2010

25.5%
$1.4 billion

$5.5B

Source: GAO analysis of Treasury data.

Unlike HUD, Treasury has not taken back any funds because the first deadline for the HFAs to disburse funds is December 31, 2010. Specifically, under Section 1602 Program rules, HFAs must commit the funding to projects by December 2010 and can continue to disburse funds to awarded projects through December 31, 2011, provided that the project owners spend at least 30 percent of the eligible project costs by December 31, 2010.[137] HFAs must disburse all Section 1602 Program funds by December 2011, or the funds the HFAs have not disbursed must be returned to Treasury. Originally, Treasury's guidance required that HFAs had to make all Section 1602 Program disbursements by December 31, 2010, or return the undisbursed funds to Treasury, but Treasury extended the disbursement deadline to December 31, 2011.

In the six previous Recovery Act reports, we have collected and reported data on programs receiving substantial Recovery Act funds in 16 selected states and the District of Columbia. These 16 states and the District of Columbia together have about 65 percent of the U.S. population and will receive an estimated two-thirds of the TCAP funds and about 60 percent of the Section 1602 Program funds. Figure 30 lists the TCAP and Section 1602

---

[137]Project owners must have, by the close of 2010, spent at least 30 percent of their total adjusted basis on land and depreciable property that is reasonably expected to be part of the low-income housing project.

Program obligations and outlays for the 16 states and the District of Columbia as of July 31, 2010.

Figure 30: HUD and Treasury Obligations and Outlays for TCAP and Section 1602 Program for the 16 States and the District of Columbia as of July 31, 2010, Compared to April 30, 2010

TCAP		July 31, 2010 Obligations	Outlays	Percentage	Apr. 30, 2010 Percentage	Section 1602 Program		July 31, 2010 Obligations	Outlays	Percentage	Apr. 30, 2010 Percentage
Arizona		$32.3	$25.0	77.5%	41.7%			$37.6	$6.0	16.0%	0.0%
California		325.9	53.3	16.4	7.8			478.1	120.3	25.2	8.9
Colorado		27.3	11.5	42.0	26.5			17.8	6.8	38.2	31.5
Washington, D.C.		11.6	7.9	67.9	49.3			33.8	4.5	13.3	0.7
Florida		101.1	46.1	45.6	16.5			580.4	61.8	10.7	3.9
Georgia		54.5	20.8	38.2	24.4			195.6	62.7	32.1	14.1
Illinois		94.7	43.6	46.1	24.2			264.5	29.5	11.2	6.4
Iowa		19.0	11.5	60.8	23.9			72.8	42.3	58.1	46.6
Massachusetts		59.6	22.8	38.3	17.1			110.3	33.3	30.2	3.8
Michigan		64.0	19.8	31.0	14.4			285.9	29.6	10.4	4.3
Mississippi		21.9	4.6	21.0	0.0			29.7	0.0	0.0	0.0
New Jersey		61.2	14.3	23.4	5.9			123.5	41.5	33.6	23.9
New York		252.7	101.7	40.3	25.2			0.0	0.0	0.0	0.0
North Carolina		52.2	4.6	8.9	5.8			95.0	66.4	69.9	51.4
Ohio		83.5	15.6	18.6	6.6			118.1	23.9	20.3	16.5
Pennsylvania		95.1	43.4	45.6	18.7			229.9	117.6	51.2	33.0
Texas		148.4	17.0	11.4	3.1			594.1	71.1	12.0	2.6
Total		1,504.9	463.7	30.8	15.1			3,267.0	717.4	22.0	10.9

Dolllars obligated (in millions)

Dollars outlayed (in millions)

Source: GAO analysis of HUD and Treasury data.

According to HUD and Treasury data, nearly all the HFAs have made progress in disbursing TCAP and Section 1602 Program funds to project owners. Figure 30 shows HUD outlays to HFAs in the 16 selected states and the District of Columbia. Because HFAs must disburse their TCAP and

Section 1602 Program funds to project owners within 3 days, these figures would closely track disbursements. As shown in figure 30, Arizona, Iowa, and the District of Columbia have drawn down more than 50 percent of their TCAP funds, and Iowa, North Carolina, and Pennsylvania have drawn down more than 50 percent of their Section 1602 Program funds as of July 31, 2010. When we reported in May, North Carolina was the only state out of the 16 selected states and the District of Columbia to have drawn down more than 50 percent of its funds from one of the programs.

However, the level of outlays, and therefore HFA spending, continues to vary considerably across the states. We previously reported that the difference in spending across the 16 states and the District of Columbia depended on when the HFA requested Section 1602 Program funds, the level of construction activity, and the HFA's implementation timeline.[138] For example, Treasury officials told us that while 40 HFAs had requested funds by September 2009, the Mississippi Home Corporation (MHC) requested funds for the first time in February 2010. According to Treasury officials, Treasury outlayed funds to MHC for the first time on August 12, 2010. MHC officials told us that they expect to close on most of their projects in August and September 2010, which is when MHC will sign agreements with project owners that will meet HFA requirements to begin disbursing funds.

TCAP and the Section 1602 Program Have Had a Strong Impact on the LIHTC Market

HFA officials, project owners, and third-party investors that we interviewed generally agreed that TCAP and the Section 1602 Program provided funds to many stalled LIHTC projects and enabled them to move forward.[139] For example, some owners of stalled projects said that their projects could not have continued without TCAP and Section 1602 Program funds. TCAP and Section 1602 Program funds also made some rural projects and special needs population projects—such as farm worker housing, housing for formerly homeless, and housing for the disabled—more feasible and attractive to third-party investors. Officials from one HFA we interviewed told us that investors scrutinize the financial outlook

---

[138]Unlike TCAP, the Section 1602 Program permits rolling applications through December 31, 2010.

[139]We interviewed a cross-section of HFAs and conducted site visits to selected projects that had received either TCAP or Section 1602 Program funds, and interviewed project owners and third-party investors involved with these selected projects. The Georgia, Ohio, Pennsylvania, Florida, and Mississippi appendixes in the e-supplement of this report provide information on our site visits (GAO-10-1000SP). We also conducted telephone interviews with the HFAs in Colorado, Iowa, Michigan, and Montana.

for rural projects because they expect that the income for these projects will be tight or non-existent. HFAs, project owners, and investors also told us that in a difficult market, investors are less likely to risk investments in these types of projects. We interviewed nine HFAs that awarded financing to 385 projects—154 (40 percent) were rural and 37 (10 percent) were special needs population projects—which may not have moved forward without the assistance of the TCAP and Section 1602 Program.

LIHTC projects that received TCAP and Section 1602 Program funds typically had less investor equity than LIHTC projects had prior to the economic downturn. The decrease in investor equity varied for each project and by state. The nine HFAs that we interviewed reported that equity in LIHTC projects prior to the economic downturn generally ranged from 50 to 80 percent of the total financing for a project. In contrast, for projects receiving TCAP and Section 1602 Program funds from the nine HFAs that we interviewed, investor equity represents on average 43 percent of a project's overall financing. For LIHTC projects receiving TCAP and Section 1602 Program funds, the decrease in investor equity has been offset by the increase in federal funds.

Some HFA officials, project owners, and third-party investors that we interviewed currently believe that demand for LIHTCs is re-emerging since the credit markets were severely disrupted in 2008. However, some of them said that third-party investor demand still was not at a level where most projects were feasible. Investor demand and tax credit prices have been picking up in some states and regions more than others. According to some investors with whom we spoke, investor demand and tax credit prices tended to be higher on the coasts than in the middle of the country. Investors also preferred certain types of projects, such as those that were larger, located in urban areas, and catered to seniors. Projects that were smaller, located in rural areas, and targeted special needs populations more often lacked third-party investors.

Since the economic downturn, the composition of third-party investors also has changed. First, Fannie Mae and Freddie Mac, which according to an investor, had bought the largest share of tax credits (40 percent in 2006) and were the primary third-party investors in special population projects, exited the marketplace. Second, according to another investor, the low tax credit prices have resulted in higher yields that in turn have attracted "yield-driven" investors, including insurance companies, large corporations, and individuals. Banks, which had invested in the tax credit markets primarily because of Community Reinvestment Act requirements, have continued to do so.[140] However, if tax credit prices continue to rise, yields will decrease, which may cause "yield-driven" investors to exit the market.

Because the LIHTC market is still rebounding and some states continue to face challenges attracting investors, the majority of HFAs that we interviewed support temporarily extending the Section 1602 Program. If the Section 1602 Program were not extended, some project owners anticipated scaling back development activities and being more selective about which projects they develop. Some HFAs and project owners who supported the extension of the Section 1602 Program believe the funds would be most useful if used to fill financing gaps, to fund rural and special needs population projects, and to provide grants or funds to nonprofits that are developing projects that target such needs.

Some HFAs and Projects May Face Challenges in Meeting HUD and Treasury Deadlines for Using Funds

Some HFAs and projects may face challenges in meeting TCAP and Section 1602 Program deadlines for reasons ranging from increased workload to the time needed to assemble financing to construction delays. Some HFAs reported that the addition of TCAP and Section 1602 Program transactions this year has increased their workloads significantly. One HFA reported that it typically closed from 18 to 22 projects annually, but this year would close 60 projects. Two other HFAs reported that they typically closed from 8 to 15 projects annually, but expected to close 50 and 85 projects this year, respectively.

Most HFAs Likely Will Meet TCAP Deadlines, but Those That Have Delayed Disbursing TCAP Funds May Face Challenges

For TCAP, the potential challenges HFAs face appear to be related to how they structured the timing of the TCAP disbursements. According to HUD officials, it is difficult to determine which states may have difficulty meeting TCAP spending deadlines because states took different

---

[140]The Community Reinvestment Act (CRA) is intended to encourage institutions that accept deposits, such as banks, to help meet the credit needs of the communities in which they operate. CRA requires regulators to evaluate periodically each insured depository institution's record in helping meet the credit needs of its entire community. That record is taken into account in considering an institution's application for deposit facilities, including mergers and acquisitions. Investing in LIHTC projects allows banks to earn positive consideration toward their regulatory ratings under CRA.

approaches to awarding funds. A few HFAs may be at a disadvantage in terms of meeting 2011 and 2012 deadlines because they chose to award TCAP funds late in the development process to ensure that commitments from other financing sources are in place and the projects will be successfully completed. As a result, these HFAs have disbursed a small percentage of their TCAP funds to date. The HFA officials we interviewed in nine states did not believe the TCAP disbursement deadline was a challenge for their projects.

Treasury Plans for Ensuring That Section 1602 Program Projects Meet Spending Deadlines Remain Unclear

According to some HFA officials, some project owners may face challenges meeting the 30 percent spending deadline (December 31, 2010) for Section 1602 Program projects, due to reasons that affected some projects allocated Section 1602 Program or TCAP funds, ranging from the timing needed to assemble or disburse funding by HFAs, litigation, and routine construction delays. According to HFA officials with whom we spoke, some projects needed to wait for FHA mortgage insurance approval or approval from other sources of subsidies before receiving final HFA approval. Officials from one HFA with whom we spoke said that while all their Section 1602 Program projects were shovel-ready, getting all parties educated and comfortable about the requirements of the new program took time. Some projects had been stalled for months, and it took time to "ramp up" all parties engaged in the projects. In addition, some projects encountered delays during the construction process due to weather or other issues typical of development projects such as waiting for construction permits from local agencies. Other projects were delayed due to legal issues unrelated to the Section 1602 Program. For example, Florida Housing Finance Corporation officials told us that as of August 2010, about $22.3 million in Section 1602 Program funds were allocated to projects involved in litigation.[141]

Furthermore, in HFAs that delayed the decision to participate in the Section 1602 Program or that had a slow start to launching the Section 1602 Program projects have collectively had less time to spend eligible funds than in other states where funds were awarded earlier. For example,

---

[141] According to the Florida Housing Finance Corporation, the litigation involves three projects for which the owners disagreed with the HFA's decision to rescind provisional awards based on an unfavorable credit underwriting review.

the MHC did not request Section 1602 Program funds from Treasury until February 2010.[142] MHC told us that it is concerned that each of its 17 projects receiving Section 1602 Program funds may not meet the 30 percent spending deadline. One HFA said that a typical LIHTC project would take about 15 months from applying for funds to closing the project and commencing construction. Our review of projects in nine states shows that these HFAs had not yet awarded Section 1602 Program funds to 75 projects as of June 30, 2010. Further, as of June 30, 2010, about 39 percent of Section 1602 Program projects (98 of 252 projects) that have been awarded funds in these nine states have not yet closed, which is the first step to being able to draw funds from entities that provide financing.

Treasury initially required HFAs to return all Section 1602 Program funds not disbursed by December 31, 2010. In a regulation of August 31, 2009, Treasury extended the deadline for disbursing Section 1602 Program funds by 1 year, provided project owners met the 30 percent spending requirement. Treasury had determined that completion of projects by December 31, 2010, was too restrictive and would preclude funding of otherwise eligible projects. Treasury officials told us that the new 30 percent requirement was put in place to assure that project owners were making some progress by the original (December 31, 2010) deadline date.

Missing the deadline for the 30 percent spending requirement could have significant implications for the viability of Section 1602 Program projects. If project owners failed to meet this spending deadline, they would not be eligible to receive any additional Section 1602 Program funds. If prevented from receiving the rest of their Section 1602 Program award, project owners might not be able to find replacement financing and committed financing sources might withdraw their funds. If projects could not secure replacement financing quickly, they would be unlikely to be completed in accordance with Section 1602 Program and LIHTC requirements and would be stalled again. Under such a scenario, the HFA would be responsible for recapturing any Section 1602 Program funds that were disbursed to the project prior to the 30 percent spending deadline.

---

[142]MHC's board delayed its request for Section 1602 Program funds to Treasury until February 2010 while it assessed program risks related to Treasury's requirements for recapture of funds. MHC is responsible for returning Section 1602 Program funds to Treasury if a project owner fails to complete the project or meet LIHTC requirements. GAO reported previously on the risks and responsibilities of recapture for HFAs under TCAP and the Section 1602 Program. See GAO, *States' and Localities' Uses of Funds and Actions Needed to Address Implementation Challenges and Bolster Accountability*, GAO-10-604 (Washington, D.C.: May 26, 2010).

Treasury officials told us that they plan to enforce the deadline requirement, and would provide written guidance to HFAs that will describe the kind and format of information to be reported to Treasury to document whether projects have met the spending deadline. Treasury officials told us that they do not plan to collect this information until after the deadline has passed. Without a plan in place for handling projects that do not meet the Section 1602 Program deadline, Treasury risks further project interruptions, including the possible loss of any job creation associated with projects that must be discontinued if alternate financing cannot be found.

TCAP and the Section 1602 Program Impose More Oversight Responsibilities on HFAs Than the LIHTC Program Alone, and HFAs Have Developed Approaches for Such Oversight

TCAP and the Section 1602 Program require HFAs to assume a greater project oversight role than in the standard LIHTC program. Under the LIHTC program, HFAs need not monitor construction disbursements, but must report that projects are completed and occupied in accordance with LIHTC requirements and deadlines. For long-term monitoring under the LIHTC program, third-party investors in the project perform long-term asset management, and HFAs perform limited compliance reviews.[143]

- HFAs must review LIHTC projects at least annually to determine project owner compliance with tenant qualifications and rent and income limits.

- Additionally, every 3 years the HFAs must conduct on-site inspections of all buildings in each LIHTC project and inspect at least 20 percent of the LIHTC units and resident files associated with those units.

However, under TCAP and the Section 1602 Program, HFAs must monitor the disbursement and use of funds throughout the construction period. HFAs also must perform long-term asset management, which imposes ongoing responsibilities on the HFAs for the viability of each project.

- An HFA's asset management activities may include monitoring current financial and physical aspects of project operations. For example, an HFA may perform analyses or approvals of operating budgets, cash flow trends, and reserve accounts and conduct physical inspections more frequently than every 3 years.

---

[143] Asset management includes many activities that relate to monitoring and planning for the long-term financial and physical health and viability of a project. Some examples of asset management are discussed in this section.

- Asset management activities also examine long-term issues related to plans for addressing a project's capital needs, changes in market conditions, and recommendations and implementation of plans to correct troubled projects.

- HFAs also ensure compliance with LIHTC requirements as part of their asset- management activities.

Moreover, HFAs are responsible for returning TCAP and Section 1602 Program funds to HUD and Treasury, respectively, if a project fails to comply with LIHTC requirements.[144]

Given the increase in responsibilities and risks to HFAs, HFAs have developed approaches for oversight during the construction period as well as long-term asset management over the 15-year tax credit compliance period. These approaches are designed to monitor the physical and financial health of projects and compliance with LIHTC affordability restrictions.

In response to an open-ended question in our survey asking about what changes in oversight activities HFAs planned to put in place to assure compliance with the TCAP and Section 1602 Program, 37 HFAs said they would make some changes in oversight activities, 11 said they would make no changes in oversight activities, and 6 said they were not sure what changes they would make or they did not answer the question.[145] Changes in activities varied across HFAs. For example, of the 37 HFAs that said they would make some changes, 13 HFAs noted that they would make changes to their disbursement process to more closely track the use of TCAP and Section 1602 Program funds, 9 HFAs said they would increase overall monitoring of projects or reporting required by project owners, and 7 HFAs planned to implement or increase the frequency of site visits or inspections. Eleven HFAs said they would not change their oversight activities, but 6 of those 11 HFAs noted that they would rely on their

---

[144]In contrast, under the conventional LIHTC program, HFAs are not liable for recapturing funds if a project owner fails to comply with LIHTC requirements. Rather, their obligation is to report any noncompliance to the IRS, and the IRS takes any further actions with respect to recapture. GAO reported previously on the risks and responsibilities of recapture for HFAs under TCAP and the Section 1602 Program. See GAO-10-604.

[145]We conducted a Web-based survey in November 2009 of all 54 HFAs that received TCAP and Section 1602 Program funds as of that date. All HFAs responded. For a copy of the survey and the compiled HFA responses, see GAO-10-1023SP.

experience in and established procedures for monitoring their lending programs or disbursement of other federal funds.

HFAs Have Increased Oversight during Construction Phase of TCAP and Section 1602 Program Projects

HFAs have been providing greater oversight during the construction period for projects that receive TCAP and Section 1602 Program funds. This oversight includes monitoring disbursements of the program funds, overseeing the construction process, and ensuring compliance by TCAP projects with federal cross-cutting requirements such as Davis-Bacon wage requirements and the National Environmental Policy Act of 1969 (NEPA).[146] For example, HFAs must review payrolls for all TCAP projects to ensure that project owners and contractors are paying prevailing wages to individuals employed in the construction of the projects. HFAs also had to ensure that all TCAP projects complied with the NEPA environmental review process prior to receiving any TCAP funds. However, according to HUD officials, up to one-third of HFAs lacked prior experience in overseeing compliance with these federal cross-cutting requirements.

Under TCAP and the Section 1602 Program, HFAs have been disbursing a greater volume of funds than in the past and, as a result, have taken additional steps to limit risk and increase monitoring. For example, one HFA we interviewed expected to disburse the same amount of funds in 1 month as it previously disbursed annually. For standard LIHTC projects, HFAs only allocate tax credits and do not disburse funds. HFAs assume greater risk by disbursing TCAP and Section 1602 Program funds because they are responsible for repaying funds to HUD and Treasury, respectively, in the event of noncompliance. The nine HFAs we interviewed are supporting an average of 23 to 62 percent of the total development costs of projects through awards of TCAP or Section 1602 Program funds. Prior to the Recovery Act, three of these HFAs typically did not provide loans or grants to LIHTC projects, but now they are providing an average of 23 to 47 percent of total project financing through TCAP and Section 1602

---

[146]The Recovery Act expressly applies section 288 of the HOME statute, which requires the state to assume responsibility for environmental review under NEPA and related federal environmental authorities and regulations at 24 C.F.R. Part 58 "Environmental Review Procedures for Entities Assuming HUD Environmental Responsibilities." In addition, under section 1606 of Division A of the Recovery Act, contractors and subcontractors hired with Recovery Act funds are required to pay prevailing wages to laborers and mechanics in compliance with the Davis-Bacon Act.

Program project awards. The remaining six HFAs typically funded up to about 33 percent of the total project financing for some LIHTC projects through other loan programs prior to the Recovery Act. HFAs have mitigated risks by broadening the scope of guarantees and by requiring project owners to certify the accuracy of the information provided.

Approaches to overseeing the construction process varied across HFAs, although most HFAs we interviewed planned to apply their existing construction oversight framework to oversee TCAP and Section 1602 Program projects. These activities include site inspections of varying frequency. For example, some HFAs we interviewed planned to conduct monthly site inspections, while two HFAs said that construction superintendents would visit project sites twice per month or more frequently if needed. Site inspections help confirm whether work performed on a project is carried out as planned and approved by the HFA. One HFA also told us that it planned to facilitate communication among project owners, investors, and other lenders by sharing information or holding more frequent meetings with these stakeholders.

HFAs and project owners told us that meeting Davis-Bacon wage reporting and NEPA environmental review requirements for TCAP projects required time and resources, and it was easier for HFAs with prior experience to meet the requirements. We previously reported that HFAs viewed Davis-Bacon and NEPA requirements as a challenge and followed up with HFAs and project owners on ways that they have been meeting the requirements. To comply with Davis-Bacon wage requirements, some HFAs developed new processes for data collection and planned to apply additional scrutiny to data received from project owners or more frequent reporting, and other HFAs developed training for project owners. To comply with NEPA requirements, some HFAs and project owners drew upon their experience administering HOME funds, which also require NEPA compliance.[147] Project owners said that in some cases they allocated additional resources to projects to complete environmental reviews ahead of project closings.

---

[147]HOME, administered by HUD, provides formula grants to states and localities that communities use—often in partnership with local nonprofit groups—to fund a wide range of activities that build, buy, or rehabilitate affordable housing for rent or homeownership or provide direct rental assistance to low-income people.

In Response to New Asset Management Responsibilities, HFAs Have Increased Long-Term Monitoring and Put in Place Stricter Requirements for Project Owners

In response to the new asset management responsibilities HFAs have accepted under TCAP and the Section 1602 Program, all HFAs we interviewed reported that they had strengthened their procedures for long-term monitoring to meet the program requirements, mitigate risks, and help ensure projects' long-term physical and financial viability. Approaches to long-term asset management varied depending on an HFA's resources, workload, and asset management experience. However, all nine of the HFAs we interviewed have implemented some oversight changes, such as increasing the number of inspection visits over the 15-year tax credit compliance period and the frequency of reporting, as well as enhancing financial monitoring of projects receiving TCAP and Section 1602 Program funds when compared with standard LIHTC projects.

Of the nine HFAs we interviewed, four HFAs said that instead of inspecting projects every 3 years as required by the LIHTC program, they will inspect projects annually or more often. Seven HFAs said that they will require reports from project owners on a monthly, quarterly, or as-requested basis that may include information such as project income statements. Five of the nine HFAs we interviewed have the ability to approve and remove the project's management agent and general partner of the project owner if the project is in noncompliance with LIHTC requirements or the terms of the HFA's agreement with the project owner. Two HFAs said that they have new software systems in place to manage asset management activities, and four said they plan to provide additional training for staff to manage the monitoring and reporting for TCAP and Section 1602 Program projects. HFAs said that they have also strengthened financial requirements for project owners. All nine HFAs require annual financial audits or reports. Other changes HFAs have made include requiring or performing capital needs assessments to determine the condition and expected life of the physical infrastructure, calculating replacement costs, and assessing whether a project's replacement reserve will be adequate to meet the expected capital needs of a project. Some HFAs also require project owners to provide guaranties that the project owner will ensure compliance with program requirements or the project owner will be personally liable to repay TCAP and Section 1602 Program funds to the HFA. Some HFAs also have strengthened requirements for financial reserves or changed how and when the reserves can be accessed to ensure that there is a source of funds to draw upon in the event the project encounters operating difficulties. Some project owners with whom we spoke said that HFAs have been careful in structuring requirements to protect the HFAs' interests and that in some cases the HFAs' requirements and plans for monitoring were stricter than those typically required by third-party investors.

Nearly all HFAs we interviewed noted that a third-party investor provides additional oversight and monitoring or financial interest in a project. TCAP requires tax credits to remain in transactions, and project owners typically sell the tax credits to third-party investors. Therefore, most TCAP projects have some level of private investment and oversight. In contrast, the Section 1602 Program allows HFAs to exchange all of the tax credits awarded to a project in return for Section 1602 Program funds. As a result, many Section 1602 Program projects do not have third-party investor oversight. However, some HFAs have required third-party investor participation in all or the majority of their Section 1602 Program projects, and they plan to work in coordination with investors on asset management activities. Based on information from our survey, 32 HFAs expected to have a total of 485 projects without third-party investors out of a total of 825 projects expected to be financed with Section 1602 Program funds.[148] In our survey, about half of the HFAs planned to outsource asset management functions for TCAP and the Section 1602 Program. Based on our interviews with nine HFAs, we found that HFAs with past asset management experience and HFAs with a smaller volume of projects often chose to conduct their own asset management activities over the 15-year compliance period. In contrast, HFAs with little asset management experience or many projects requiring oversight often chose to hire a third-party contractor to perform asset management activities. However, one HFA in each of these categories chose to work in coordination with individual investors on asset management activities rather than relying solely on its own asset management efforts or the work of outsourced asset managers.

Five of the nine HFAs we interviewed are conducting their own asset management activities because they have significant experience managing loan portfolios or because the number of projects is manageable. One HFA we interviewed has 35 years of asset management experience, and two have 20 years of asset management experience. One of these HFAs also conducts asset management for HUD's performance-based contract

---

[148]These data do not include projects financed with a combination of Section 1602 Program funds and TCAP funds.

administration program and has won awards for its asset management systems. Six HFAs we interviewed said they have or are developing policies, procedures, or "watch lists" to assess project performance and identify projects that may be in need of additional monitoring.

One of the two HFAs we interviewed planning to outsource asset management activities has contracted with a national syndicator to provide asset management for its projects without private investment.[149] The syndicator has said that it will provide the same asset management services to the HFA as it would provide to investors in its LIHTC investment funds. The HFA has a staff person that is receiving an asset management certification and will work closely with the syndicator to ensure that asset management functions are performed in accordance with the syndicator's scope of work. The syndicator's scope of work covers both the leasing and asset management phases and includes activities such as providing quarterly project performance reports that rate the risk of the project based on market conditions and project owner capacity, conducting annual property inspections, and performing annual long-term financial analysis. The syndicator said that it helped the HFA structure a more comprehensive scope of work because it felt that the asset management activities started too late to ensure project success.

HFAs noted a range of challenges associated with asset management. One HFA we interviewed said that explaining the HFA's new asset management role to developers has been a challenge because the HFA does not usually act as a lender or party with long-term interests in the projects. Rather, the agency's primary role is that of tax credit allocation with compliance monitoring as required by IRS. HFAs also noted the cost of asset management as a challenge. A few HFAs are charging low or no fees for asset management because of the stress the fee puts on the project budgets. Other HFAs have estimated a fee based on market research and costs associated with their current operations, but they are not sure the fee will be sufficient to cover costs. Most HFAs we interviewed estimated that their initial asset management costs would be highest during the first

[149]This HFA told us that it did not have asset management experience and chose to outsource asset management on projects that did not have investor participation (6 projects) and coordinate with investors on projects that have investor participation (74 projects). The other HFA we interviewed that has hired an outside asset manager has a large volume of projects (89 projects) and will use the outside services to supplement its own financial monitoring of projects. Two HFAs we interviewed have required investor participation in all transactions, and they said they will coordinate with investors to ensure asset management is performed on all projects.

years implementing TCAP and the Section 1602 Program, including the initial construction monitoring period. For example, one HFA estimated that 20 - 30 percent of its asset management costs would be incurred within the first 2 years of overseeing TCAP and Section 1602 Program projects. However, some HFAs and investors noted future challenges as projects age. They said that between the fifth to twelfth year of a project's life, projects may begin to show signs of physical and financial stress due to capital replacement needs, diminishing reserves, or resident turnover. One investor said that HFAs may not have the financial resources to support troubled projects in the same way as an investor would.

HUD Strategy for Monitoring TCAP Does Not Fully Consider Project Risks

HUD officials told us that the agency has been relying on existing monitoring systems to determine whether funds have been spent properly or to track projects that have not been complying with the terms and conditions of TCAP agreements. The monitoring systems consist of HUD Office of Inspector General (OIG) audits (thus far ongoing in three states), HUD Office of Fair Housing and Equal Opportunity (OFHEO) reviews in 10 states, HOME reviews done by HUD field offices when projects include both TCAP and HOME funds, and HFA reviews. HUD officials told us that they can rely on existing Office of Community Planning and Development (CPD) field staff to carry out HUD's monitoring and also would plan to look for patterns of problems identified by the OIG, OFHEO, CPD staff, or HFAs during oversight and review activities. HUD officials noted that the agency's emphasis so far has been on the obligation, outlay, and tracking of funds to the HFAs and their disbursement to project owners.

As well as HFAs, HUD officials also expect that third-party investors will monitor TCAP projects for compliance in the same way that these stakeholders have been responsible for monitoring LIHTC projects. TCAP requires tax credits to remain in transactions, and project owners typically sell the tax credits to third-party investors. However, we found that in some cases projects included a limited amount of LIHTCs and project owners chose not to sell these credits to a third-party, thereby limiting or precluding third-party oversight of these projects. In traditional LIHTC projects, third-party investors play an important role in ensuring compliance with tax credit program requirements because they risk losing their ability to claim the tax credits if the project is not in compliance with these requirements. Some HFAs told us that they will coordinate with and rely on reviews and audits that investors and private construction lenders perform to satisfy the HFAs' asset management obligations under TCAP.[150] In cases when an HFA is coordinating with a third-party investor, the investor may provide early warning information that would be useful to the HFA if the HFA had to act quickly to assist the project or ensure compliance with TCAP requirements. But, some TCAP projects received a nominal amount of tax credits, and project owners chose not to sell the tax credits. These projects lack the additional oversight provided by third-party investors. In these cases, HFAs may be the sole monitor, other than HUD, ensuring that funds are spent properly and that the project owners comply with TCAP terms and conditions.

HUD officials acknowledged that in the absence of a significant third-party investment, the amount of overall scrutiny a TCAP project would receive is reduced; however, HUD officials told us that at this point in time they were not aware of how many projects either had nominal LIHTC awards or lacked third-party investors. Our limited review showed that some TCAP projects in Florida received a nominal amount of tax credits and lacked third-party investors that otherwise would provide an added layer of oversight for compliance with TCAP requirements. Specifically, we found that 13 of 25 projects (52 percent) that were allocated TCAP funds in Florida had received a nominal amount of LIHTCs. The Florida Housing Finance Corporation (FHFC) explained that it had awarded $100 in LIHTCs to each of these projects and that the project owners made $650 equity investments to the projects in return for the tax credit awards instead of selling the tax credits to a third-party investor.[151] FHFC plans to institute oversight activities for all of its TCAP and Section 1602 Program projects.[152] Nonetheless, HUD has not required HFAs to enhance their oversight or take other actions to account for the absence or limited involvement of third-party investors. Without the oversight provided by third-party investors and with the limited monitoring planned by HUD, these TCAP projects may constitute a higher risk to HUD and to the HFAs

---

[150]Some HFAs are coordinating with and relying on reviews and audits that investors and private construction lenders perform in order to satisfy the HFAs' asset management obligations under the Section 1602 Program as well.

[151]FHFC officials said they set $650 as the required equity investment for these projects by using the average market price for LIHTCs in Florida at the time of the TCAP award, which was 65 cents per dollar of tax credits. Because LIHTCs are claimed over a ten-year period, the total equity investment for $100 of tax credits priced at 65 cents is $650.

[152]See the Florida appendix in the e-supplement of this report for a description of FHFC's activities (GAO-10-1000SP).

that they will become troubled or fall out of compliance with LIHTC requirements.

In addition, although HUD's monitoring strategy relies partly on monitoring by third-party investors and HOME program reviews, HUD officials told us that they will not know how many TCAP projects have third-party investors or how many also have HOME funds until projects are completed and HFAs submit final reports on the projects. Therefore, HUD cannot currently determine the number of projects that are being monitored by others. Additionally, HUD does not currently know how many TCAP projects will be covered through HOME reviews. According to HUD officials, once projects are complete and all project information has been reported to HUD, it plans to use that information to tailor a monitoring plan to these projects. It will be important for HUD's TCAP monitoring strategy to recognize the differences in risk for projects without third-party investor oversight and those with investor oversight as well as those projects not covered by HOME reviews.

As discussed above, HUD officials said they have been focused on getting Recovery Act funds to HFAs. Since beginning TCAP, HUD has drawn upon limited staff resources in headquarters to administer and track the spending of TCAP funds—its Office of Affordable Housing Programs administers TCAP, and four existing headquarters staff from the HOME program work on TCAP (three part-time and one full-time). HUD officials noted that the Recovery Act does not set aside administrative resources to HUD to either implement the TCAP program, which was performed by existing HOME program staff, or to monitoring HFAs for compliance. In comparison, the Recovery Act provided additional resources for monitoring under the Neighborhood Stabilization Program, which HUD's CPD also performs.

Without a plan for identifying projects without third-party investor oversight and ensuring sufficient oversight when investors are absent, HUD will face constraints in ensuring that TCAP projects remain in compliance with program requirements, some of which apply for 15 years or more. Furthermore, without knowing whether projects involve third-party investors, HUD cannot focus its limited monitoring resources on the projects with the least oversight by others.

Treasury Developed a Risk-Based System for Monitoring HFAs

Unlike HUD, which relies on existing program oversight resources, Treasury has developed a system to conduct compliance reviews to ensure that the HFAs are following the terms and conditions of the Section 1602 Program agreement, and are providing oversight over the project owners receiving the awards. Treasury officials told us that their Office of Fiscal Assistant Secretary received $3 million to administer the Section 1602 Program and the Section 1603 Renewable Energy Program from the total funds appropriated to Treasury for administrative expenses under the Recovery Act. According to Treasury officials, they have designed a risk-based system in which they plan to conduct compliance monitoring on-site for 23 HFAs and remote monitoring for the remainder of the HFAs by the end of calendar year 2010. Whether monitoring is conducted on-site or remotely depends on factors such as identified risks and the size of the grant. The review generally consists of an interview, followed by a review of program files, a review of a sample of project files, a review of financial management information, and a cross-check to the records held at Treasury. After the review is completed, if there are any findings, staff request a corrective action or action plan, depending on the nature and severity of the noncompliance. According to Treasury officials, if staff recommend a corrective action or action plan, Treasury will follow up to ensure that the HFA takes the necessary corrective action. If the agency fails to take the corrective action, Treasury will take steps to bring the HFA into compliance and, if necessary, recapture funds.

As of August 2010, Treasury officials told us that they had completed nine compliance monitoring reviews and have been conducting six additional HFA reviews. Treasury officials said that the kinds of issues they found in their reviews relate to failure to properly document files, lack of a policy to handle fraud by project owners, and, in one case, unresponsiveness to Treasury's request for documentation. Treasury officials told us that these issues were often resolved during the compliance review, but that some issues required additional follow-up with the HFAs. In the case of the unresponsive HFA, Treasury officials said they have put a hold on the HFA's Section 1602 Program funds until they are sure the HFA has provided all materials required to satisfy Treasury's requests.

TCAP Reporting Requirements Have Been More Complex Than Section 1602 Program Requirements

Recovery Act recipient reporting requirements are different and more complex for TCAP than for the Section 1602 Program. More specifically, the Recovery Act describes recipient reporting requirements, including that of estimated jobs created and retained.

The Recovery Act recipient reporting requirements apply only to programs under Division A of the Recovery Act, which includes TCAP. The Section 1602 Program is under Division B of the Recovery Act, and, therefore, not subject to recipient reporting requirements.

As Recovery Act-funded recipients, HFAs must file quarterly reports through FederalReporting.gov on a number of data elements, including the number of full-time equivalent jobs funded by TCAP funds during that quarter. Jobs must be counted in accordance with methodology provided by OMB. OMB guidance limits the number of jobs reported to the actual use of the funds in each quarter. In cases of construction funding based on a mix of financing sources, HFAs can count the jobs created or retained based on the proportion of TCAP funds. In addition to reporting through FederalReporting.gov, HFAs report information on TCAP projects through two HUD systems. HFAs use HUD's Integrated Disbursement and Information System to report on the selection of TCAP projects by HFAs as well as disbursement of TCAP funds. HFAs also use the Recovery Act Management and Performance System to report on project compliance with environmental reviews.

Although not subject to recipient reporting, Treasury chose to collect project information through quarterly performance reports submitted by HFAs on an Excel spreadsheet. HFAs need only make one report of all jobs created or retained by Section 1602 Program funds for each project. HFAs submit estimated information on the number of FTE jobs to be created or retained by the entire project with the first quarterly report for each project. The number of jobs reported to Treasury need not be reduced to reflect parts of the project not funded under the Section 1602 Program. Except for requiring the use of FTEs, Treasury has not issued detailed guidance specifying job estimation methodology under the Section 1602 Program.

Job counts between the programs and across HFAs are not comparable. About two-thirds of the HFAs in our survey said that they will conduct a review of the information being provided by the project owners, but others said that they relied on signed statements from the project owners attesting to the accuracy of the jobs estimates. Furthermore, because of the differences in job reporting methodology for TCAP and the Section 1602 Program, job counts reported for the programs varied widely. We previously reported that some HFAs were concerned about underreporting jobs that TCAP funds created because of OMB's requirement that they count only jobs directly funded by TCAP.[153] They said that because projects funded under TCAP would not have moved forward without TCAP funds, all the jobs associated with the projects

---

[153]See GAO-10-604.

should be counted. For example, $2 million in TCAP funds could enable an $8 million project to be constructed that otherwise would not have been built, but only the jobs directly related to the $2 million TCAP expenditure would be reported.

Conclusions

Although constrained by limited resources or time, HUD and Treasury developed two new programs, TCAP and the Section 1602 Program, respectively, that are designed to provide capital investment to LIHTC projects hit hard by the economic crisis. TCAP and the Section 1602 Program have had a strong impact on the LIHTC market. However, our review identified two areas of concern: one that relates to HUD's identification of higher-risk TCAP projects and another that relates to challenges that some project owners may face in meeting a December 2010 deadline for spending funds in Treasury's Section 1602 Program.

Under TCAP, HFAs have increased responsibilities for asset management and monitoring compliance of project owners with the terms and conditions of the program. However, some projects with a nominal amount of tax credits may lack the benefit of oversight by third-party investors. Nonetheless, HUD has not identified projects that lack this additional level of oversight and thus may be at higher risk of noncompliance with TCAP and LIHTC requirements. Although HUD relies in part on HFAs to provide oversight, HUD does not know the extent to which the HFAs will provide additional oversight for projects that lack third-party investors. HUD is relying on existing monitoring systems and resources, but has not fully identified those projects that may be subject to review under its existing system (such as TCAP projects that also have HOME funds) or developed additional guidance or oversight of TCAP projects where there is little or no third-party oversight. HUD could take a more active role in monitoring TCAP projects—first by identifying those projects that may present a higher risk of noncompliance, and second by identifying those projects that also have HOME funds. HUD could also more effectively use limited oversight resources by using a risk-based approach that considers whether a TCAP project has third-party investors and whether HFAs are providing enhanced oversight. Likewise, by gathering information about the number of the projects that have TCAP and HOME funding, HUD could more effectively plan reviews and deploy staff. Without a more rigorous approach to oversight, HUD will be limited in its efforts to ensure that TCAP projects meet program requirements and continue to provide a source of affordable housing.

Treasury's regulations require project owners to spend 30 percent of eligible project costs by December 31, 2010, to continue receiving additional Section 1602 Program funds in 2011. However, some of the HFAs and project owners expressed concerns about meeting the 30 percent requirement because of unexpected delays stemming from the time needed to assemble funding, litigation, or construction or permitting issues. For instance, as of June 30, 2010, about 39 percent of Section 1602 Program projects that we reviewed have yet to close, leaving little time to meet the spending deadline. Projects that do not meet the deadline would not be eligible to receive any additional Section 1602 Program funds. In response, other sources of funding might withdraw from the projects, and project owners would face difficulty finding replacement financing. Thus, the 30 percent spending requirement might stop projects already under way—an unintended irony for a program designed to jumpstart stalled projects. Should there be a significant number of such projects, Treasury will be challenged in ensuring that the program achieves its intended goals. Specifically, although Treasury has been developing guidance for how HFAs should monitor project spending, it has yet to develop contingency plans in the event that significant numbers of projects stall again.

Recommendations for Executive Action

Because the absence of third-party investors reduces the amount of overall scrutiny TCAP projects would receive and HUD is currently not aware of how many projects lack third-party investors, HUD should develop a risk-based plan for its role in overseeing TCAP projects that recognizes the level of oversight provided by others.

Treasury should expeditiously provide HFAs with guidance on monitoring project spending and develop plans for dealing with the possibility that projects could miss the spending deadline and face further project interruptions.

Agency Comments and Our Evaluation

We provided a draft of this report to HUD for review and comment. HUD responded by saying it will identify projects that are not funded by HOME funds and projects that have a nominal tax credit award. HUD said it will make these identifications after projects are complete and develop a monitoring plan tailored to these projects. It will be important to ensure that HUD's approach includes a risk-based plan. We revised our section to recognize actions that HUD proposed in their response. HUD also provided technical comments that we incorporated as appropriate.

We provided a draft of this report to Treasury for review and comment. Treasury responded by saying that it has taken a number of steps to ensure HFAs and project owners have a complete understanding of the 30 percent deadline and are prepared to comply with that requirement.

Further, Treasury said it plans to continue monitoring the impact of the 30 percent spending deadline on the program and to provide additional guidance necessary to address unforeseen or unexpected circumstances. In our review of nine HFAs, we found that about 39 percent of the projects awarded funds in those nine states had not yet closed, which is the first step to being able to draw funds from entities that provide financing. Treasury's development of timely guidance may be particularly important because the December 31 deadline for spending 30 percent of program funding is quickly approaching. Treasury also provided technical comments that we incorporated as appropriate.

Many Recipients Are Citing Greater Ease Meeting Recovery Act Reporting Requirements, but Some Recipients Continue to Face Difficulties Calculating Jobs

According to Recovery.gov, as of August 24, 2010, recipients reported on close to 200,000 awards indicating that the Recovery Act funded approximately 750,000 jobs during the quarter beginning April 1, 2010, and ending June 30, 2010.[154] As reported by the Recovery Accountability and Transparency Board (the Board), the job calculations are based on the number of hours worked in a quarter and funded under the Recovery Act and expressed in FTEs.[155] Officials from many states reported that the recipient reporting process was, by this fourth round, becoming routine. Given that no new reporting guidance was issued by OMB during the quarter and that a time extension was again granted by the Board, recipients indicated they had few problems reporting.[156] The FTE calculations, however, continue to be difficult for some recipients as evidenced by our field work in selected jurisdictions covering two energy programs.

---

[154]Under the continuous corrections period, recipients were able to modify this round of submissions from August 3, 2010, through September 20, 2010. The final update of this round of recipient reported data should occur on September 22, 2010.

[155]Under the Recovery Act, recipients are to file reports for any quarter in which they receive Recovery Act funds directly from the federal government. Reporting requirements apply to nonfederal recipients of funding, including entities such as state and local governments, educational institutions, nonprofits, and other private organizations. These requirements apply to recipients who receive funding through the Recovery Act's discretionary appropriations, not recipients receiving funds through entitlement programs, such as Medicaid, or tax provisions. Certain other exceptions apply, such as for individuals. Recovery Act, div. A, § 1512, 123 Stat. at 287–288.

[156]Under the Recovery Act, recipients are required to submit reports no later than 10 days after the end of each calendar quarter. The Board extended the reporting deadline by several days for all four rounds of reporting.

Fourth Round Data Indicate Progress in Linking of Recipient Reports, Which Can Facilitate Tracking Across Quarters

We reviewed 74,249 prime recipient report records from Recovery.gov for this fourth round. This was 3,592 more than submitted in the previous quarter and represents about a 5 percent increase from round three. For our analyses, in addition to the round four recipient report data, we also used the round one, round two, and round three data as posted on Recovery.gov as of July 30, 2010.

We examined recipient reports to identify the extent to which progress was being made in addressing several key limitations we had found in our prior reports, including

- the inability to link reports for the same project across quarters;
- reporting errors;
- unusual values, such as award amounts of zero, or relationships between values requiring further review because they are unexpected; or
- flaws in the data logic and consistency, such as reports marked final that show a significant portion of the award amount not spent.

Linking Reports for the Same Projects across Quarters

Our analysis showed better linkage of reports across quarters, but we still found instances where it appears reporting on projects was discontinued and may indicate possible issues with linking. The ability to link reports across quarters is critical to tracking project funding and FTEs that are key indicators of project results. For example, if two consecutive quarterly reports on the same project are not linked, they become identified as two separate records, having an impact on the cumulative funding calculation and the ability to associate FTEs reported in the separate quarters with one another. Similarly, mislinked reports would result in funding and FTEs from two different projects being incorrectly associated with one another. For the data in Recovery.gov, the award key data field is used to track recipient reports across quarters.[157]

In our previous report, we performed a series of matching operations between the three rounds of prime recipient reports using the award key data field. We extended these matches to the current fourth round of prime recipient reports to continue reviewing the tracking of reports from one quarter to the next and to identify potential mismatches of reports. We

---

[157]An award key is a derived field that identifies an award. This field is derived using a distinct combination of the following component fields: Award_type, Prime_DUNS, Award_id and Order_number.

identified 1,111 fourth round prime recipient reports—1.3 percent of the fourth round prime recipient reports—that reflected a break in reporting (e.g., recipient reports that appeared in rounds one and four but not rounds two and three or, similarly, appeared in rounds two and four but not round three, etc.). Even though the number of prime recipient reports has increased for this fourth round, this is a smaller number of reports showing a break in reporting than we observed in the previous quarter. In our previous match across three rounds of reports, we identified 1,358 prime recipient reports that appeared in rounds one and three but not round two.

We performed another analysis using the final report and project status indicator fields that also suggested some concerns with missing linkages or potential errors in one of the reporting fields. As before, we identified recipient reports that only appeared in prior rounds, but not in round four. For prime recipients whose last report appeared in one of the prior three rounds, we examined the final report status and the project status fields, as those would presumably be the last reports from these projects. As shown in table 11, of the total 14,542 prime recipients that did not report in round four, overall, 34 percent of their last prior round reports were not marked as final and 27 percent showed project status as being less than 50 percent complete or not started. These data suggest that, among other reasons, the projects may not have been completed, or they should have been linked to a report in a subsequent quarter, or that recipients were locked out of the reporting system.

The percentage not marked as final is less than we observed in our previous analysis. However, the number of recipient reports from round three that did not appear in round four, with no indication that the round three report was final or that it was not close to completion, is quite similar to the number of discrepancies found in our last report. Based on these results showing projects that were not marked as final and indicating that they were in the earlier stages of implementation, it seems reasonable to expect that a fourth round quarterly report should have been filed, but the necessary linkage has not been made. Alternatively, these fields may not show the correct status.

Table 11: Number, Final Report Designation, and Project Status of Prime Recipient Reports Not Appearing in Round Four

Prime recipient reports last reported in:	Number of reports	Percent not marked as final report	Percent project status is "not started" or "less than 50 percent complete"
Round 1	2,671	50	43
Round 2	5,983	30	23
Round 3	5,888	30	23
Total	14,542	34	27

Source: GAO analysis of Recovery.gov data as of July 30, 2010.

During the most recent reporting quarter, recipients were able to reorganize unlinked or mislinked reports between rounds three and four. This may have facilitated the reduction in the proportion of reports that did not appear in round four, but that were not marked as a final report.[158]

Reporting Errors

In addition to our examination of report linking across quarters, we continued our monitoring of errors or potential problems by repeating many of the analyses and edit checks reported in our earlier reports using the fourth reporting period data. The results of such analyses can help improve the accuracy and completeness of the Recovery.gov data and inform planning for analyses of recipient reports over time. In general, the overall results were similar to what we observed in the previous round.

For example, we identified a mismatch of 128 reports for Treasury Account Symbol (TAS) codes and 115 for Catalog of Federal Domestic Assistance (CFDA) numbers.[159] This is a small increase from the previous round, where 117 reports for TAS codes and 112 reports for CFDA number

---

[158]This function was provided to recipients at FederalReporting.gov in order to achieve more accurate tracking and analyses of reports across quarters. The function, however, did not allow users to link current reports submitted in round four to ones submitted in round one or round two. Since there is no information on the downloadable recipient reports about the use of this function by recipients, we are unable to assess the extent to which this function was applied.

[159]Both TAS and CFDA values are linked to specific agencies and their programs. The TAS codes identify the Recovery Act funding program source. The two leftmost characters of each TAS code form a data element, which is identical with the two-digit numerical code used in the federal budgetary process to identify major federal organizations. The CFDA is a governmentwide compendium of federal programs, projects, services, and activities that provide assistance or benefits. It contains assistance programs administered by departments. Each program is assigned a unique number where the first two digits represent the funding agency.

were mismatched to the agency name fields. We also checked the data fields on the number and total amount of small subawards of less than $25,000 and identified 443 reports where the amount reported in both small subawards and small subawards to individuals were the same. This may be an indicator of improper keying of data or inaccurate placement of award data in a data field, both of which negatively affect data accuracy. The 443 reports is a small increase from the 436 reports identified in the previous round. However, the number of reports where the same value was entered for the number of subawards and the total dollar value of subawards was reduced, from 110 in round three to 101 in round four.

Unusual or Atypical Data Values

Unusual or atypical data values alert the analyst to potential inaccuracies. We checked unusual or atypical data values by identifying reports where the award amount was zero or less than $10. We know that it is highly improbable that grants were awarded in these small amounts. Finding numbers like these suggests improper keying of data or a misinterpretation of the guidance for FederalReporting.gov, both of which negatively affect data quality. We determined that the number of reports where this occurred was reduced to 37 reports in this round out of the 74,249 prime recipient report records, down from 74 reports in round three.

Flaws in Data Logic and Consistency

Data logic and consistency inform the analyst about whether the data are believable, given program guidelines and objectives. To assess consistency in the range between award amount and amounts reported as received or expended, we repeated our analyses of reports marked as final to identify possible over or underspending or misreporting by identifying final reports where the amount received or expended by the recipient was less than 75 percent of the award amount or exceeded the award amount by 10 percent or more. If the final report status is correct, this check can help agencies identify where award funds were not being spent, which may indicate project implementation problems. If more funds were spent than were awarded, it may indicate problems with project financial accounts or controls. Similar to round three, 3 percent of the round four reports marked as final showed an amount received or expended that was not within 75 percent of the award amount, and no reports exceeded the award amount by 10 percent or more.

Many State Officials Cited Increased Ease Compiling and Reporting Recipient Data

Many state officials noted that the reporting process is starting to become routine. They highlighted the fact that guidance remained stable for this round of reporting and that the early decision to extend the reporting deadline from July 10 to July 14 contributed to the success of the reporting process. For example, officials in California stated that the fourth round of recipient reporting went a lot smoother than prior rounds; further, the extension of the deadline to July 14 allowed many of the state agencies to obtain more complete data through the end of the month of June and report this to FederalReporting.gov. Similarly, officials in Colorado reported that the deadline extension to July 14 allowed for three additional working days for recipients to review their submissions and make necessary corrections, which they felt improved the data quality. Officials in the District of Columbia reported that in general there are no difficulties in the District's recipient reporting process and the process has become smoother with each subsequent reporting period, while officials in Illinois stated that with the reporting guidance remaining the same, their agencies are becoming familiar with the reporting process. Officials in Georgia noted that they did not hear negative feedback from the state agencies regarding the recipient reporting process or the FederalReporting.gov Web site during this round.

A Few States Are Preparing for Changes in Leadership

A number of the states we reviewed are anticipating leadership changes in the upcoming gubernatorial elections. In preparation, a few states noted that they are planning or are undertaking changes in procedures to ensure continuity during a transition. For example, Michigan Economic Recovery Office officials told us that because of anticipated changes to the state's administration, they moved to a decentralized process during this round of reporting to allow time for state agencies to adjust to reporting. Michigan state agencies submitted quarterly recipient reports directly to the federal government via FederalReporting.gov rather than to the state's Economic Recovery Office, which had previously served as a centralized reporting point. The officials told us that the decentralized reporting process for the quarter ending June 30, 2010, went as smoothly as they had anticipated, and the quality of the data submitted by state agencies to FederalReporting.gov has improved over time. The governor's office in Colorado is in the initial planning phase of transitioning to a new administration. Colorado state officials commented that the recipient reporting process has become a stable activity that should be able to move into a new administration with relatively little disruption. Officials in Georgia did not have any real concerns regarding a transition in administration, as the state now has recipient reporting systems and processes in place. California officials stated that steps have already been taken to ensure continuity in recipient reporting for the duration of the

Recovery Act, while New Jersey officials noted that there were not many challenges related to recipient reporting amid a transition to a new administration in their state.

States Focus Their Recovery Act Web Sites on Providing Information to the Public and Continue to Enhance Web Site Features

Many states noted that their Web sites were designed to provide information about Recovery Act programs, funding, and eligibility to the people of their states. For example, officials in California commented that the state Web site was designed for use by the average Californian to keep citizens informed about the Recovery Act's impact in California. Officials in Arizona noted that their Web site was designed to provide transparency to the public on how stimulus funds are being spent in the state. Several state Web sites were also used to provide potential applicants information on how to obtain grants, assistance, and contracts. For example, officials in the District of Columbia noted that their Web site provides information about Recovery Act funding received by the city and is a resource for people and organizations who are seeking opportunities to apply for grant funding, assistance, and potential contracts involving Recovery Act funds.

A number of state officials reported that they are continuing to add content to their Web sites. For example, Ohio's Recovery Act Web site recently added an interactive searchable map of funds awarded by location and enhanced information on the use of funds that are not covered by recipient reporting requirements. Officials in Texas said that enhancements in the past year have included new tracking reports to follow dollars, an interactive county map, and disbursement information. As another example, the Massachusetts Recovery and Reinvestment Office recently created a new Recovery Act Web site using an outside firm to help develop the most important features. An official from that office felt that the Recovery Act data collection and reporting effort will positively affect state government by improving policy and management discussions through the use of data.

Most DOE EECBG and Weatherization Program Recipients We Interviewed Followed OMB's FTE Calculation Guidance, and DOE's Recovery Operations' Data Quality Efforts Continue to Develop

EECBG Program

The EECBG program is administered within DOE and was funded for the first time with the passage of the Recovery Act. Because over 2,300 state, local, and tribal governments are eligible for direct formula EECBG grants and the grants are also awarded on a competitive basis, the program has many different types and sizes of recipients. For example, each state-level recipient must use at least 60 percent of its allocation to provide subgrants to local government units that are not eligible for direct grants, making the state the prime recipient while the local government unit is a subrecipient. Larger local government units receive grants directly from DOE, making them prime recipients.[160] For the fourth round of reporting, 2,116 prime recipients of the program reported, as of July 30, 2010, that they created or retained about 2,265 FTEs funded by the Recovery Act.

We interviewed 13 EECBG state-level and 19 local government recipients from our 17 selected jurisdictions about their FTE calculations for the fourth round of reporting. Given that the EECBG program is new, some of them had not yet reported. For example, District of Columbia officials from the District's Department of the Environment told us that their work under the EECBG program had not started in time for them to report for the period that ended on June 30, 2010. California Energy Commission officials noted that they had only a few EECBG recipients for the last reporting round, but there were 50 or 60 recipients for this fourth round. Another recipient commented that reporting was fairly easy now because they were only reporting internal data they controlled, as compared to contractor data, but the official anticipated more complexity as the program expands.

---

[160]Prime recipients are nonfederal entities that receive Recovery Act funding as federal awards in the form of grants, loans, or cooperative agreements directly from the federal government. Subrecipients are nonfederal entities that are awarded Recovery Act funding through a legal instrument from the prime recipient.

Officials from all of the state-level government units we interviewed that had FTEs to report said they followed OMB's December 18, 2009, guidance on FTE calculations. Specifically, they collected the number of hours worked that were funded by the Recovery Act and divided that total by the number of hours in a full-time work schedule, with defined processes in place to collect the EECBG recipient reported data. For example, Arizona Department of Commerce officials said that their office is responsible for reporting EECBG recipient data to the state's Office of Economic Recovery centralized reporting team. The Office of Economic Recovery works closely with the Arizona Department of Commerce to ensure that the reporting data are accurate. Additionally, Arizona officials said there is a review and approval process in place to check that the hours reported by the program's subrecipients are accurate. Officials in the Colorado state energy office noted that it has been easier collecting hours worked from EECBG subrecipients because DOE requires reporting the hours worked and the same data is used to convert hours to FTEs for OMB reporting. However, officials from a few other states said that generating the most comprehensive and complete job numbers available from subrecipients is still a challenge. The same challenge surfaced in education and housing programs that we previously reviewed.[161]

A few local government EECBG recipients we interviewed used methods other than the OMB guidance to estimate their number of FTEs, possibly resulting in over or undercounting. For example, while DOE guidance explicitly states that the job-year estimate issued by the Council of Economic Advisers for job creation potential is not appropriate in determining direct jobs created or retained and should not be used for reporting to either OMB or DOE, a New Jersey recipient informed us that she planned to use this number to estimate her township's FTEs. We informed the recipient that this was incorrect. In New York, a county official said that an EECBG contractor was conducting work under a Recovery Act contract, but the county did not report any FTEs in its most recent quarterly report because the official did not think the contractor had any documented jobs created or saved. Related to the problem with complete FTE numbers, several EECBG recipients reported confusion about including data from subrecipients on jobs, which OMB guidance states should be included. For example, officials from a county in California stated they received conflicting information about including jobs from subrecipients and vendors in their recipient reports. The

---

[161]GAO-10-604, pp. 195-211.

officials said that the conflicting information emanated from different levels within DOE and between DOE's and OMB's guidance. The county officials believed they did not get a clear answer from DOE as to the difference between subrecipients and vendors. Deciding that it was better to over report jobs than to under report jobs, they included subrecipient and vendor hours that could be project-related in their recipient reports.

Based on the recipients we interviewed, there was some evidence that larger EECBG direct grant recipients seemed to conduct more thorough recipient reporting data quality reviews than smaller direct grant recipients, possibly due to their enhanced administrative capacity. For example, a large EECBG grant recipient in Georgia reported that it improves data accuracy by prepopulating reports for subrecipients so they only need to include job numbers and vendor disbursements. In some instances, it also compares the subrecipient data to other documents, such as invoices and Davis-Bacon reports. However, according to a city official in Georgia, for their small grant, no specific data quality reviews are conducted other than a city official reviewing the hours worked. Colorado state officials said that communities that received under $2 million in direct formula grants have more difficulty administering EECBG grants and meeting the reporting requirements because they have limited staff resources. As an example, they mentioned a Colorado city, which received approximately $1 million in its EECBG grant. Because of limited resources, the city has the person who administers its housing programs also administer the EECBG grant. The Colorado state officials believed that in the case of smaller communities, it would work better if the state administered the EECBG grants and could report for the locality.

According to DOE officials, their EECBG program project officers have as minimum responsibilities making sure the recipients that need to report are reporting, reviewing the quality of the recipient reporting data submitted, and ensuring that recipients correct the data if the project officers detect errors. DOE monitors grant recipients primarily through its project officers, and project officers work directly with recipients to provide guidance and evaluate performance. Project officers also gather and analyze information about project planning and implementation and outcomes to help ensure data quality and to ensure that statutory requirements are met. DOE stated that it has updated the checklist that project officers use to monitor recipients, and it is also developing guidance that includes best practices on how states should monitor their subrecipients. Such increased attention to monitoring recipients, including the quality of their data, could likely reduce the errors made by recipients.

Weatherization Assistance Program	During the fourth round of recipient reporting, 58 prime recipients of DOE's Weatherization Assistance Program submitted their quarterly data to FederalReporting.gov, and as of July 30, 2010, reported approximately 12,980 FTEs funded by the Recovery Act. We interviewed 8 state-level and 17 local weatherization assistance recipients from our 17 selected jurisdictions about their FTE calculations for the fourth round of reporting. As with the EECBG grants, we found that most of the weatherization assistance recipients we interviewed followed OMB's December 18, 2009, guidance regarding FTE calculations. A few recipients, however, did not estimate the number of FTEs correctly for this round of reporting, resulting in under or over counting. For example, in one case, subrecipients in Florida did not include the hours worked by contractors who performed weatherization work at individual homes, which they attributed to a lack of awareness of the requirement to report the hours. In California, a local weatherization assistance provider also expressed confusion regarding reporting subcontractor hours. In Pennsylvania, a state official indicated some weatherization subrecipients experienced difficulties, at least in their initial reports, in submitting FTE information through a new Web-based reporting system that collects and calculates FTE information from the subrecipients. The Pennsylvania weatherization recipients report hours through this system to the Department of Community and Economic Development, but the system does not currently provide a method for subrecipients to certify the accuracy of what they report.

A few states had processes in place to help ensure weatherization assistance recipient reporting accuracy. For example, a District of Columbia official said the weatherization program staff and Recovery Act grant managers review submitted recipient reporting data from community-based organizations on a monthly basis before it is reported into the District's centralized reporting system. A New York official reported reviewing data submitted by a sample of subrecipients and comparing jobs data to contract and payment information in the program base, while in Georgia, the state weatherization program officials reviewed each provider's submission and called each provider to discuss their numbers. This process resulted in some changes to vendor information and the number of jobs created or retained.

DOE's Recipient Reporting Data Quality Review	According to DOE officials, during the quarter ending June 30, 2010, 3,988 DOE recipients submitted reports, an increase of about 7 percent from the quarter ending March 31, 2010, and an increase of about 28 percent from the 2009 year-end reporting period. DOE stated that only eight recipients

are considered nonreporters for this quarter, the majority of whom belong to a group with consistent challenges in reporting.

According to a senior DOE official in the department's Recovery Operations Group, the department's data quality review process for fourth round recipient reports was enhanced by several factors. The DOE official noted that access to FederalReporting.gov during the reporting period helped DOE identify recipients who had not yet filed and helped assist those who had unsuccessfully filed, entered the wrong awarding agency code, or confused the reporting required by OMB with DOE's system. In addition, he said that communicating the extended time frame for reporting before the reporting period actually began alleviated last-minute confusion or frustration on the part of recipients or reviewers, causing fewer recipients to wait until the last minute to file. Also, the official commented that the July 14 to July 20, 2010, late submission period, during which recipients were still allowed to file, allowed recipients experiencing access issues to FederalReporting.gov to submit reports. During this time period, DOE staff was also able to identify and assist with issues such as Central Contractor Registration numbers and getting new passwords for the last approximately 100 recipients filing reports. The DOE official noted that while the continuous correction provision has added to the workload of the DOE team, the period allows them greater time to review more recipient reported data than previously, identify potential errors, and work with agency reviewers and recipients to improve data quality.

The senior official listed a number of frustrations DOE encountered during the fourth round of reporting, most of which are in areas where they felt FederalReporting.gov is technologically limited. For example, according to the official, FederalReporting.gov lacks some basic logic tests for matching award numbers, with most of the mismatches resulting from prefix differences. The lack of this matching capability creates extra work for the DOE staff, but the Board declined to run separate matching routines for each agency.

In an April 2010 audit report of DOE's efforts to ensure the accuracy and transparency of reported Recovery Act results, the DOE Inspector General's (IG) office found that the department had taken a number of actions designed to do so and made two recommendations, which DOE had already started to address.[162] For example, recipient reported data elements are compared to information maintained in the department's financial systems. The IG recommended that DOE adjust the quality assurance process to include adding comparisons of other data elements, and a senior DOE official reported that for this round of reporting, the department has added several data elements to the original four that were reviewed centrally by the headquarters Recovery Operations Group. Now reviewers compare recipient reports in FederalReporting.gov against DOE systems to identify recipient information that falls outside expected results in seven different areas. According to DOE, these areas are key project markers being tracked by the public, the administration, Congress, and within the department to determine if the high-level goals of stimulating the economy and creating jobs outlined in the Recovery Act are being met. The DOE official said that increased attention has been placed on data quality within DOE systems as a result of this review process, which has created new communication channels and processes to identify issues and correct them. In line with the other IG recommendation, DOE developed a training program for officials responsible for reviewing recipient data submissions that includes detailed steps and procedures for officials to follow when reviewing recipient quarterly data for significant reporting errors and material omissions.

The Inspector General Community Has a Series of Efforts Aimed at Increasing Recipient Reported Data Quality

The IG community is also performing data quality audits of federal agencies' data quality review efforts for their recipient reports. In June, an IG-led Board review of the effectiveness of the agencies' data quality review processes was completed.[163] To identify material omissions and significant errors that were not identified by the reviewed agencies for the quarter ending December 31, 2009, the IGs performed reviews of the recipient reported data on FederalReporting.gov and attempted to compare that data with the data available in the agency-owned systems. In general, the IGs found that the agency systems were legacy systems that had been developed, designed, and implemented prior to the Recovery Act. As a result, data elements were not always consistent and at times

---

[162]U.S. Department of Energy, Office of Inspector General, Office of Audit Services, *Accounting and Reporting for the American Recovery and Reinvestment Act by the Department of Energy's Funding Recipients*, OAS-RA-10-06 (Washington, D.C., Apr. 1, 2010).

[163]U.S. Department of Agriculture, Office of Inspector General, *American Recovery and Reinvestment Act—Review of the Effectiveness of Department/Agency Data Quality Review Processes* (Washington, D.C., June 25, 2010).

were nonexistent, making matching the data difficult if not impossible. The final report provided three recommendations to the Board to pursue discussions with the appropriate government entities regarding improving the effectiveness of agency data quality reviews. These recommendations included establishing a uniform and consistent governmentwide award numbering system; making mandatory the suggested data logic checks identified in OMB guidance; and issuing guidance to better define material omissions and significant errors. Although consensus was not reached among the IGs regarding the award numbering system, there was general consensus regarding the logic checks and guidance recommendations. The next effort aimed at recipient reported data quality includes a Board review focusing on key data reporting elements and the factors contributing to errors in the recipient reports.

Intergovernmental Interaction Is a Critical Component of Recovery Act Operations and Will Likely Have Implications beyond the Act

The new procedures and tools developed to implement the Recovery Act are reshaping intergovernmental interactions and ways that governments collect, maintain, and report information. For example, the federal government built a huge data warehouse, FederalReporting.gov, which is populated by thousands of governments and other Recovery Act fund recipients, to ensure that the public receives as much information as possible on the implementation of the Recovery Act. Because such a wide variety of information is required and since some elements are being reported for the first time, OMB used a variety of methods to train federal agencies and recipients of Recovery Act funding on how to comply with their reporting responsibilities. OMB and federal agencies provided several types of clarifying information to recipients, as well as opportunities to interact and ask questions or receive help with the reporting process. These included weekly phone calls between OMB and groups representing the state budget and comptrollers offices, weekly calls between state reporting leads, webinars, a call center, and e-mail outreach. In addition, the Board recently reported that, along with the IG community, they have provided more than 2,000 training and outreach sessions to federal, state, and local government employees and to private sector individuals involved in Recovery Act implementation.

According to many of the state officials we interviewed, the Recovery Act's reporting requirements also promoted more interaction between state and federal agencies, state agencies, and within departments of these state agencies. For example, Ohio officials stated that the governor's stimulus office had established contacts with OMB, administration officials, and other federal agency contacts through work on Recovery Act implementation and monitoring. Officials from Illinois noted that recipient reporting was one of the few efforts that brought their otherwise very independent state agencies together. Colorado state officials reported that the program and accounting staffs within each state agency are working together closely to help ensure the accuracy and quality of the Recovery Act data. A few state officials, however, commented that although communication with federal agencies and other entities has increased due to the recipient reporting requirements, the communication is aimed primarily at dispelling confusion and is not necessarily positive. For example, Texas state officials commented that the one change that has been prompted by recipient reporting is the significant effort required to communicate reporting requirements to subrecipients and to collect, review, and submit the data.

Officials from a number of states expressed hopes that the increase in intergovernmental interactions resulting from the Recovery Act reporting requirements will continue after the act's reporting requirements expire. For example, District of Columbia Recovery Act coordinators schedule a weekly teleconference for all District agencies receiving Recovery Act funds to provide status updates and have discussions relating to the Recovery Act. They intend to continue scheduling the meetings after the Recovery Act funds are expended in order to maintain communication on other grant-related topics. Michigan officials reported that state agencies are working with each other in a way they have not before. They said the Recovery Act has facilitated collaboration, citing that the act removed some barriers to interaction between state agencies because the timeline for complying with Recovery Act requirements has been so short that agencies must work together to meet requirements, which has yielded many positive effects. Michigan officials noted that they hope the changes will be long-standing. As another example, a representative from a state association described Recovery Act-related problem solving between the audit and technology communities. These interactions included discussions where there was a flow of information at the policy, technological, and political levels that they would like to see continued.

A recent report issued by the National Association of State Budget Officers echoed the responses from many of the state officials we interviewed.[164] The report noted that during the months before recipient reporting began in October 2009 and in the months since, the Recovery Act helped to foster

---

[164]National Association of State Budget Officers, *Intergovernmental Communication and the Recovery Act* (Washington, D.C., July 28, 2010).

movement toward a more open and communicative atmosphere between both the federal government and states, as well as between individual states, while also providing important lessons currently being used in the implementation of the Federal Funding Accountability and Transparency Act of 2006 and the recent health care legislation. The report maintained that states have noted that increased transparency on government spending is a worthy goal which they support, as long as the federal government maintains a level of communication that allows for the effective and efficient implementation of any accountability requirements.

Oversight and Accountability Efforts

Actions Are Needed to Improve Single Audit and Federal Follow-up as Oversight Accountability Mechanisms

OMB has indicated that Single Audits play a key role in the achievement of its accountability objectives over Recovery Act funds, which include helping to ensure whether Recovery Act funds are used for authorized purposes and that risks of fraud, waste, error, and abuse are mitigated. A Single Audit includes the auditor's schedule of findings and questioned costs, internal control and compliance deficiencies, and the auditee's corrective action plans along with a summary of prior audit findings that includes planned and completed corrective actions. We identified significant concerns with the Single Audit process that (1) diminish the effectiveness of the Single Audit as an oversight accountability mechanism and (2) could allow risks associated with Recovery Act funds to persist. The Single Audit Act[165] and related OMB Circular No. A-133 *Audits of*

---

[165]Congress passed the Single Audit Act, as amended, 31 U.S.C. ch. 75, to promote, among other things, sound financial management, including effective internal controls, with respect to federal awards administered by nonfederal entities. The Single Audit Act requires states, local governments, and nonprofit organizations expending $500,000 or more in federal awards in a year to obtain an audit in accordance with the requirements set forth in the act. A Single Audit consists of (1) an audit and opinions on the fair presentation of the financial statements and the Schedule of Expenditures of Federal Awards; (2) gaining an understanding of and testing internal control over financial reporting and the entity's compliance with laws, regulations, and contract or grant provisions that have a direct and material effect on certain federal programs (i.e., the program requirements); and (3) an audit and an opinion on compliance with applicable program requirements for certain federal programs. The Single Audit Act requires that recipients submit their financial reporting packages, including the Single Audit report, to the federal government's audit clearinghouse no later than 9 months after the end of the period being audited. As a result, an audited entity may not receive feedback needed to correct an identified internal control deficiency over compliance until the latter part of the subsequent fiscal year.

States, Local Governments, and Non-Profit Organizations[166] do not adequately address the risks associated with the current environment in which billions of dollars in federal awards are being expended quickly through new and existing programs associated with the Recovery Act. In our prior bimonthly reports, we made several recommendations to improve OMB's oversight of Recovery Act-funded programs through the use of Single Audits. OMB has implemented some, but not all, of our recommendations.[167]

OMB's Single Audit Internal Control Project (project) highlighted areas where significant improvements in the Single Audit process are needed. OMB encouraged auditors from states that volunteered to participate in the project to communicate internal control deficiencies[168] over compliance for selected Recovery Act programs earlier than required under statute. The project has been a collaborative effort between volunteer states receiving Recovery Act funds, their auditors, and the federal government. One of the project's goals was to achieve more timely communication of internal control deficiencies for higher-risk Recovery Act programs so that corrective action can be taken more quickly. GAO assessed the results of the project and found that it met several of its objectives and that the project was helpful in identifying critical areas where further OMB actions are needed to improve the Single Audit process over Recovery Act funding. The project also required that auditee management provide, 2 months earlier than required under statute, plans for correcting internal control deficiencies to the cognizant agency for audit for immediate distribution to the appropriate federal awarding agency. The federal agency was then to have provided its concerns relating to management's plan of corrective actions in a written decision.

---

[166]This circular is issued pursuant to the Single Audit Act and sets forth standards for obtaining consistency and uniformity among federal agencies for the audit of states, local governments, and nonprofit organizations expending federal awards.

[167]See *Recovery Act: States' and Localities' Uses of Funds and Actions Needed to Address Implementation Challenges and Bolster Accountability*, GAO-10-604 (Washington, D.C.: May 26, 2010) for a status of OMB's implementation of GAO's recommendations.

[168]Internal control deficiencies refer to significant deficiencies and material weaknesses as defined by generally accepted auditing standards issued by the American Institute of Certified Public Accountants and *Government Auditing Standards*, issued by the Government Accountability Office. A material weakness is a significant deficiency or combination of significant deficiencies that result in more than a remote likelihood that a material misstatement of the subject matter will not be prevented. Auditors report internal control deficiencies over compliance requirements applicable to the major programs in accordance with OMB Circular No. A-133.

We found, however, that (1) most federal awarding agencies did not issue their management decisions about the corrective actions within the project's required time frames, (2) the current reporting time frames for the Single Audit process are not conducive to the timely identification and correction of internal control deficiencies, and (3) OMB's Single Audit guidance is not timely—specifically for 2010 audits, as well as guidance for a subsequent project. In our May 2010 bimonthly report, we recommended that OMB issue its Single Audit guidance, including guidance for future projects, in a timely manner so that auditors can efficiently plan their audit work, and OMB concurred with our recommendation. According to several state auditors who participated in the project, OMB's issuance of its guidance in an untimely manner adversely impacts the auditors' ability to plan and conduct their Single Audits. They added that untimely project guidance would also hinder their ability to participate in future OMB projects intended to provide earlier communication and correction of internal control deficiencies identified in Recovery Act programs.

We recommend that the Director of OMB strengthen the Single Audit and federal follow-up as oversight accountability mechanisms by (1) shortening the timeframes required for issuing management decisions by federal awarding agencies to grant recipients and (2) issuing the OMB Circular No. A-133 Compliance Supplement no later than March 31 of each year.

Single Audits as an Oversight Accountability Mechanism for Recovery Act Programs

OMB has indicated that Single Audits would serve as important oversight accountability mechanism for Recovery Act programs, which have considerable risks. The most significant of these risks are associated with

- new programs that may not have the internal controls and accounting systems in place to help ensure that funds are distributed and used in accordance with program regulations and objectives,
- Recovery Act funding increases for existing programs that may exceed the capacity of existing internal controls and accounting systems,
- the more extensive accountability and transparency requirements for Recovery Act funds that require the implementation of new controls and procedures, and
- increased risks because of the need to spend funds quickly.

We reported in our previous bimonthly reports that we were concerned that, as federal funding of Recovery Act programs accelerates, the Single Audit process may not provide the timely accountability and focus needed to assist recipients in making necessary adjustments to internal controls to provide assurances that the money is being spent as effectively as possible to meet program objectives. We also reported that the Single Audit reporting deadline is too late to provide audit results in time for the audited entity to take action on internal control deficiencies noted in Recovery Act programs.

In those prior reports, we made several recommendations to OMB for improving the Single Audit Process to address the increased risks by helping ensure that Recovery Act funds are not used for unauthorized purposes and that risks of fraud, waste, error, and abuse are mitigated. OMB has implemented some, but not all, of these recommendations. In response to one of our recommendations, in October 2009 OMB implemented a project to encourage earlier reporting and timely correction of internal control deficiencies identified in Single Audits that included Recovery Act programs. OMB's guidance for the project stated that this earlier communication of internal control deficiencies over compliance would allow participating auditees to correct internal control deficiencies related to Recovery Act funds in a timely manner, thereby reducing potential future unallowable costs.

We assessed the results of the project and found that the project met its original objectives of (1) achieving more than 10 volunteer states participating in the project, (2) having the participating auditors issue interim internal control reports for the selected programs at least 3 months earlier, and (3) having auditee management issue corrective action plans to resolve internal control deficiencies at least 2 months earlier than required by OMB Circular No. A-133. The project also increased the level of awareness by the auditors of some of the risks associated with Recovery Act funds and, in some cases, increased the communication and interaction between the auditors, program officials, and the cognizant agency for audit concerning internal control deficiencies related to Recovery Act funds. For example, many of the auditors who responded to our survey stated that the project increased awareness of internal control deficiencies and focused attention on the need for federal agencies to be more involved in pursuing corrective actions to develop more timely corrective action plans for internal control deficiencies related to programs receiving Recovery Act funding.

The project also called for federal awarding agencies to actively work with auditees to resolve high-risk findings in the most expeditious manner. One of the project's goals was to achieve more timely communication of internal control deficiencies for higher-risk Recovery Act programs so that corrective action could be taken more quickly. The implementation of corrective actions of internal control deficiencies will help to ensure that Recovery Act funds are used as intended.

Most Federal Awarding Agencies Did Not Provide Their Management Decisions within the Prescribed Time Frames

The project's guidelines called for the federal awarding agencies to complete two steps by April 30, 2010: (1) perform a risk assessment of the internal control deficiency and identify those with the greatest risk to Recovery Act funding, and (2) identify corrective actions taken or planned by the auditee. OMB guidance called for this information to be included in a management decision that the federal agency was to have issued to the auditee's management, the auditor, and the cognizant agency for audit. As of April 30, 2010, most federal awarding agencies had not provided their management decisions on the states' corrective action plans as required under the project's guidelines. Several of the state auditors and state program officials we surveyed emphasized the need for more timely communication from the federal awarding agencies, which is important for state agencies to gain a clear understanding of needed corrective actions. It is also important for auditors so that they can monitor progress towards addressing Single Audit results. OMB Circular No. A-133 requires management decisions to be issued by federal awarding agencies within 6 months of receipt of the audit report. However, the project's guidelines required the federal awarding agencies to issue a management decision as promptly as possible and not later than 90 days after the date that the corrective action plan was received by the cognizant agency for audit.

The internal control reports for the project identified internal control deficiencies in at least 24 Recovery Act programs awarded by seven federal agencies by December 31, 2009.[169] Moreover, under the project's guidelines, most corrective action plans were completed by January 31, 2010, 2 months earlier than the time frames under OMB Circular No. A-133 and were concurrently provided to the federal awarding agencies. Despite the federal awarding agencies having the internal control reports and

---

[169]One of the states that participated in the project has a fiscal year that ends on August 31 rather than on June 30. Therefore, OMB gave this state until March 1, 2010, to report on its fiscal year 2009 internal control deficiencies. OMB made this change so that the state's auditors would have the same amount of time to complete their test work as the other project participants did. All of the other states that participated fiscal year ended on June 30, 2009, and OMB required them to report by December 31, 2009.

corrective action plans in January 2010,[170] only three of the seven federal awarding agencies had submitted some of the relevant management decisions on corrective actions by May 14, 2010. We asked OMB officials to provide us with an update of the number of management decisions that had been submitted by the federal awarding agencies through August 5, 2010. OMB provided a summarized list of the total number of management decisions by agency where the auditee and the federal agency had agreed on action to be taken to address the report findings but had not traced these totals to the detailed documentation to verify the summary information.

It is important to note that an awarding agency's issuance of a management decision does not mean that internal control deficiencies have been corrected; rather, the management decision reflects the agency's approval of the auditee's proposed corrective action. Although some corrective actions can be implemented quickly, others can take months or years to implement. The issuance of timely management decisions by federal agencies is important because it can affect the timeliness of the auditees' implementation of corrective actions to address internal control deficiencies concerning Recovery Act programs. For example, according to an HHS Office of Inspector General official, auditees sometimes wait until they receive a management decision before taking corrective action on internal control deficiencies.[171] On March 22, 2010, OMB issued memorandum M-10-14, *Updated Guidance on the American Recovery and Reinvestment Act*, which among other things, instructs federal agencies to take immediate action as appropriate to review and act on Single Audit findings. However, as indicated by the project's results, further efforts by OMB are needed to help ensure that federal agencies provide their management decisions on the corrective action plans in a timely manner.

---

[170]The project's second milestone required that auditee management provide the interim communication report and a corrective action plan to the cognizant federal agency by January 31, 2010. For 10 of the 13 states that submitted the required internal control report, the corrective action plans were included in the interim communication report. In three instances, the plans were provided in a separate report.

[171]HHS, the cognizant agency for audit, has designated the HHS Office of the Inspector General to perform certain responsibilities relating to Single Audits.

Time Frames of the Single Audit Process Do Not Facilitate the Timely Identification and Correction of Audit Findings in Recovery Act Programs

Under the current time frames for identifying and correcting audit findings provided by the Single Audit Act and OMB Circular No. A-133, it could take years to correct significant deficiencies and material weaknesses that expose Recovery Act funds to misuse or fraud. For example, in accordance with current requirements, a material weakness that has been identified by the auditor for an entity that has a June 30, 2009, fiscal year-end is to be reported in the Single Audit report to be issued by March 31, 2010, along with the auditee's corrective action plan. The federal awarding agency would have 6 months or until September 30, 2010, from receipt of the Single Audit report to communicate a written management decision to the auditee.[172] As a result, it may take 15 months or more since the end of the fiscal year in which the audit finding was initially identified before any work is begun. Auditee's management reports their progress in taking corrective action in the schedule of prior audit findings where the status of the finding is reported as either corrected (closed) or not (open). The auditor then reviews this schedule and it is included in the next Single Audit reporting package. If the awarding agency delayed issuing a management decision to the auditee, it is possible that corrective action on the finding was also delayed, and, as a result, the finding may have remained open. In addition, several state auditors have expressed frustration regarding Single Audit findings that remain open years after they were initially identified, without the auditee or the federal awarding agency taking action. The lack of attention to ensuring prompt corrective action impairs the federal government's ability to ensure that unallowable costs have been repaid or that internal control deficiencies have been corrected. Shortening the timeframes required for issuing management decisions by federal agencies and monitoring the auditee's implementation of timely corrective actions by the federal agency will help to ensure that appropriate audit follow-up and resolution are achieved.

Figure 31 illustrates an example of the Single Audit reporting time frames.

---

[172]According to OMB Circular No. A-133, *Audits of States, Local Governments, and Non-Profit Organizations*, (June 27, 2003 and June 26, 2007) section .400 (c) (5) and section .405 (a) – (e), the federal agency is responsible for issuing a management decision on audit findings within 6 months after receipt of the audit report. Additional OMB guidance to federal agencies focused specifically on audit follow up is found in OMB Circular No. A-50, *Audit Follow-up* (September 29, 1982).

Figure 31: Illustration of the Single Audit Reporting Time Frames for Entities with a June 30, 2009, Fiscal Year-End

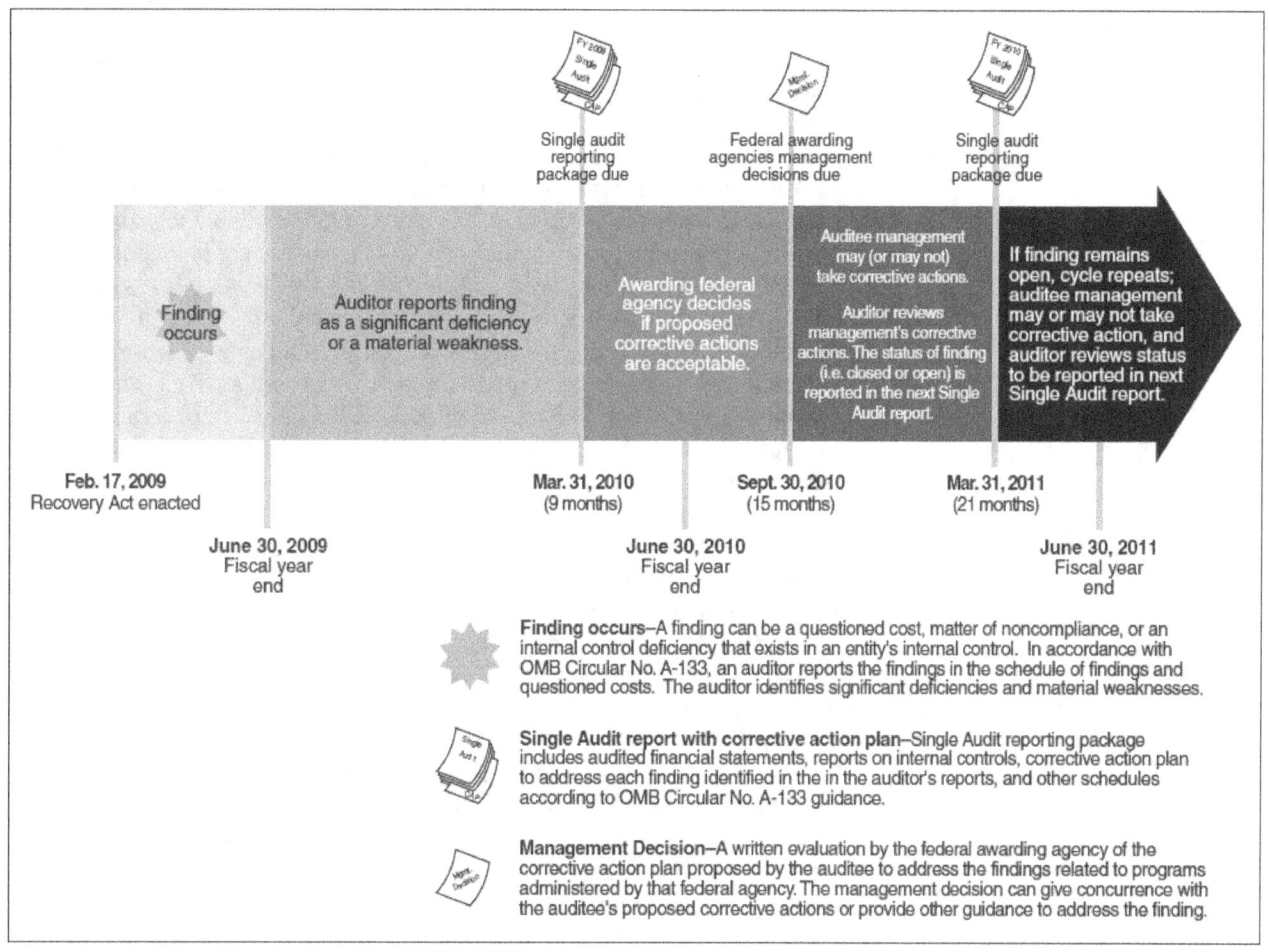

Source: GAO.

As we reported in prior Recovery Act reports, the problem that the Single Audit reports are not due until 9 months after the fiscal year-end was exacerbated by the extensions to the deadline to file Single Audit reports. The federal awarding agencies, consistent with OMB guidance, had routinely granted such extensions. In February 2010, HHS, the cognizant agency for audit, adopted a policy of no longer approving requests for such extensions. Further, in March 2010, OMB issued a memorandum, in response to our recommendation, that directed federal agencies to not grant any requests made to extend the Single Audit reporting deadlines for fiscal years 2009 through 2011. Despite this guidance, we found that the

Federal Audit Clearinghouse (FAC) did not receive Single Audit reporting packages for fiscal year ending 2009 from 5 of the 16 selected states and the District of Columbia within the 9-month time frame provided by statute.[173] Single Audit reporting packages include a schedule of internal control deficiencies and the auditee's plans for correcting them. Thus, when submissions of reporting packages are late, the auditees' efforts to correct internal control deficiencies may be delayed. According to OMB guidance, late submissions of the Single Audit to FAC in either of the 2 prior fiscal years would prevent the auditor from attaining low-risk auditee status, which could likely result in an increase in the scope of audit coverage to address the additional risk for the subsequent year's audit of the auditee. While the focus of our bi-monthly reports has been on Recovery Act funds, in general, the Single Audit pertains to federal expenditures awarded from the Recovery Act as well as from other federal sources; thus, internal control deficiencies identified in a program expending Recovery Act funds would generally affect all other sources of federal funds for that program as well.

As of August 5, 2010, five of the states participating in the project did not submit their completed fiscal year 2009 Single Audit reports to FAC by the March 31 due date; one of these states had not yet submitted its fiscal year 2009 Single Audit Report as of August 24, 2010.[174] While these states were able to meet the project's reporting deadline, they were not able to meet the deadline to submit the state's Single Audit reporting package.

Single Audit Guidance Continues to Be Issued in an Untimely Manner

We identified other concerns through our review of the project that point to the need for OMB to issue all Single Audit guidance in a more timely manner. Specifically, 12 of the 14 participating state auditors who responded to our survey stated that guidance for any future OMB projects should be more timely. In addition, more than half of the auditors who

---

[173]The five states are Arizona, Illinois, New Jersey, Ohio, and Pennsylvania. Although the FAC received initial Single Audit reporting packages from Colorado, Georgia, and Massachusetts by the March 31 due date, the FAC received subsequent information, which completed the reporting requirements from these states, after the March 31 due date.

[174]According to OMB data, as of August 5, 2010, five of the 16 states that participated in the OMB Single Audit Internal Control Project (Colorado, Georgia, Ohio, South Dakota, and Tennessee) did not file their completed Single Audit reporting package by the March 31, 2010, due date. Although FAC received the initial Single Audit reporting packages from Colorado and Georgia by the March 31 due date, FAC received subsequent information which completed the reporting requirements from these states after the March 31 due date. As of August 24, 2010, the FAC had not yet received Tennessee's reporting package for the fiscal year 2009 Single Audit.

responded to our survey indicated that they had concerns with timeliness issues relating to the release of OMB's 2009 Circular No. A-133 Compliance Supplement. OMB issued the Compliance Supplement in two stages, the initial one in May 2009 and an addendum in August 2009. This guidance was issued after the Single Audits for entities with a June 30, 2009, fiscal year-end were already under way. Most of the participating auditors told us that they needed the information as early as February 2009, or at least by April 2009, to effectively plan their work. Some of these state auditors stated that the OMB guidance was issued too late, causing inefficiencies and disruptions in the planning of audit procedures.

OMB officials told us that they planned to issue the 2010 Compliance Supplement in late May 2010. In our May 2010 bi-monthly report, we recommended that OMB issue its Single Audit guidance, including guidance for future projects, in a timely manner so that auditors can efficiently plan their audit work. OMB concurred with our recommendation. However, OMB issued the 2010 Compliance Supplement on July 29, 2010—again after the audit planning and work for Single Audits for entities with a June 30, 2010, fiscal year end was already under way. OMB officials stated that the delay in issuing the 2010 Compliance Supplement was primarily due to the additional attention needed to include more Recovery Act programs in the Compliance Supplement and information regarding the audit procedures for reviewing Recovery Act reporting requirements. OMB had provided the American Institute of Certified Public Accountants (AICPA) Governmental Audit Quality Center and the National Association of State Auditors, Comptrollers and Treasurers (NASACT) with draft Single Audit guidance in May 2010. AICPA and NASACT posted the draft to its Web sites for auditors to use for planning their work. However, some auditors we spoke with stated that because the guidance was not in a final form, it still impacted their ability to efficiently plan and conduct their work.

We also reported that OMB initiated the first project in October 2009 well after most of the audit work had been underway, resulting in some of the project's benefits not being realized. The project's guidance called for the auditors to complete their internal control work as of November 30, 2009, and to report internal control deficiencies by December 31, 2009. The project's guidelines included incentives to provide the participating auditors with some relief in their workload to encourage them to participate in the project. Under the project's guidelines, auditors were not required to perform risk assessments of smaller federal programs that they would otherwise need to complete. However, since most of the auditors had already completed the risk assessments by the time the project had started, most of the participating auditors stated that they did not experience any audit relief.

OMB has stated that it plans to have a second phase of the Single Audit Internal Control Project for fiscal year 2010. However, as of August 5, 2010, OMB had not yet defined the parameters of the project and issued guidance for potential volunteer participants. OMB has not provided detailed guidance that would explain incentives for volunteering to participate in the project, types of entities that will be permitted to participate, the scope of the project (including the specific programs that participants could select from), the number of participants it is seeking, or the time frames for beginning and ending the project.

We continue to report concerns about the Single Audit process because it does not provide a means for the timely identification and correction of internal control deficiencies or other findings relating to Recovery Act programs. This limits the effectiveness of the Single Audit process as an oversight accountability mechanism and exposes Recovery Act funds to increased risk of misuse or fraud. We recommend that the Director of OMB strengthen the Single Audit and federal follow-up as oversight accountability mechanisms by (1) shortening the timeframes required for issuing management decisions by federal awarding agencies to grant recipients, and (2) issuing the OMB Circular No. A-133 Compliance Supplement no later than March 31 of each year.

Fraud, Waste, and Abuse Allegations GAO Has Received That Are Related to the Recovery Act

As of August 11, 2010, we have received 224 allegations of Recovery Act wrongdoing from the public. We have closed 137 of these cases because the allegations were nonspecific or lacked information about fraud, waste, or abuse. Another 44 were investigated further and closed by us or the appropriate agency inspector general (IG) when no violations were found. Of allegations that are open, 16 are being handled by us and 27 by an IG. We generally refer allegations to an IG when that office is already pursuing the same or a similar complaint. We periodically contact the IGs to determine the status of our referrals. We will continue to evaluate all Recovery Act allegations received through FraudNet and provide updates in future reports.

Recovery Accountability and Transparency Board Initiatives

The Recovery Accountability and Transparency Board (the Board) continues to take steps to identify and report on potential areas for risk to fraud, waste, and mismanagement of Recovery Act funds. The Board recently published its third report in its series of reviews regarding recipient reporting data quality. In addition, the Board continues to augment its various initiatives for detecting potential instances of risk in Recovery Act contracting and turn over information regarding such instances to the appropriate inspectors general for further review. The Board also continues to organize coordinated reviews performed by its inspectors general working group aimed at further assessments of the management and oversight of Recovery Act spending. The Board is also planning to expand on some of its initiatives to strengthen future oversight as implementation of the Recovery Act continues.

Board Reports Focus on Data Quality

In June 2010, the Board reported on the third of three phases of its inspectors general working group's review of actions taken by agencies to improve the quality of data that recipients of Recovery Act funds are providing for posting to the public Web site.[175] Working in conjunction with the Board, six inspectors general reported that their agencies had issued policies and general procedures that follow OMB's guidance; however, the implementation of their respective guidance differed significantly among the agencies and their subunits.[176] We discuss the results of the inspectors general work in more detail under the recipient reporting section of this report.

Current Board Initiatives

The Board continues to use a variety of initiatives to monitor Recovery Act spending in an effort to identify potential areas at risk for fraud, waste, and abuse. The Board's current oversight initiatives include the following:

- maintaining a Fraud Hotline, which receives complaints of potential fraud, waste, and abuse from the public, and referring potential cases to the respective inspector general for further review.

---

[175]Recovery Accountability and Transparency Board, *American Recovery and Reinvestment Act—Review of the Effectiveness of Department/Agency Data Quality Review Processes* (Washington, D.C., June 25, 2010).

[176]The six inspectors general participating in the review were the Department of Housing and Urban Development, the Department of Defense, the General Services Administration, the Environmental Protection Agency, the National Science Foundation, and the Department of Agriculture.

- performing data analyses on publicly available information about Recovery Act recipients. The Board continues to modify its analytical efforts to provide insights on potential risk areas for the oversight community. The Board increased its staff, added more software, and obtained new public data sources to provide for additional analyses.

As of July 31, 2010, the Board had received 2,398 Fraud Hotline complaints.[177] As a result of these complaints as well as the Board's data analyses, the Board had referred 184 leads to various inspectors general as of July 31, 2010. Over half of these leads involved the potential misappropriation of funds or nonperformance of services.

Board Coordination and Monitoring of Inspectors General Initiatives

The Board continues to coordinate audits carried out by the inspectors general working group and monitor the independent efforts of the inspectors general related to the Recovery Act. The inspectors general working group has one audit under way reviewing the accuracy of selected fields of recipient reporting data. In addition, the working group is beginning a review of potential fraud indicators for grants programs in September 2010.

The Board continues to review monthly reports submitted by the inspectors general on the number and status of Recovery Act-related audits and investigations each has initiated. As of July 31, 2010, the inspectors general received 3,806 complaints related to the Recovery Act and reported that they have 424 active investigations; 141 investigations closed without action; and 474 audits, inspections, evaluations, or reviews in process. The inspectors general also reported they have completed 689 work products on Recovery Act-related issues since the act was passed— 534 of which are published on Recovery.gov and 155 of which are not publicly available since they contain proprietary or sensitive information.[178] In addition, the inspectors general, in conjunction with the Board, reported that they have conducted 2,231 training and outreach sessions related to Recovery Act issues.

---

[177]According to the Board staff, the majority of the complaints received via the fraud hotline did not contain any actionable information; for example, some complaints contained a generalized comment on the Recovery Act rather than any specific allegation of wrongdoing. The Board refers those that are actionable to the appropriate inspector general when there is a specific allegation of wrongdoing or multiple factors indicate a possible area of risk.

[178]According to a Board official, 63 of the 534 inspectors general products published on Recovery.gov are interim reports published to raise important issues with agency management in an expedited manner.

Impact of the Board and Inspectors General Efforts	According to Board representatives, an outcome of the Board and its work has been to shift the focus of the inspectors general community to the prevention of fraud, rather than just the identification and correction of it. As discussed earlier, the Board's data analysis capabilities provides the inspectors general with leads regarding potential risks associated with Recovery Act funds and recipients. In addition, over half of the training sessions provided have been focused on preventing fraudulent use of Recovery Act funds. According to Board representatives, the Board's work has also resulted in changes in the data to provide for better visibility over the use of federal funds. For example, a data field was added in FedBizOpps for recording a company's DUNS number;[179] a DUNS number is an important data element in tracking companies' transactions with the government, and including this information is expected to enhance data matching capabilities.
Board Plans for the Future	Board representatives explained that the Board and its predictive analysis capabilities are considered a template for changing how the government does business. In the short-term, the Board would like to develop predictive analysis tools for federal agencies' use, such as a list of databases to search and steps to be taken to identify risks. In addition, the Board is considering plans for the transition of its analytic capabilities elsewhere in the federal government when the Board's authorization expires at the end of fiscal year 2013.
Recovery Independent Advisory Panel	In February 2009, the Recovery Act provided for a Recovery Independent Advisory Panel to make recommendations to the Board on ways to prevent fraud, waste, and abuse relating to Recovery Act funds.[180] Four members of the Advisory Panel were appointed by the President in March 2010. At its first public meeting in Cambridge, Massachusetts, in August 2010, state and City of Boston officials presented information and addressed the panel's questions about their actions to prevent fraud, waste, and abuse. In addition, they discussed the content and structure of the state Recovery Act Web site, as well as continuity among state and

[179]The DUNS—Data Universal Numbering System—number is a unique 9-digit identification number provided by Dun and Bradstreet, Inc., for each physical location of a business or organization. The DUNS number is a unique identifier for an organization and is used to identify which business or organization is submitting reporting information to the government for federal contracts.

[180]Recovery Act, div. A §§ 1541-1546, 123 Stat. at 295-296.

local Web sites with the federal government's Recovery.gov Web site. The panel also held a closed session to discuss techniques to investigate fraud. Currently, the panel plans to hold a series of public meetings across the United States, and has tentatively planned its next public meeting for November 2010.

Audit Activities Involving Recovery Act Funds Continue at the State and Local Levels

State and local oversight and audit entities across the 16 selected states and the District continue to actively audit Recovery Act funds. As mentioned in our May 2010 report, many of these audits are conducted through the state Single Audit process—an accountability mechanism for overseeing federal funds at the state and local levels. These audits spanned many programs and primarily focused on programs that have been assessed as having higher risk of noncompliance with federal program requirements, such as weatherization, transportation, and Medicaid. However, according to officials from several of our selected states and the District, budget and staffing constraints have limited the number of Recovery Act audit reviews they could perform. Audit report findings have covered various areas including financial management and compliance laws or regulations. In some cases, the audits of Recovery Act funds identified and reported audit findings that were subsequently addressed by audited entities. In other cases, audits of Recovery Act funds did not identify or report findings.

Examples of audit findings relating to financial management practices identified in audits of Recovery Act funds include the following:

- In California, the State Auditor found that cash management practices were not in compliance with federal rules in the state's Weatherization Assistance Program.

- The Illinois Office of Internal Audit reported on the failure of state agencies to minimize the time between drawdowns of federal funds and expenditure of those funds and failure to charge hours worked to the proper federal grant at one agency.

- In Iowa, auditors found that a local school district possibly commingled Recovery Act funds with other school district revenue, which led to the replacement of the district's accounting supervisor.

- In New Jersey, an audit of the Weatherization Assistance Program found inadequate policies and controls in place to ensure that federal financial reporting was properly completed, supported by adequate documentation, and reviewed by a supervisor prior to submission.

- In Ohio, the Auditor of the State identified deficiencies related to unallowable expenditures and inadequate cash management in some programs funded through the Recovery Act.

Examples of audit findings relating to program compliance with laws and regulations that were identified in various audits of Recovery Act funds include the following:

- In Arizona, Single Audits found that the Arizona Department of Education failed to have current central contractor registrations on file prior to awarding Recovery Act ESEA Title I grants to LEAs but have developed a corrective action plan to correct these findings.

- In Colorado, a local government audit revealed that some Federal Transit Formula Grant funds had been spent without a check on whether the vendor had been suspended or debarred from participating in federal programs.

- In Florida, state auditors found that the program officials were unable to document that certain individuals were eligible for Medicaid benefits as required by law, and that their procedures did not ensure that all health care providers receiving Medicaid payments had provider agreements in effect.

- In Massachusetts, the state auditors found that the actual number of youths being reported as participating in the state's WIA summer jobs program was overstated, that the calculation of job numbers needed to be monitored more closely, and that compliance with participation levels needed to be reviewed.

- In Michigan, the Single Audit of the Medicaid program found that the Michigan Department of Community Health did not fully monitor its Medicaid payments to ensure that such claims are paid promptly. Failure to comply with the "prompt pay" requirements could result in Michigan not being eligible to receive increased FMAP for certain claims.

- In Mississippi, auditors found many instances of noncompliance with recipient reporting requirements. In these cases, state agencies were not providing clear and consistent guidance to subrecipients.

- In North Carolina, the state auditor's office found that a state department did not consistently perform effective monitoring to ensure that subrecipients of Recovery Act funds were in compliance with Davis-Bacon wage-rate requirements.

- In Texas, the Single Audit for fiscal year 2009 identified program weaknesses in determining eligibility in Medicaid, Temporary Assistance for Needy Families, and the Supplementary Nutrition Assistance Program.

In addition to audits of Recovery Act funds, several states took steps to strengthen their accountability efforts to help to ensure appropriate uses of Recovery Act funds by implementing new work groups or entities to help manage and oversee Recovery Act-funded programs. In addition, these new entities have helped state and local governments address the new requirements associated with Recovery Act funding, coordinate efforts among the accountability community, and inform the public. Other activities performed by these entities included maintaining a Recovery Act Web site, providing technical assistance, tracking the use of funds, issuing advisories, conducting training on internal controls, and providing assistance with recipient reporting. Examples of such activities are as follows:

- In California, the Recovery Task Force meets regularly with state agencies receiving Recovery Act funds, maintains a Recovery Act Web site as a central repository of information, and has issued more than 30 Recovery Act bulletins providing instructions and guidelines to state agencies. Also, the Recovery Act Inspector General published an advisory which included steps to ensure that contractors perform in accordance with contract terms and to reduce the potential of fraud.

- In Georgia, the State Accounting Office launched an internal control initiative to enhance accountability for Recovery Act funds that began in June 2010 and provided internal control training to 28 state agencies.[181] More specifically, these agencies completed a self-assessment tool covering internal controls in areas such as financial reporting, revenue, and Recovery Act funds.

---

[181]The State Accounting Office also provided the training to several universities and technical colleges.

- In Massachusetts, the City of Boston contracted auditor is developing a computerized worksheet in which Recovery Act fund recipients will submit their reporting data in a standardized format that will be centrally stored at the City Auditor's office. According to city officials, this will make the managing of subrecipients and the reporting process easier and more efficient.

- In New Jersey, the Recovery Accountability Task force is responsible for monitoring the distribution of Recovery Act funds in the state and promoting the effective and efficient use of those funds. The task force discusses issues related to the oversight of Recovery Act funds and receives updates from state agencies to ensure funds are dispersed with the goals of the Recovery Act in mind.

- In New York, the Governor created a Stimulus Oversight Panel which meets biweekly to examine the use of Recovery Act funds by each of the 22 state agencies designated to receive them. In addition to other responsibilities, individual panel members also conduct reviews and audits in their areas of expertise.

- In North Carolina, the Office of Economic Recovery and Investment (OERI) tracks, monitors, and reports on Recovery Act funds and works with state agencies on corrective action plans to help resolve Recovery Act-related findings. OERI also conducted several technical assistance seminars around the state and provides resources such as webinars and checklists on its Web site to help agencies comply with Recovery Act requirements.

- In Pennsylvania, the Governor appointed the Chief Accountability Officer to help oversee reporting and transparency for Recovery Act activities of state agencies. For the quarter ending June 30, 2010, the office filed 371 recipient reports on behalf of state agencies and posted them to the state's Recovery Act Web site.

- In Texas, the Governor's Stimulus Working Group, which includes representatives from state agencies receiving significant amounts of Recovery Act funding, is a vehicle for sharing information. This group has been used to inform state agencies about recipient reporting requirements, help focus auditing and monitoring efforts, and address program concerns.

Observations on States' Use of Contracts and Contract Outcomes

During our Recovery Act reviews, we tracked and observed 208 contracts awarded by state and local governments. While this is a small number of contracts, our observations indicate that state and local governments receiving Recovery Act funds reported that they are generally using competition and fixed-price contracts, and are not facing major issues with cost, schedule, or contractor performance.

State and Local Recovery Act Contracts Generally Are Reported to Use Competition and Fixed-Price Arrangements

Between July 2009 and March 2010, we selected and subsequently analyzed contracts from a variety of programs and held discussions with state and local officials to gain an understanding of the extent to which they believe contracts were awarded competitively and used pricing structures, particularly fixed-price contracts, which reduced the government's financial risk.[182] The use of competition is generally considered a fundamental tenant of public procurement. In addition, fixed-price contracting generally places the maximum amount of risk on the contractor because the government pays a fixed price even if actual costs of the product or service exceed the contract price. Of the 208 contracts we reviewed, 86 percent were reported by state and local officials as being competed and 79 percent were reported as fixed-price contracts.[183] Further, in five states all of the contracts we reviewed were reported as being competed, and in four states all of the contracts we reviewed were reported as being fixed-price contracts. Almost all contracts for highway projects were reported as competed, and all public housing contracts as fixed-price. Table 12 shows the number of contracts reported by officials as being competed and awarded with fixed prices in the various programs we are monitoring across the selected states.

---

[182]The states and the District of Columbia have varying definitions and procedures relating to competition and contract types. Therefore, we relied on state and local officials to verify whether a particular contract was awarded competitively and considered to be fixed-price under state or local contracting definitions and procedures.

[183]In some instances, state officials further identified these contracts as having fixed-unit pricing arrangements, where, according to state officials, unit prices for contract items are fixed, but total quantities of items may vary, if needed. Some officials characterized this type of arrangement as fixed-price, while others reported that it was other-than- fixed-price. As such, contracts with fixed-unit pricing arrangements are included in both the fixed-price and other-than-fixed-price totals identified in this section of the report.

Table 12: Number of Contracts Reported as Competed and Fixed Price, by Program Area as of June 2010

Program area	Total contracts reviewed	Contracts reported as competed	Contracts reported as fixed-price
Public Housing Authority officials	55	52	55
Highway programs—state level	52	51	35
Weatherization	27	17	21
Workforce Investment Act Youth Program—local level	19	14	7
Highway Programs—local project	16	16	12
Title I, Part A of the Elementary and Secondary Education Act of 1965—local level	15	6	14
Transit programs	12	11	10
Other	12	11	11
Total	208	178	165

Source: GAO analysis of data reported by state and local officials.

State and local officials cited various reasons why some contracts were awarded noncompetitively. For instance, officials reported that, for several contracts, the contractors provided a unique service and were the only source available. In another instance, officials said that the state was granted a waiver of some competition requirements in order to, in part, expedite the delivery of goods and services. Officials also gave various reasons why some contracts were not awarded as fixed-price contracts. For instance, officials reported that, for many contracts, fixed-price contracts were not used because use of another contract type was the agency's standard practice for a particular type of project. In other cases, officials stated that other contract types enabled the program to award a contract and begin performance faster than a fixed-price contract would.

As part of our overall body of work on the Recovery Act, in July 2010 we reported on the level of insight and oversight regarding the use of noncompetitive Recovery Act contracts in 5 of the 16 states covered in our bimonthly reviews: California, Colorado, Florida, New York, and Texas.[184] We found that the five states varied on the type and amount of data routinely collected on noncompetitive Recovery Act contracts and that the states do not routinely provide state-level oversight of contracts awarded

[184]See GAO, *Recovery Act: Contracting Approaches and Oversight Used by Selected Federal Agencies and States*, GAO-10-809 (Washington, D.C.: July 15, 2010).

at the local level, where a portion of Recovery Act contracting occurs.[185] According to state officials, they were generally following the contracting policies and practices for awarding and overseeing contracts that were in place prior to passage of the Recovery Act. Officials from the selected states' audit organizations said that if they were to address Recovery Act contracting issues, it could be done through the annual Single Audit or other reviews of programs that involve Recovery Act funds.

Majority of State and Local Recovery Act Contracts Are Reported to Be on Cost and Schedule and Performing Satisfactorily

Between March and June 2010, we followed up with state and local officials to understand whether the contracts we had selected were achieving the key acquisition outcomes of delivering on cost, on schedule, and with satisfactory performance. State and local officials reported that most of the Recovery Act contracts we reviewed are meeting these goals. According to state and local officials, of the 208 contracts we reviewed, 51 percent had no change to overall contract cost, 12 percent had decreased costs, and 1 percent had changes to cost and prices but remained within the contracts' total cost permitted. Approximately one-third of the contracts reported cost increases. In addition, officials reported that 52 percent of contracts had no change to schedule and 11 percent delivered early. The remaining 36 percent of contracts reported schedule delays. Thirty-six percent—or 74 contracts—had no changes to either cost or schedule.[186] Table 13 shows the number of contracts reported by officials as having cost or schedule changes by the various programs we are monitoring across the selected states.

---

[185]For the purposes of the report, we considered state-level oversight as centralized state government offices with purview over more than one state agency or department. This included each governor's office and state controller offices.

[186]We were unable to determine whether overall costs had increased, decreased, or remained the same for four contracts. In addition, we were unable to determine whether the schedule had increased, decreased, or remained the same for three contracts.

Table 13: Number of Contracts Officials Reported as Having Cost or Schedule Changes, by Program Area as of June 2010

Program area	Total contracts reviewed	Contracts reporting no cost or schedule changes	Contracts reporting increased costs	Contracts reporting decreased costs	Contracts reporting schedule delay	Contracts reporting early delivery
Public Housing Authority	55	12	23	4	27	3
Highway programs—state level	52	7	20	13	23	15
Weatherization	27	18	4	0	7	0
Workforce Investment Act Youth Program—local level	19	9	3	4	6	1
Highway programs—local project	16	4	10	1	5	1
Title I, Part A of the Elementary and Secondary Education Act of 1965—local level	15	13	0	1	0	1
Transit programs	12	5	7	0	4	1
Other	12	6	3	1	3	0
Total	**208**	**74**	**70**	**24**	**75**	**22**

Source: GAO analysis of data reported by state and local officials.

Note: Some contracts fell into more than one category, so figures do not total across each program.

For three-quarters of the 70 contracts where price increased, state and local officials attributed these increases to conditions that were not anticipated at the time of contract award. For example, officials reported that total costs increased by over $300,000 for one public housing project because materials containing asbestos were found on boilers, which had to be taken apart to remove asbestos before they could be demolished, and several boilers intended to be repaired or reused needed to be replaced instead. The most common factors state and local officials pointed to for schedule delays were circumstances beyond the control of the contractor and conditions not anticipated at the time of contract award. For instance, in several cases, officials noted that severe weather caused schedule delays.

According to state and local officials, 91 percent of the contracts we reviewed had no contractor work performance issues that adversely impacted the work being performed or deliverables being provided. Only

14 of 208 contracts we reviewed reported that there had been issues with contractor performance.[187] Of those, seven were highway construction projects at the state and local level and three of the contracts were for public housing projects. While the nature of these issues varied, in most cases officials reported that the contractor was able to satisfactorily continue or complete the project. In some of these cases, the contractor was assessed fees to compensate for the contractor's performance issues. Officials reported only two instances where the contractor ceased to perform the remaining work, which will now be performed by another contractor or the agency's staff.

Local Governments' Use of Recovery Act Funds

For this report, we continue our focus on the use of Recovery Act funds at the local government level while updating our review of states' uses of Recovery Act funds in proposed and enacted budgets. As shown in figure 32, we visited 24 local governments in our 16 selected states and the District to collect information regarding their use of Recovery Act funds. Similar to the approach taken for our May 2010 report,[188] we identified localities representing a range of types of governments (cities and counties), population sizes, and economic conditions (unemployment rates greater and less than the state's overall unemployment rate). We balanced these criteria with other considerations, including other scheduled Recovery Act work, local contacts established during prior reviews, and the geographic proximity of the local government entities. Officials from the 24 local governments we interviewed ranged in population from 258 in Steward, Illinois, to approximately 2.5 million in Miami-Dade County, Florida. Unemployment rates in our selected localities ranged from 6.7 percent in Round Rock, Texas, to 13.4 percent in Redding, California.[189]

---

[187]For three contracts, officials did not provide any response regarding contractor performance issues, and for two contracts officials responded that they "don't know."

[188]GAO, *Recovery Act: States' and Localities' Uses of Funds and Actions Needed to Address Implementation Challenges and Bolster Accountability*, GAO-10-604 (Washington, D.C.: May 26, 2010).

[189]See appendix IV for a complete list of population and unemployment rates for the selected local governments.

Figure 32: Selected Local Governments Included in Our September 2010 Review

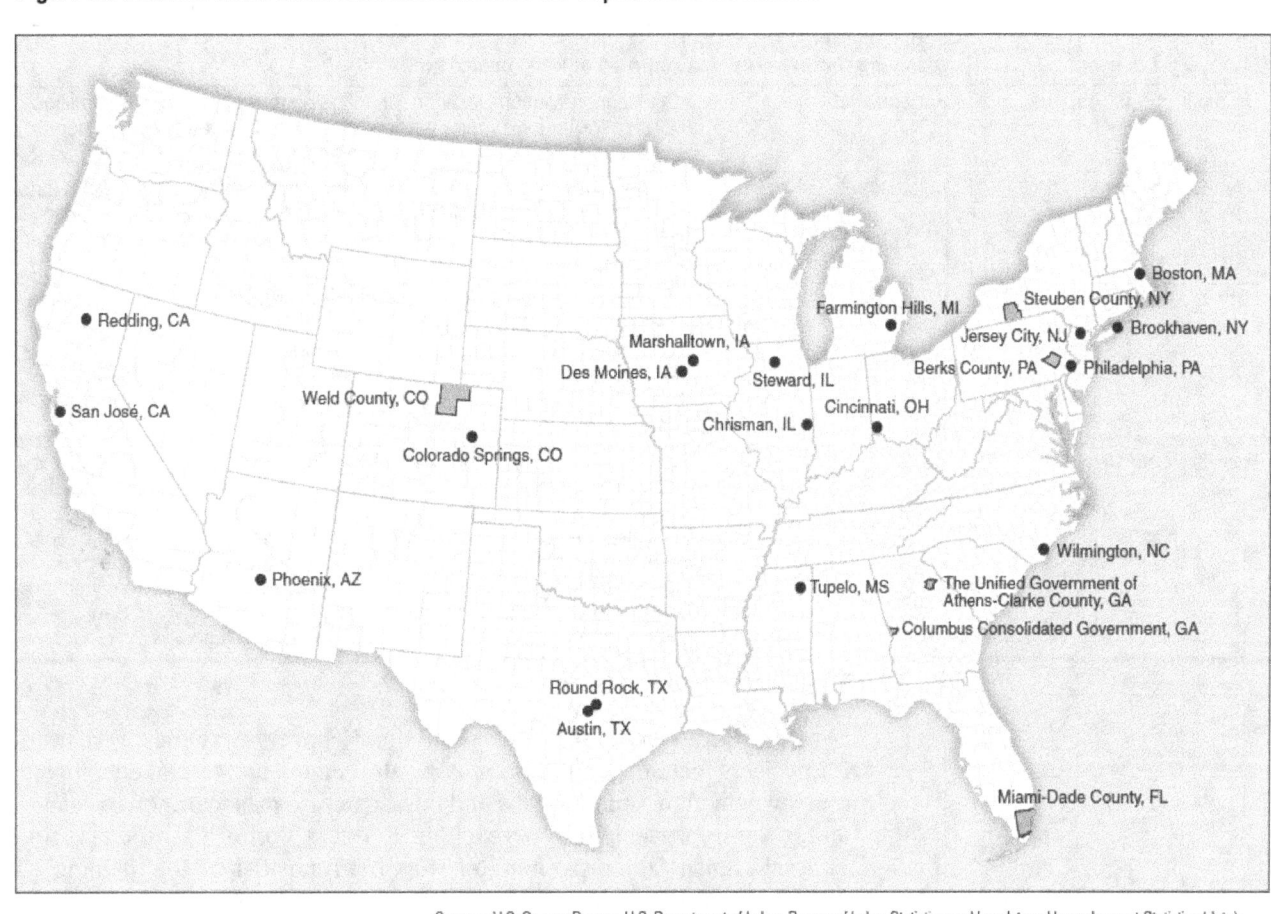

Sources: U.S. Census Bureau, U.S. Department of Labor, Bureau of Labor Statistics, and Local Area Unemployment Statistics (data); MapInfo (map).

Local Governments Continue to Use Recovery Act Funds to Initiate One-Time Projects, Provide Services, and Support Staff, While Fiscal Challenges Persist

Local officials reported their governments' continued use of Recovery Act funds in a range of program areas such as public safety (Community Oriented Policing Services (COPS) and Edward Byrne Memorial Justice Assistance Grants (JAG)), energy (EECBG), housing (Homelessness Prevention and Rapid Re-housing Program (HPRP) and Community Development Block Grant (CDBG)), and transportation and transit. Other Recovery Act funds received by the selected localities include grants for lead mitigation, wastewater treatment, and airport improvement. Some examples of the uses of Recovery Act funds appear in table 14.

Table 14: Selected Examples of Local Governments' Uses of Recovery Act Funds

Recovery Act grant	Local government receiving funds	Examples of local use of funds
Grants-in-Aid for Airports	Phoenix, AZ	The Phoenix Aviation Department obligated approximately $10.4 million in Grants-in-Aid for Airports funds to construct Taxiway C at the Phoenix Sky Harbor Airport to improve traffic flow.
Lead-Based Paint Hazard Control Program	Marshalltown, IA	The City of Marshalltown was awarded approximately $2.6 million to fund lead-mitigation efforts, including eliminating lead-based paint, repainting affected homes, replacing leaded windows, and housing citizens affected by renovations in temporary quarters.
Highway Infrastructure Investment grant	Wilmington, NC	Wilmington received a $4 million highway surface transportation grant to construct a multiuse trail linking key city resources and providing access to shopping, recreational, cultural, and educational destinations. The grant is expected to allow the city to complete 75 percent of the trail by 2011. The city had previously estimated completion by 2030 without federal funding.
Retrofit Ramp-Up	Austin, TX	The City of Austin was awarded $10 million for use of the Retrofit Ramp-Up program (part of the EECBG program) which may provide alternative financing options for property owners to make energy-efficiency improvements to their property, such as installing solar panels and roof water heating mechanisms. Alternative financing options include new financing mechanisms, interest rate buy-downs, and on-bill repayment. Austin city officials said they are coordinating with the City of San Antonio, which also received competitive EECBG funds.

Source: GAO analysis of local governments' reported use of funds.

Several local government officials said that Recovery Act funds were used for projects including purchase of law enforcement and transit equipment and investment in public works and infrastructure projects such as road and sewer improvements. For example, Redding, California, officials said Federal Transit Administration Recovery Act funds helped the Redding Area Bus Authority (RABA) accelerate the purchase of three new buses and nine new paratransit vans, thus allowing RABA to avoid implementing service cuts and fare increases. Officials in Farmington Hills, Michigan, reported using Recovery Act funds from the JAG program to purchase a range of public safety equipment, such as radio equipment, digital camcorders, undercover transmitters, and a Digital Eyewitness Media Manager Server System that otherwise would not have been purchased. Officials in Athens-Clarke County, Georgia, reported using Recovery Act funds from the Clean Water State Revolving Fund program to help construct four sewer inceptors. Columbus, Georgia, officials said they were using Recovery Act funds to enhance the implementation of transportation projects including the construction of a bike/pedestrian trail and streetscape improvements.

The use of Recovery Act funds also helped several local governments continue to provide local services. Philadelphia, Pennsylvania, officials said that the use of Recovery Act funds from the COPS Hiring Recovery Program (CHRP) grant helped support community policing and crime prevention efforts by allowing the city to hire 50 additional police officers. Similarly, officials in Colorado Springs, Colorado, reported using Recovery Act funds from the JAG program to fund the salaries of community service officers. Officials in Austin, Texas, reported using Recovery Act funds from the Edward Byrne Memorial Justice Assistance Grant program to fund 12 new emergency dispatchers. With regard to local services provided, officials in Weld County, Colorado, and Boston, Massachusetts, reported using Recovery Act funds from the Congregate Nutrition Services program to provide meal deliveries to low-income senior citizens. Officials in Berks County, Pennsylvania, said the county would not have been able to provide rent and utility assistance to persons at risk of becoming homeless without Recovery Act funds from the HPRP grant.

In most localities we visited, government officials reported working in partnership with other local entities, such as nonprofit organizations, the private sector, transit authorities, and other local jurisdictions to apply for or administer Recovery Act funds. For example, officials in Round Rock, Texas, said the city partnered with the Capital Area Metropolitan Planning Organization to apply for a Transit Capital Assistance Recovery Act grant. The application was successful with Round Rock receiving $2 million to construct a transit facility consisting of bus lanes, a transit pavilion, bicycle racks, and more than 100 parking spaces. Officials in Marshalltown, Iowa, reported that the city worked extensively with partners from surrounding counties, educational institutions, and other agencies to administer funds for the Lead-Based Paint Hazard Control Program. In Miami-Dade County, Florida, the local officials said the county partnered with private commercial farmers to administer Recovery Act funds from the National Clean Diesel Assistance Program. This program provided $2 million to farmers to purchase approximately 300 more efficient diesel motors used in portable and fixed irrigation equipment.

Most local governments we contacted for this review reported experiencing fiscal challenges due to revenue declines or reductions in state aid. In Jersey City, New Jersey, officials said the city faces an $80 million budget deficit and an estimated $27.5 million reduction in state aid for fiscal year 2011. Officials in Steuben County, New York, reported a decline in all categories of revenue receipts and state funding cuts of $858,000. Officials also noted that delays in state reimbursements have resulted in substantial use of county reserves. Officials in Miami-Dade

County, Florida, said a decrease in property and sales tax revenue combined with a reduction in state funding contributed to a $426 million budget gap for 2010. Officials in San José and Redding, California, also cited budget gaps for the current fiscal year and reductions in revenue from property taxes and other sources as examples of their governments' fiscal challenges. In Colorado Springs, Colorado, officials said their fiscal condition has slightly improved due to an unanticipated 4 percent increase in 2010 sales tax revenue over actual 2009 revenue. Despite this increase, Colorado Springs is not planning to expand services in 2010. Officials from the city of Austin reported an increase in sales tax revenue and declines in other revenue sources, such as fees and charges for commercial and residential development. Specifically, Austin, Texas, officials reported a 3.2 percent sales tax revenue increase and anticipate using this revenue to help address the city's budget gap of between $11 million and $28 million.

Officials in several localities reported that they are developing plans to continue funding Recovery Act programs using local government funds or by pursuing other funds after Recovery Act funding ends. For example, Cincinnati, Ohio, officials said the city hopes to continue funding the 50 police officers hired under the 3-year CHRP grant by using city revenues to cover expenditures after 2012. Officials in Wilmington, North Carolina, reported that the city intends to replace JAG funding for law enforcement equipment and services with general funds and other grant funds. San José, California, officials said the city plans to pursue other grant opportunities in order to continue funding city infrastructure projects currently benefiting from the use of Recovery Act funds. In contrast, officials in a number of localities said that because Recovery Act funds were primarily used for one-time projects they do not need to develop a specific plan to prepare for the end of Recovery Act funding. For example, officials in Farmington Hills, Michigan, reported that the city used Recovery Act funds for one-time expenditures, such as equipment purchases and energy-efficiency upgrades, and therefore does not need to develop an exit strategy. Similarly, in Tupelo, Mississippi, officials said the city used Recovery Act funds for infrastructure-related, "stand-alone" projects requiring minimal or no long-term financial support and specifically avoided applying for a CHRP grant because of the requirement to retain officers hired under the grant after Recovery Act funding ends. A few local governments reported that they plan to end Recovery Act-funded projects or reduce staff or funding for these programs after Recovery Act funding ends.

States' Use of Recovery Act Funds for Programs and Services Continues to Prevent Deeper Budget Cuts

Recovery Act funds continued to help states maintain services in areas such as education, health care, and transportation. A few states reported that they recently received additional Recovery Act funding in other areas. For example, New Jersey received $8 million for an energy rebate program and $14 million for energy-efficiency programs. Michigan received $30 million in Recovery Act funds to provide energy-efficiency retrofits for residential, commercial, industrial, and public buildings. Many of our selected states, as well as the District, reported that the Recovery Act continues to have a positive effect on their fiscal stability. As an example, Arizona state officials told us that Recovery Act funds helped their state through the worst part of the recession by preventing deeper cuts in social programs, and giving officials breathing room to figure out what fiscal steps to take in the long term. Officials in Ohio credit the over $7.9 billion in Recovery Act funds they have received as of August 1, 2010, with helping to protect jobs and continue services in their state. Officials in Illinois and the District said that they would be in more dire fiscal condition without SFSF and the increased FMAP funds from the Recovery Act. In Iowa, Recovery Act funds received in fiscal year 2011 helped officials balance their fiscal year 2011 budget while avoiding tax increases and reducing the amount by which officials needed to draw down the state's reserve fund. Recovery Act funds also reduced the need in Massachusetts to use more of the state's authorized fiscal year 2010 rainy-day reserve funds to balance the budget, according to state officials. City officials told us that Recovery Act funds helped the District maintain a balanced budget for fiscal year 2011 without tapping into the city's rainy-day fund.

Several states and the District contacted for this review reported that they incorporated measures to prepare for the end of Recovery Act funding in their fiscal year 2011 budget or in budgets in prior cycles.[190] For example, in Mississippi officials told us the legislature sharply reduced spending to offset reductions in Recovery Act funding. According to city officials, the District's fiscal year 2010 budget, as well as the mayor's proposed fiscal year 2011 budget, reflects the reduction in revenues that will result from the reduction in Recovery Act funds in fiscal year 2011. Officials in some states reported they were planning for the end of Recovery Act funding. For example, Florida officials told us they were in the early stages of

---

[190]Not all jurisdictions have the same fiscal year. Most of the states we visited have fiscal years beginning July 1, with the following exceptions: New York's fiscal year begins on April 1; the fiscal year for Texas begins on September 1; and the fiscal year for the District of Columbia and Michigan begins on October 1.

developing their fiscal year 2012 budget which will include a plan to address the phasing out of Recovery Act funds. According to Michigan officials, they have made some structural changes such as reforms to the public school employees' retirement plan and are working to devise solutions for when the Recovery Act funds run out in fiscal year 2012. In Georgia, officials said they are preparing for the cessation of Recovery Act funds by planning additional budget reductions. They also are projecting moderate revenue growth. New York officials told us that they will address the phasing out of Recovery Act funds this fall when they develop the budget for the next fiscal year.

State officials reported mixed assessments of changes to their states' fiscal conditions since we contacted them for our May 2010 report. Officials in several states noted that they continue to face difficult budget challenges. Several states told us that their fiscal condition has generally remained the same since our May report. Some states have seen signs that their fiscal condition is shifting and showing signs of improvement. For example, state officials reported that tax revenue collections in Massachusetts during the last 2 months of fiscal year 2010 were above revenue estimates by $191 million and $149 million respectively, and the commonwealth ended fiscal year 2010 with tax collections above budget estimates. State officials in Pennsylvania also reported that revenues were $58 million ahead of estimates in June—the first month since December 2007 that revenues exceeded estimates. Arizona officials also told us that their April and May revenues were much better than they had projected, however, they noted that the trend did not continue in June and July. In another example, Michigan officials told us that in June 2010, total wage and salary employment was up 23,400 jobs compared to June 2009. This was the first year-over-year increase in total wage and salary employment in Michigan since March 2005. These signs of improvement, in contrast to revenue declines, are consistent with national trends reported in the June 2010 *Fiscal Survey of States* issued by the National Governors Association and the National Association of State Budget Officers.[191] According to the Fiscal Survey, states are projecting a slight rise of 3.9 percent in tax collections for fiscal year 2011 recommended budgets relative to fiscal year 2010 estimates. However, states estimate that their 2010 tax revenues will represent an almost 12 percent decline in states' sales, personal

---

[191]National Governors Association and the National Association of State Budget Officers, *The Fiscal Survey of States* (Washington, D.C., June 2010). The survey is based on survey responses from all 50 states' governors' budget offices collected from March through May 2010.

income, and corporate income tax collections since fiscal year 2008, the last fiscal year in which states were not significantly affected by the national recession. The Fiscal Survey attributes reduced state sales, personal income, and corporate income tax collections to the lack of economic expansion and job losses.

New and Open Recommendations; Matters for Congressional Consideration

For this report, GAO both updates the status of agencies' efforts to implement GAO's 25 open recommendations and makes 5 new recommendations to the Departments of Transportation (DOT), Housing and Urban Development (HUD), Labor, Energy (DOE), Health and Human Services, and Treasury, and to the Environmental Protection Agency (EPA), and to the Office of Management and Budget (OMB).[192] Agency responses to our new recommendations are included in the program sections of this report. Lastly, we update the status of our Matters for Congressional Consideration.

Department of Transportation

New Recommendations

To ensure that Congress and the public have accurate information on the extent to which the goals of the Recovery Act are being met, we recommend that the Secretary of Transportation direct FHWA to take the following two actions:

---

[192]GAO, *Recovery Act: As Initial Implementation Unfolds in States and Localities, Continued Attention to Accountability Issues Is Essential*, GAO-09-580 (Washington, D.C.: Apr. 23, 2009); *Recovery Act: States' and Localities' Current and Planned Uses of Funds While Facing Fiscal Stresses*, GAO-09-829 (Washington, D.C.: July 8, 2009); *Recovery Act: Funds Continue to Provide Fiscal Relief to States and Localities, While Accountability and Reporting Challenges Need to Be Fully Addressed*, GAO-09-1016 (Washington, D.C.: Sept. 23, 2009); *Recovery Act: Recipient Reported Jobs Data Provide Some Insight into Use of Recovery Act Funding, but Data Quality and Reporting Issues Need Attention*, GAO-10-223 (Washington, D.C.: Nov. 19, 2009); *Recovery Act: Status of States' and Localities' Use of Funds and Efforts to Ensure Accountability*, GAO-10-231 (Washington, D.C.: Dec. 10, 2009); *Recovery Act: One Year Later, States' and Localities' Uses of Funds and Opportunities to Strengthen Accountability*, GAO-10-437 (Washington, D.C. Mar. 3, 2010); and *Recovery Act: States' and Localities' Uses of Funds and Actions Needed to Address Implementation Challenges and Bolster Accountability*, GAO-10-604 (Washington, D.C.: May 26, 2010).

- Develop additional rules and data checks in the Recovery Act Data System, so that these data will accurately identify contract milestones such as award dates and amounts, and provide guidance to states to revise existing contract data.

- Make publicly available—within 60 days after the September 30, 2010, obligation deadline—an accurate accounting and analysis of the extent to which states directed funds to economically distressed areas, including corrections to the data initially provided to Congress in December 2009.

Open Recommendations

To better understand the impact of Recovery Act investments in transportation, we believe that the Secretary of Transportation should ensure that the results of these projects are assessed and a determination made about whether these investments produced long-term benefits. Specifically, in the near term, we recommend the Secretary direct FHWA and FTA to determine the types of data and performance measures they would need to assess the impact of the Recovery Act and the specific authority they may need to collect data and report on these measures.

Agency Actions

In its response, DOT noted that it expected to be able to report on Recovery Act outputs, such as the miles of road paved, bridges repaired, and transit vehicles purchased, but not on outcomes, such as reductions in travel time, nor did it commit to assessing whether transportation investments produced long-term benefits. DOT further explained that limitations in its data systems, coupled with the magnitude of Recovery Act funds relative to overall annual federal investment in transportation, would make assessing the benefits of Recovery Act funds difficult. DOT indicated that, with these limitations in mind, it is examining its existing data availability and, as necessary, would seek additional data collection authority from Congress if it became apparent that such authority were needed. While we are encouraged that DOT plans to take some steps to assess its data needs, it has not committed to assessing the long-term benefits of Recovery Act investments in transportation infrastructure. We are therefore keeping our recommendation on this matter open.

Open Recommendation

The Secretary of Transportation should gather timely information on the progress they are making in meeting the maintenance-of-effort requirement and to report preliminary information to Congress within 60 days of the certified period (September 30, 2010), (1) on whether states met required program expenditures as outlined in their maintenance-of-effort certifications, (2) the reasons that states did not meet these certified levels, if applicable, and (3) lessons learned from the process.

Agency Actions

DOT concurred in part with our March 2010 recommendation that it gather and report more timely information on the progress states are making in meeting the maintenance-of-effort requirements. Because more timely information could better inform policymakers' decisions on the usefulness and effectiveness of the maintenance-of-effort requirements and is important to assessing the impact of Recovery Act funding in achieving its intended effect of increasing overall spending, we are leaving this recommendation open and plan to continue to monitor DOT's actions.

In its August 2010 response, DOT officials stated that DOT will encourage states to report preliminary data for the certified period ending September 30, 2010, and deliver a preliminary report to Congress within 60 days of the certified period. DOT officials said they have developed a timeline for obtaining information to produce this report and will issue guidance by October 1, 2010, requesting that states update actual aggregate expenditure data and provide the data to DOT by November 15, 2010. DOT officials said they will use this information to develop the report to Congress, and it will submit the report no later than November 30, 2010.

Department of Housing and Urban Development

New Recommendation

Because the absence of third-party investors reduces the amount of overall scrutiny TCAP projects would receive and HUD is currently not aware of how many projects lacked third-party investors, HUD should develop a risk-based plan for its role in overseeing TCAP projects that recognizes the level of oversight provided by others.

Department of Labor

Open Recommendations

To enhance Labor's ability to manage its Recovery Act and regular WIA formula grants and to build on its efforts to improve the accuracy and consistency of financial reporting, we recommend that the Secretary of Labor take the following actions:

- To determine the extent and nature of reporting inconsistencies across the states and better target technical assistance, conduct a one-time assessment of financial reports that examines whether each state's reported data on obligations meet Labor's requirements.

- To enhance state accountability and to facilitate their progress in making reporting improvements, routinely review states' reporting on obligations during regular state comprehensive reviews.

Agency Actions

Labor agreed with both of our recommendations and has begun to take some actions to implement them. To determine the extent of reporting inconsistencies, Labor plans to conduct an assessment of state financial reports to determine if the data reported is accurate and reflects Labor's guidance on reporting of obligations and expenditures. After the assessment, Labor plans to provide technical assistance to states that need further instruction and guidance. To enhance states' accountability and facilitate their progress in making improvements in reporting, Labor has instructed all its regional offices to begin routinely reviewing state's reporting on obligations during state comprehensive reviews. In addition, Labor plans to issue guidance on the definitions of key financial terms such as obligations, provide online training to ensure that the terms are accurately and consistently applied, and conduct workshops on financial and administrative management.

Open Recommendation

Our September 2009 bimonthly report identified a need for additional federal guidance in two areas—measuring the work readiness of youth and defining green jobs —and we made the following two recommendations to the Secretary of Labor:

- To enhance the usefulness of data on work readiness outcomes, provide additional guidance on how to measure work readiness of youth, with a goal of improving the comparability and rigor of the measure.

- To better support state and local efforts to provide youth with employment and training in green jobs, provide additional guidance about the nature of these jobs and the strategies that could be used to prepare youth for careers in green industries.

Agency Actions

Labor agreed with both of our recommendations and has begun to take some actions to implement them. With regard to the work readiness measure for WIA Youth summer employment activities, Labor issued guidance on May 13, 2010 for the WIA Youth Program that builds on the experiences and lessons learned during implementation of Recovery Act-funded youth activities in 2009. Labor broadly identified some additional requirements for measuring work readiness of youth that it plans to address in future guidance. This includes having the employer observe and assess workplace performance and determine what worksite skills are necessary to be successful in the workplace.

Regarding our recommendation on the green jobs, Labor told us that the Bureau of Labor Statistics published a Federal Register Notice on March 16, 2010 for comment on a proposed definition for measuring green jobs, which includes an approach for identifying environmental industries and counting associated jobs. Labor officials hope this will inform state and local workforce development efforts to identify and target green jobs and their training needs. In addition, Labor is using the Recovery Act-funded green jobs training grants to document lessons learned on designing and providing green jobs training.

Department of Energy

Open Recommendations

Given the concerns we have raised about whether program requirements are being met, we recommend that DOE, in conjunction with both state and local weatherization agencies, develop and clarify weatherization program guidance that

- establishes best practices for how income eligibility should be determined and documented and issues specific guidance that does not allow the self-certification of income by applicants to be the sole method of documenting income eligibility.

- clarifies the specific methodology for calculating the average cost per home weatherized to ensure that the maximum average cost limit is applied as intended.

- accelerates current DOE efforts to develop national standards for weatherization training, certification, and accreditation, which is currently expected to take 2 years to complete.

- develops a best practice guide for key internal controls that should be present at the local weatherization agency level to ensure compliance with key program requirements.

- sets time frames for development and implementation of state monitoring programs.

- revisits the various methodologies used in determining the weatherization work that should be performed based on the consideration of cost-effectiveness and develops standard methodologies that ensure that priority is given to the most cost-effective weatherization work. To validate any methodologies created, this effort should include the development of standards for accurately measuring the long-term energy savings resulting from weatherization work conducted.

- considers and addresses how the weatherization program guidance is impacted by the introduction of increased amounts of multifamily units.

In addition, given that state and local agencies have felt pressure to meet a large increase in production targets while effectively meeting program requirements and have experienced some confusion over production targets, funding obligations, and associated consequences for not meeting production and funding goals, we recommend that DOE clarify its production targets, funding deadlines, and associated consequences while providing a balanced emphasis on the importance of meeting program requirements.

Agency Actions

In our May 2010 report, we provided eight recommendations and raised concerns about whether program requirements were being met. DOE generally agreed with all of our recommendations and has begun to take several steps in response. For example, DOE reported that it has drafted national workload standards to address our concerns regarding training, certification, and accreditation. DOE plans to issue these standards to recipients in October 2010. DOE is still in the process of considering our recommendations and will provide additional information on how they plan to fully implement our recommendations at a later date.

Environmental Protection Agency

Open Recommendation

We recommend that the EPA Administrator work with the states to implement specific oversight procedures to monitor and ensure subrecipients' compliance with the provisions of the Recovery Act-funded Clean Water and Drinking Water SRF program.

Agency Actions

In response to our recommendation, EPA provided additional guidance to the states regarding their oversight responsibilities, with an emphasis on enhancing site specific monitoring and inspections. Specifically, in June 2010, the agency developed and issued an oversight plan outline for Recovery Act projects that provides guidance on the frequency, content, and documentation related to regional reviews of state Recovery Act programs and regional and state reviews of specific Recovery Act projects. For example, EPA's guidance states that regions and states should be reviewing the items included on the EPA "State ARRA Inspection Checklist" or use a state equivalent that covers the same topics. The plan also describes EPA headquarters role in ongoing Recovery Act oversight and plans for additional webcasts. EPA also reiterated that contractors are available to provide training and to assist with file reviews and site inspections.

Department of Health and Human Services: Office of Head Start

Our May 2010 bimonthly report identified the need for improved management information on regional offices and grantees' decisions and activities to consistently oversee the rapid expansion and program performance of Head Start and Early Head Start under the Recovery Act. We made three recommendations to the Director of the Office of Head Start (OHS), part of the Department of Health and Human Services' Administration for Children and Families. In May, HHS disagreed with our conclusion that a lack of management information limits its ability to consistently oversee the rapid expansion of Head Start and Early Head Start under the Recovery Act. We provided a draft of all materials related to Head Start and Early Head Start to OHS and HHS for comment, but they did not provide comments in time for us to consider them in this report.

Open Recommendation

To provide grantees with appropriate guidelines on their use of Head Start and Early Head Start grant funds, and enable OHS to monitor the use of these funds, the Director of OHS should direct regional office staff to stop allocating all grant funds to the "other" budget category, and immediately revise all financial assistance awards (FAAs) in which all funds were allocated to the "other" category.

Open Recommendation	To facilitate understanding of whether regional decisions regarding waivers of the program's matching requirement are consistent with Recovery Act grantees' needs across regions, the Director of OHS should regularly review waivers of the nonfederal matching requirement and associated justifications.
Open Recommendation	To oversee the extent to which grantees are meeting the program goal of providing services to children and families and to better track the initiation of services under the Recovery Act, the Director of OHS should collect data on the extent to which children and pregnant women actually receive services from Head Start and Early Head Start grantees.

Department of Treasury

New Recommendation	Treasury should expeditiously provide HFAs with guidance on monitoring project spending and develop plans for dealing with the possibility that projects could miss the spending deadline and face further project interruptions.

Executive Office of the President: Office of Management and Budget (OMB)

New Recommendation	To strengthen the Single Audit and federal follow up as oversight accountability mechanisms, we recommend that the Director of OMB (1) shorten the timeframes required for issuing management decisions by federal awarding agencies to grant recipients, and (2) issue the OMB Circular No. A-133 Compliance Supplement no later than March 31 of each year.
Open Recommendation	To leverage Single Audits as an effective oversight tool for Recovery Act programs, in our prior bimonthly reports, we recommended that the Director of OMB should

1. provide more direct focus on Recovery Act programs through the Single Audit to help ensure that smaller programs with higher risk have audit coverage in the area of internal controls and compliance;
2. take additional efforts to provide more timely reporting on internal controls for Recovery Act programs for 2010 and beyond; and
3. evaluate options for providing relief related to audit requirements for low-risk programs to balance new audit responsibilities associated with the Recovery Act.
4. issue Single Audit guidance in a timely manner so that auditors can efficiently plan their audit work; and
5. explore alternatives to help ensure that federal awarding agencies provide their management decisions on the corrective action plans in a timely manner.

Agency Actions

OMB has taken several steps in response to our recommendations. Its efforts, however, are ongoing, and further actions are needed to fully implement our recommendations to help mitigate risks related to Recovery Act funds. We include a summary of OMB's efforts to implement these recommendations.

To focus auditor risk assessments on Recovery Act-funded programs and to provide guidance on internal control reviews for Recovery Act programs, OMB worked within the framework defined by existing mechanisms—Circular No. A-133 and the Circular No. A-133 Compliance Supplement (Compliance Supplement).[193] In this context, OMB has made limited adjustments to its Single Audit guidance. OMB issued the Compliance Supplement in May 2009, which focused risk assessments on Recovery Act-funded programs. In August 2009, OMB issued the Circular No. A-133 Compliance Supplement Addendum I, which provided additional guidance for auditors and modified the Compliance Supplement to, among other things, focus on new Recovery Act programs and new program clusters.

In October 2009, OMB began a Single Audit Internal Control Project (project), which is nearing its completion as of May 14, 2010. One of the project's goals is to encourage auditors to identify and communicate significant deficiencies and material weaknesses in internal control over

---

[193]The Compliance Supplement is issued annually to guide auditors on what program requirements should be tested for programs audited as part of the Single Audit.

compliance for selected major Recovery Act programs 3 months sooner than the 9-month time frame currently required under OMB Circular No. A-133. OMB plans to analyze the results to identify the need for potential modifications to improve OMB guidance related to Single Audits.

Although OMB noted the increased responsibilities falling on those responsible for performing Single Audits, it has yet to issue proposals or plans to address this issue. States that volunteered to participate in the project were eligible for some relief in their workloads because OMB modified the requirements under Circular No. A-133 to reduce the number of low-risk programs for inclusion in the Single Audits.

Open Recommendation

To provide more direct focus on Recovery Act programs through the Single Audit with regard to smaller programs with higher risk, OMB provided guidance in the 2009 OMB Circular No. A-133 Compliance Supplement that required auditors to consider all federal programs with expenditures of Recovery Act awards to be considered higher risk programs when performing the standard risk-based tests for selection of programs to be audited. OMB also issued clarifying information on determining risk for programs with Recovery Act expenditures. However, since most of the funding for Recovery Act programs will be expended in 2010 and beyond, we remain concerned that some smaller programs with higher risk would not likely receive adequate audit coverage. One approach for OMB to consider in helping to ensure that smaller programs with higher risk have audit coverage is to explore various options to provide auditors with the flexibility needed to select programs that are considered high risk, even though the federal expenditures for a smaller program may be less than the expenditure threshold provided under the Single Audit Act.

With regard to taking additional efforts to provide more timely reporting on internal controls for Recovery Act programs for 2010 and beyond, OMB has not yet put into place measures to achieve earlier communication of the reporting of internal control deficiencies for fiscal years 2010 and beyond—years where considerable amounts of Recovery Act funds will be expended. OMB officials have stated in August 2010, that they plan to initiate a subsequent Single Audit Internal Control Project for fiscal year 2010. Similar to the 2009 project, one of the project's goals will be to encourage more timely identification and earlier communication of internal control deficiencies in selected programs expending Recovery Act funding.

OMB designed its Single Audit Internal Control Project to grant some relief to the auditors for the states that volunteered to encourage participation in the project. Specifically, participating auditors were not required to perform risk assessments of smaller federal programs. OMB had also modified the requirements under Circular No. A-133 to reduce the number of low-risk programs that must be included in some project participants' Single Audits. Although the project which began in October 2009, was designed to provide the auditors some relief in their workload, many auditors had already completed their risk assessment for audits with fiscal years ending June 30, 2009. As a result, the auditors did not experience the audit relief intended by the project.

With regard to issuing Single Audit Guidance in a timely manner, we reported in May 2010 that OMB officials told us that they had planned to issue the Compliance Supplement in late May 2010. However, OMB did not issue the Compliance Supplement until July 29, 2010. Several of the auditors that we surveyed stated that they needed the information as early as February, or at least by April, to effectively plan their work. OMB officials stated that the delay in issuing the 2010 compliance supplement was primarily due to the additional attention needed to include more Recovery Act programs in the Compliance Supplement and information regarding the audit procedures for reviewing Recovery Act reporting requirements. In May 2010, OMB provided the American Institute of Certified Public Accountants (AICPA) Governmental Audit Quality Center and the National Association of State Auditors, Comptrollers and Treasurers (NASACT) with draft Single Audit guidance in May 2010. AICPA and NASACT posted the draft to its Web sites for auditors to use for planning their work. However, some auditors we spoke with stated that because the guidance was not in a final form, it still impacted their ability to efficiently plan and conduct their work. In addition, OMB has stated that it plans to have a second phase of the Single Audit Internal Control Project for fiscal year 2010. However, as of August 5, 2010, OMB had not yet defined the parameters of the project and issued guidance for potential volunteer participants. OMB also has not provided detailed guidance that would explain incentives for volunteering to participate in the project, types of entities that will be permitted to participate, the scope of the project (including the specific programs that participants could select from), the number of participants it is seeking, or the timeframes for beginning and ending the project.

OMB officials have stated that they have discussed alternatives for helping to ensure that federal awarding agencies provide their management decisions on the corrective action plans in a timely manner but have yet to decide on the course of action that they will pursue to implement this recommendation.

Open Recommendation

As we noted in our July 2009 report, reporting on Recovery Act performance results is broader than the employment-related reporting required by the act. We continue to recommend that the Director of OMB—perhaps through the Senior Management Councils—clarify what other program performance measures recipients are expected to report on to demonstrate the impact of Recovery Act funding.

Matters for Congressional Consideration

Matter

To the extent that appropriate adjustments to the Single Audit process are not accomplished under the current Single Audit structure, Congress should consider amending the Single Audit Act or enacting new legislation that provides for more timely internal control reporting, as well as audit coverage for smaller Recovery Act programs with high risk.

GAO continues to believe that Congress should consider changes related to the Single Audit process.

Matter

To the extent that additional coverage is needed to achieve accountability over Recovery Act programs, Congress should consider mechanisms to provide additional resources to support those charged with carrying out the Single Audit Act and related audits.

GAO continues to believe that Congress should consider changes related to the Single Audit process.

Matter

To provide housing finance agencies (HFA) with greater tools for enforcing program compliance, in the event the Section 1602 Program is extended for another year, Congress may want to consider directing Treasury to permit HFAs the flexibility to disburse Section 1602 Program funds as interest-bearing loans that allow for repayment.

GAO continues to believe that Congress should consider directing Treasury to permit HFAs the flexibility to disburse Section 1602 Program funds as interest-bearing loans that allow for repayment.

We are sending copies of this report to the Office of Management and Budget and the Departments of Health and Human Services (Centers for Medicare and Medicaid Services), Education, Transportation, Energy, and Housing and Urban Development. In addition, we are sending sections of the report to officials in the 16 states and the District and the 24 local governments covered in our review. The report is available at no charge on the GAO Web site at http://www.gao.gov.

If you or your staffs have any questions about this report, please contact me at (202) 512-5500. Contact points for our Offices of Congressional Relations and Public Affairs may be found on the last page of this report. GAO staff who made major contributions to this report are listed in appendix V.

Gene L. Dodaro
Acting Comptroller General of the United States

List of Addressees

The Honorable Nancy Pelosi
Speaker of the House of Representatives

The Honorable Daniel K. Inouye
President Pro Tempore of the Senate

The Honorable Harry Reid
Majority Leader
United States Senate

The Honorable Mitch McConnell
Republican Leader
United States Senate

The Honorable Steny Hoyer
Majority Leader
House of Representatives

The Honorable John Boehner
Republican Leader
House of Representatives

The Honorable Daniel K. Inouye
Chairman
The Honorable Thad Cochran
Vice Chairman
Committee on Appropriations
United States Senate

The Honorable Dave Obey
Chairman
The Honorable Jerry Lewis
Ranking Member
Committee on Appropriations
House of Representatives

The Honorable Joseph I. Lieberman
Chairman
The Honorable Susan M. Collins
Ranking Member
Committee on Homeland Security and Governmental Affairs
United States Senate

The Honorable Edolphus Towns
Chairman
The Honorable Darrell E. Issa
Ranking Member
Committee on Oversight and Government Reform
House of Representatives

Appendix I: Objectives, Scope, and Methodology

This appendix describes our objectives, scope, and methodology for this seventh of our bimonthly reviews on the American Recovery and Reinvestment Act of 2009 (Recovery Act). A detailed description of the criteria used to select the core group of 16 states and the District of Columbia (District) and programs we reviewed is found in appendix I of our April 2009 Recovery Act bimonthly report.[1]

Objectives and Scope

The Recovery Act specifies several roles for GAO, including conducting bimonthly reviews of selected states' and localities' use of funds made available under the act. As a result, our objectives for this report were to assess (1) selected states' and localities' uses of and planning for Recovery Act funds, (2) the approaches taken by the selected states and localities to ensure accountability for Recovery Act funds, and (3) state activities to evaluate the impact of the Recovery Act funds they have received to date. We selected programs for review primarily because they have begun disbursing funds to states or because they have known or potential risks. The risks can include existing programs receiving significant amounts of Recovery Act funds or new programs. In some cases, we have also collected data from all states and from a broader array of localities to augment the in-depth reviews.

Our teams visited the 16 selected states, the District, and a nonprobability sample of entities (e.g., state and local governments, local educational agencies, public housing authorities) during the period from May 2010 through September 2010. As with our previous Recovery Act reports, our teams met with a variety of state and local officials from executive-level and program offices. During the discussions with state and local officials, teams used a series of program review and semistructured interview guides that addressed state plans for management, tracking, and reporting of Recovery Act funds and activities. We also reviewed state statutes, legislative proposals, and other state legal materials for this report. Where attributed, we relied on state officials and other state sources for descriptions and interpretation of state legal materials. Appendix IV details the states and localities visited by GAO. Criteria used to select localities within our selected states follows below.

---

[1]GAO, *Recovery Act: As Initial Implementation Unfolds in States and Localities, Continued Attention to Accountability Issues Is Essential*, GAO-09-580 (Washington, D.C.: Apr. 23, 2009).

The act requires that nonfederal recipients of Recovery Act-funded grants, contracts, or loans submit quarterly reports on each project or activity including information concerning the amount and use of funds and jobs created or retained.[2] The first of these recipient reports covered cumulative activity since the Recovery Act's passage through the quarter ending September 30, 2009. The Recovery Act requires us to comment on the estimates of jobs created or retained after the recipients have reported. We issued our initial report related to recipient reporting, including recommendations for recipient report improvements, on November 19, 2009.[3] A second major focus of the current report is to provide updated information concerning recipient reporting in accordance with our mandate for quarterly reporting.[4]

States' and Localities' Uses of Recovery Act Funds

Using criteria described in our earlier bimonthly reports, we selected the following streams of Recovery Act funding flowing to states and localities for review during this report: Medicaid Federal Medical Assistance Percentage (FMAP) grant awards; the State Fiscal Stabilization Fund (SFSF); Title I, Part A of the Elementary and Secondary Education Act of 1965 (ESEA); Parts B and C of the Individuals with Disabilities Education Act (IDEA); the Federal-Aid Highway Surface Transportation and Transit Capital Assistance programs; the State Energy Program (SEP); the Energy Efficiency and Conservation Block Grant program (EECBG); the Weatherization Assistance Program; the Public Housing Capital Fund; the Tax Credit Assistance Program (TCAP); and Grants to States for Low-Income Housing Projects in Lieu of Low-Income Housing Credits Program under Section 1602 of the Recovery Act (Section 1602 Program). We also reviewed how Recovery Act funds are being used by states and localities. In addition, we analyzed www.Recovery.gov data on federal spending.

---

[2]Recovery Act, div. A, §1512, 123. We will refer to the quarterly reports required by Section 1512 as recipient reports.

[3]GAO, *Recovery Act: Recipient Reported Jobs Data Provide Insights into Use of Recovery Act Funding, but Data Quality and Reporting Issues Need Attention,* GAO-10-223 (Washington, D.C.: Nov. 19, 2009).

[4]The Recovery Act requires recipients of funding from federal agencies to report quarterly on jobs created or retained with Recovery Act funding. The first recipient reports filed in October 2009 cover activity from February through September 30, 2009. This bimonthly report incorporates recipient reports covering activity through June 30, 2010.

Federal Medical Assistance Percentage

To examine Medicaid enrollment, states' efforts to comply with the provisions of the Recovery Act, states' uses of the grant awards, and other related information, we conducted a Web-based survey, asking the 16 states and the District to provide new information, as well as to update information they had previously provided to us. To establish the reliability of our Web-based survey data, we pretested the survey with Medicaid officials in two states and also conducted follow-up with sample states as needed. For the increased FMAP grant awards, we obtained increased FMAP grant and draw down figures for each state in our sample and the District from the Centers for Medicare & Medicaid Services (CMS). We discussed with CMS issues related to the agency's oversight of increased FMAP grant awards and its guidance to states on Recovery Act provisions. To assess the reliability of increased FMAP draw down figures, we previously interviewed CMS officials on how these data are collected and reported. Based on these steps, we determined that the data provided by CMS and submitted by states were sufficiently reliable for the purposes of our engagement.

SFSF, ESEA Title I, and IDEA

To obtain national level information on how Recovery Act funds made available by the U.S. Department of Education under SFSF, ESEA Title I, and IDEA were used at the local level, we designed and administered a Web-based survey of local education agencies (LEAs) in the 50 states and the District of Columbia. We surveyed school district superintendents across the country to learn how Recovery Act funding was used and what impact these funds had on school districts. We conducted our survey between March and April 2010, with a 78 percent final weighted response rate. We selected a stratified[5] random sample of 575 LEAs from the population of 16,065 LEAs included in our sample frame of data obtained from Education's Common Core of Data (CCD) in 2007-08.

We took steps to minimize nonsampling errors by pretesting the survey instrument with officials in 5 LEAs in January and February 2010. Because we surveyed a sample of LEAs, survey results are estimates of a population of LEAs and thus are subject to sampling errors that are associated with samples of this size and type. Our sample is only one of a large number of samples that we might have drawn. As each sample could

---

[5]We stratified the population into strata based on size and urban status. Regarding size, we identified the 100 largest LEAs in the country. The 33 geographic districts comprising the New York City Public Schools were treated as one school district and that one district was placed in the 100 largest LEAs stratum.

have provided different estimates, we express our confidence in the
precision of our particular sample's results as a 95 percent confidence
interval (e.g., plus or minus 10 percentage points). We excluded 16 of the
sampled LEAs for various reasons – because they were no longer
operating in the 2009-10 school year, were a duplicate entry, or were not
an LEA — and therefore were considered out of scope. All estimates
produced from the sample and presented in this report are representative
of the in-scope population and have margins of error of plus or minus 7
percentage points or less for our sample, unless otherwise noted.

To obtain specific examples of how LEAs are using Recovery Act funds,
we selected LEAs in each of the following states: California,
Massachusetts and Michigan to visit and interview LEA officials. We
selected these states from among the 16 states and the District of
Columbia in our review based on geographic diversity and varying state
budget situations for K-12 education.

Within the selected states, we identified a mix of local districts that would
represent urban, rural, and suburban districts, LEAs among the 100 largest
LEAs as well as districts that were not as large, and local districts with
different budget situations. We also obtained selected additional
information from LEA officials in New York. In addition to interviewing
local officials, we interviewed selected state officials. Specifically, we
interviewed ESEA Title I officials in states with relatively low Recovery
Act Title I drawdown rates to assess to what extent state officials in these
states are monitoring LEA obligations and also discussed implementation
of School Improvement Grants. We also interviewed officials at the U.S.
Department of Education (Education) and reviewed relevant laws,
guidance, and communications to the states. Further, we obtained
information from Education's website about the amount of funds these
states have drawn down from their accounts with Education. We also
reviewed data on state level funding changes from the National
Association of State Budget Officers (NASBO). To assess the reliability of
the NASBO data, we (1) reviewed existing documentation related to the
data sources and (2) interviewed knowledgeable agency officials about the
data. We determined that the data are sufficiently reliable for the purposes
of this report.

Federal-Aid Highway Surface Transportation Program

For highway infrastructure investment, we reviewed status reports and guidance to the states and discussed these with the U.S. Department of Transportation and Federal Highway Administration (FHWA) officials. We obtained funding data for each of the 16 states and the District in our review. We also reviewed data related to contracts and economically distressed areas—submitted by states—in the FHWA Recovery Act Data System (RADS) for completeness and compliance with FHWA guidance. We also interviewed or obtained information from state department of transportation officials in Arizona, California, Florida, Illinois, Massachusetts, Mississippi, North Carolina, Pennsylvania, and Texas. Specifically, we discussed rates of deobligations in suballocated and nonsuballocated areas, accuracy of contract data entered into RADS, and rates of spending from regular FHWA highway program during the period of the Recovery Act.

Transit Capital Assistance Program

For public transit investment, we reviewed status reports and guidance to the states and transit agencies and discussed these with U.S. Department of Transportation and Federal Transit Administration (FTA) officials as part of our review of the Transit Capital Assistance Program and Fixed Guideway Infrastructure Investment program. We obtained funding data on the amounts of funding transferred from FHWA to FTA and funding levels used for transit operating expenses for each of our urbanized and nonurbanized areas. We also interviewed FTA officials about operating expense data. Finally we interviewed or obtained information from state and transit agency officials in California, Illinois, Massachusetts, Michigan, New Jersey, and Texas regarding these issues.

State Energy Program, Energy Efficiency Conservation Block Grant, and Weatherization Assistance Program

For the State Energy Program (SEP), the Energy Efficiency and Conservation Block Grant program (EECBG), and Weatherization Assistance Program, we reviewed relevant regulations and federal guidance and interviewed Department of Energy officials who administer the programs at the federal level. Specifically, for the SEP and the EECBG programs, we collected information from 6 and 12 of our selected states and the District, respectively.[6] Also, we conducted semistructured interviews of officials in state and local agencies that administer the programs and with local subrecipients who received Recovery Act funds. These interviews covered the respective state's and locality's usage of funds, internal controls, and reporting procedures. We also collected data on the number and types of projects funded with Recovery Act money for the SEP and EECBG programs. In addition, for this report, we collected updated information from seven of our selected states and the District on their weatherization programs.[7] We conducted semistructured interviews of officials in the states' agencies that administer the weatherization program and with local service providers responsible for weatherization production. We interviewed officials at local service providers in the District and the seven states, and reviewed local agencies' client case files for homes weatherized with Recovery Act funds. We also conducted site visits to interview local providers of weatherization and to observe weatherization activities. For all three programs, we collected data about each state's total allocation under the Recovery Act, as well as the allocation already provided to the states and the obligations and expenditures-to-date.

Public Housing Capital Fund

For public housing, we obtained data from HUD's Electronic Line of Credit Control System on the amount of Recovery Act funds that have been obligated and expended by each housing agency in the country that received Public Housing Capital Funds. To monitor progress on how housing agencies are using these funds, we visited 12 housing agencies in nine states.[8] For each state, we selected at least 1 public housing agency

---

[6]For SEP, the six states we collected information from are: Arizona, California, Colorado, Iowa, New York, and Pennsylvania. For EECBG, the 12 states we collected information from are: Arizona, California, Colorado, Florida, Georgia, Iowa, Massachusetts, Michigan, New Jersey, New York, Pennsylvania, and Texas.

[7]The nine states we collected information from are: Arizona, California, Florida, Georgia, Iowa, New York, Ohio, Pennsylvania, and Texas.

[8]The states we visited are Arizona, California, Georgia, Illinois, Masschusetts, Mississippi, New Jersey, Pennsylvania, and Texas.

from a list of 47 housing agencies visited for previous Recovery Act
reports to update the status of their grant projects. At the selected housing
agencies, we interviewed housing agency officials and conducted site
visits of Recovery Act projects. We also interviewed officials of the U.S.
Department of Housing and Urban Development (HUD) to follow up on
HUD's efforts in monitoring public housing agency obligations and uses of
Recovery Act funds and to understand HUD's capacity to administer
Recovery Act funds. Further, we interviewed HUD officials to understand
their procedures for reviewing data that housing agencies reported to
FederalReporting.gov.

Tax Credit Assistance Program

To further assess state implementation of the Tax Credit Assistance
Program (TCAP) and Section 1602 program, we asked managers of state
housing finance agencies in all 50 states, the District, Puerto Rico, Guam,
and the U.S. Virgin Islands to complete a Web survey. Our questionnaire
asked about the status of program delivery, program design, safeguards
and controls, expected results, and challenges to implementation. We
designed and tested the self-administered questionnaire in consultation
with experts, representatives of housing finance stakeholders, and state
agency managers. Survey data collection took place in November and
early December of 2009. We received usable responses from all 54
agencies.

While all state agencies returned questionnaires, and thus our data is not
subject to sampling or overall questionnaire nonresponse error, the
practical difficulties of conducting any survey may introduce other errors
in our findings. We took steps to minimize errors of measurement,
question-specific nonresponse, and data processing. In addition to the
questionnaire development activities listed above, and pretesting the
questionnaire with four state agency officials before the survey, GAO
analysts also recontacted selected respondents to follow up on answers
that were missing or that required clarification. In addition, GAO analysts
resolved respondent difficulties in answering our questions during the
survey. Before the survey, we also contacted each agency to determine
whether our originally identified respondent was the most appropriate and
knowledgeable person to answer our questions, and made changes to our
contact list as necessary. Finally, analysis programs and other data
analyses were independently verified.

Head Start and Early Head Start

Owing to the focus on Early Head Start expansion under the Recovery Act, we visited nine Early Head Start expansion grantees in four states: Florida, Georgia, North Carolina, and Ohio. Due to time and resource considerations, we chose these states based on GAO staff expertise in Head Start. For each state, all but one Early Head Start grantee selected had received a grant above the median for all Recovery Act expansion funds awarded in each state in order to focus our limited resources on relatively sizable grants. We also included four grantees that had been awarded expansion funds for constructing or renovating facilities. The grantees we visited included grantees that had not previously provided an Early Head Start program but that had provided Head Start, as well as experienced Early Head Start grantees. For each selected grantee, we reviewed federal assistance award information, enrollment data, proposals for the use of Quality Improvement funds, and facilities under construction or renovation. We conducted structured interviews with grantee officials covering updates on the use of Recovery Act funds, challenges to spending funds within Office of Head Start (OHS) deadlines, OHS monitoring of grantees, and grantees' interpretation of enrollment and attendance requirements. We also reviewed files on-site at each grantee on enrollment, income eligibility, and health screening. The grantees we visited were purposefully chosen and are not a representative sample of all expansion grantees. The information gathered from these site visits is not generalizable to the population of Early Head Start expansion grantees.

Recipient Reporting

The recipient reporting section of this report responds to the Recovery Act's mandate that we comment on the estimates of jobs created or retained by direct recipients of Recovery Act funds. For our review of the fourth submission of recipient reports, covering the period from April 1, 2010, through June 30, 2010, we built on findings from our three prior reviews of the reports, covering the period from February 2009 through March 30, 2010. We performed edit checks and basic analyses on the fourth submission of recipient report data that became publicly available at Recovery.gov on July 30, 2010. We interviewed federal agency officials from the Department of Energy, who have responsibility for ensuring a reasonable degree of quality across their programs' recipient reports. We also interviewed representatives from a variety of state associations, such as the National Association of State Auditors, Comptrollers, and Treasurers and the National Association of State Budget Officers, to obtain their views on whether the process of recipient reporting has had an effect on intergovernmental interactions.

From the fourth submission of recipient reports, we reviewed reports for
two energy programs, EECBG and the Weatherization Assistance Program,
to determine whether they had used Office of Management and Budget
(OMB) guidance for calculating their full-time equivalents (FTE) funded by
the Recovery Act. We interviewed 13 EECBG state-level and 19 local
government recipients from our 17 selected jurisdictions about their FTE
calculations for the fourth round of reporting. We also interviewed 8 state-
level weatherization assistance recipients and 17 local government
weatherization assistance subrecipients from our 17 selected jurisdictions
about their FTE calculations. In some instances, we reviewed supporting
documentation with quarterly FTE reports, and assessed the validity of
those calculations in complying with OMB guidance. Due to the limited
number of recipients reviewed and the judgmental nature of the selection,
GAO's FTE findings are not generalizable beyond the programs examined.
In addition, state teams also interviewed government officials from our 16
selected states and the District to discuss issues that arose in the fourth
reporting period statewide, specifically related to any difficulties they
encountered during the fourth round of reporting, development of their
state Web sites, and their views on whether the recipient reporting
requirements have affected intergovernmental interactions. We also asked
these officials about ongoing state plans for managing, tracking, and
reporting on Recovery Act funding and activities and solicited feedback
from state officials regarding how states are using data generated from the
recipient reporting effort and ways the recipient reporting process could
be improved.

Single Audit as an Accountability and Oversight Mechanism

To perform our audit work, we interviewed federal officials, state auditors,
and officials from the cognizant agency for audit from the Department of
Health and Human Services (HHS). We examined documents related to
Single Audits, including the 2010 OMB Circular No. A-133 *Audits of States,
Local Governments, and Non-Profit Organizations Compliance
Supplement*,[9] OMB's and HHS's evaluations of the OMB Single Audit
Internal Control project, and related federal agency management
decisions. We reviewed Federal Audit Clearinghouse documents, such as
selected Single Audit reports. We also conducted a survey of the state
auditors and state program and finance officials that participated in the
OMB Internal Control Single Audit Project. We analyzed and summarized

---

[9]The 2010 OMB Circular No. A-133 *Audits of States, Local Governments, and Non-Profit
Organizations Compliance Supplement* was issued on July 29, 2010.

the responses to our survey.[10] We conducted our surveys in March 2010 and interviewed several state auditors, officials from the Department of Health and Human Services, which is the cognizant agency for audit, and officials from awarding federal agencies whose programs were selected for audit under the project. We also participated in an OMB-led discussion of the project's participants to obtain their views on the project.

Recovery Accountability and Transparency Board Initiatives

To determine the status and results of oversight activities of the Recovery Accountability and Transparency Board (the Board), we met with representatives of the Board to discuss the initiatives they have taken to coordinate and monitor the efforts of the inspectors' general oversight activities as well as the Board's initiatives to prevent and detect fraud, waste, and abuse of Recovery funds. We reviewed available documentation related to the Board's efforts.

Observations on States' Use of Contracts and Contract Outcomes

To provide observations on selected states' use of competitive procedures and fixed prices in awarding contracts for Recovery Act funds, between July 2009 and March 2010, we met with state and local officials to discuss the contract award process for a sample of 208 contracts in 16 states and the District. Between March and June 2010, we met again with the officials responsible for these same contracts to discuss the extent to which there had been cost or schedule changes or contractor performance issues. The contracts we reviewed with state officials were selected based on a combination of several factors to obtain a mix of various programs and dollar values that varied among the states. Our methodology for selecting these contracts does not allow for reported information to be generalized.

State and Local Accountability

To assess actions taken by the state and local audit community to monitor the use of Recovery Act funds, we have interviewed selected state and local auditors and state inspectors general about their ongoing and planned audit activities. We have also reviewed state and local audit reports. We have also spoken to some of the Recovery Act oversight entities created in many of the selected states such as New Jersey's Recovery Accountability Task Force and the Recovery Task Force in

---

[10]For additional information about our survey and our analysis of responses, see *Recovery Act: States' and Localities' Uses of Funds and Actions Needed to Address Implementation Challenges and Bolster Accountability*, GAO-10-604 (Washington, D.C.: May 26, 2010).

California. In addition, in an effort to update the audit community
concerning our Recovery Act work and participate in information sharing
about Recovery Act issues, we are working with state and local auditors
and their associations to facilitate routine telephone conference calls to
discuss Recovery Act issues with a broad community of interested parties.
The conference call participants include the Association of Government
Accountants; the Association of Local Government Auditors; the National
Association of State Auditors, Comptrollers, and Treasurers; OMB; the
Board; federal inspectors general; the National Governors Association; and
the National Association of State Budget Officers. In an effort to ensure
information sharing about allegations of fraud, we are also working with
state and local auditors to develop plans for routine sharing of
information.

State and Local Budget

We continued our review of the use of Recovery Act funds for the 16
selected states, the District, and selected localities. We conducted
interviews with state budget officials and reviewed proposed and enacted
budgets and revenue forecasts to update our understanding of the use of
Recovery Act funds in the 16 selected states and the District. To update
our understanding of local governments' use of Recovery Act funds, we
met with finance officials and city administrators at the selected local
governments.

The topics covered in our meetings included what Recovery Act funds the
states and localities received, how they used the funds, and their exit
strategy to prepare for the phasing out of Recovery Act funding. In the
course of our discussions with officials we explored the extent to which
the receipt of Recovery Act funds has stabilized state and local
government budgets. We also reviewed reports and analyses regarding the
fiscal conditions of states and localities.

The selected states and the District for our review contain about 65
percent of the U.S. population and are estimated to receive collectively
about two-thirds of the intergovernmental grant funds available through
the Recovery Act. To select local governments for our review, we
identified localities representing a range of jurisdictions (cities and
counties) and variations in population sizes and economic conditions
(unemployment rates greater than or less than the state's overall
unemployment rate). In making our selections, we also considered
proximity to our other scheduled Recovery Act work and local contacts
established during prior reviews. The GAO teams visited a total of 24 local
governments in our 16 selected states that ranged in population from

approximately 258 in Steward, Illinois, to approximately 2.5 million in
Miami-Dade County, Florida. Unemployment rates in our selected
localities ranged from 6.7 percent in Round Rock, Texas, to 13.4 percent in
Redding, California.[11] Due to the small number of jurisdictions visited and
judgmental nature of their selection, GAO's findings are not generalizable
to all local governments.

The list of local governments selected in each state is found in appendix
IV.

Data and Data Reliability

We collected funding data from www.Recovery.gov and federal agencies
administering Recovery Act programs for the purpose of providing
background information. We used funding data from www.Recovery.gov—
which is overseen by the Board—because it is the official source for
Recovery Act spending. Except as may be noted with regard to specific
analyses appearing in other sections of this report and based on our
examination of this information thus far, we consider these data
sufficiently reliable with attribution to official sources for the purposes of
providing background information on Recovery Act funding for this
report. Our sample of states, localities, and entities has been purposefully
selected and the results of our reviews are not generalizable to any
population of states, localities, or entities.

We conducted this performance audit from May 27, 2010, to September 20,
2010, in accordance with generally accepted government auditing
standards. Those standards require that we plan and perform the audit to
obtain sufficient, appropriate evidence to provide a reasonable basis for
our findings and conclusions based on our audit objectives. We believe
that the evidence obtained provides a reasonable basis for our findings
and conclusions based on our audit objectives.

---

[11]See appendix IV, for a complete list of population and unemployment rates for the
selected local governments.

Appendix II: Implemented and Closed Recommendations

The following are 31 GAO recommendations that Departments of Transportation (DOT), Housing and Urban Development (HUD), Education, Treasury, and the Office of Management and Budget (OMB) have implemented since we began conducting bimonthly reviews in April 2009.[1] We have also closed 2 recommendations.

Department of Transportation

Implemented Recommendation

To ensure that the public has accurate information regarding economically distressed areas, we also recommend that the Secretary of Transportation direct FHWA to issue guidance to the states advising them to update information in the Recovery Act Data System to reflect current DOT decisions concerning the special-need criteria. Projects in areas currently lacking documentation showing that the areas meet the criteria to be designated as economically distressed should be reported as a project in a noneconomically distressed area.

Agency Actions

In July 2010, FHWA directed Arizona, California, and Illinois to revise their designations and to report these projects as being in noneconomically distressed areas. FHWA also directed all states to ensure that future Recovery Act Data System entries be coded as economically distressed only if FHWA division and headquarters offices had approved the designation.

---

[1]GAO, *Recovery Act: As Initial Implementation Unfolds in States and Localities, Continued Attention to Accountability Issues Is Essential*, GAO-09-580 (Washington, D.C.: Apr. 23, 2009); *Recovery Act: States' and Localities' Current and Planned Uses of Funds While Facing Fiscal Stresses*, GAO-09-829 (Washington, D.C.: July 8, 2009); *Recovery Act: Funds Continue to Provide Fiscal Relief to States and Localities, While Accountability and Reporting Challenges Need to Be Fully Addressed*, GAO-09-1016 (Washington, D.C.: Sept. 23, 2009); *Recovery Act: Recipient Reported Jobs Data Provide Some Insight into Use of Recovery Act Funding, but Data Quality and Reporting Issues Need Attention*, GAO-10-223 (Washington, D.C.: Nov. 19, 2009); *Recovery Act: Status of States' and Localities' Use of Funds and Efforts to Ensure Accountability*, GAO-10-231 (Washington, D.C.: Dec. 10, 2009); and *Recovery Act: One Year Later, States' and Localities' Uses of Funds and Opportunities to Strengthen Accountability*, GAO-10-437 (Washington, D.C. Mar. 3, 2010); *Recovery Act: States' and Localities' Uses of Funds and Actions Needed to Address Implementation Challenges and Bolster Accountability*, GAO-10-604 (Washington, D.C. May 26, 2010).

Implemented Recommendation
Recipients of highway and transit Recovery Act funds, such as state departments of transportation and transit agencies, are subject to multiple reporting requirements. Both DOT and OMB have issued implementation guidance for recipient reporting. Despite these efforts, state and local highway and transit officials expressed concerns and challenges with meeting the Recovery Act reporting requirements. We recommended in our September 2009 report that the Secretary of Transportation should continue the department's outreach to state departments of transportation and transit agencies to identify common problems in accurately fulfilling reporting requirements and provide additional guidance, as appropriate.

Agency Actions

In September 2009, in responding to our recommendation, DOT said that it had conducted outreach, including providing technical assistance, training, and guidance to recipients, and will continue to assess the need to provide additional information. For example, in February 2010, FTA continued three training webinars to provide technical assistance in complying with reporting requirements under section 1201(c) of the Recovery Act. In addition, on February 1, 2010, FTA issued guidance to transit agencies instructing them to use the same methodology for calculating jobs retained through vehicles purchased under section 1201 as they had been for the recipient reporting. This reversed previous guidance that had instructed transit agencies to use a different methodology for vehicle purchases under sections 1201 and recipient reporting.

Implemented Recommendation
DOT and FHWA have yet to provide clear guidance regarding how states are to implement the Recovery Act requirement that economically distressed areas (EDA) are to receive priority in the selection of highway projects for funding. We found substantial variation both in how states identified EDAs and how they prioritized project selection for these areas. To ensure states meet Congress's direction to give areas with the greatest need priority in project selection, we recommended in our July 2009 report that the Secretary of Transportation develop clear guidance on identifying and giving priority to EDAs that are in accordance with the requirements of the Recovery Act and the Public Works and Economic Development Act of 1965, as amended, and more consistent procedures for FHWA to use in reviewing and approving states' criteria.

Agency Actions

In August 2009, in response to our recommendation, FHWA, in consultation with the Department of Commerce, developed guidance that addresses our recommendation. In particular, FHWA's August 2009 guidance defines "priority," directing states to give priority to projects that are located in an economically distressed area and can be completed within the 3-year time frame over other projects. In addition, FHWA's guidance sets out criteria that states may use to identify economically distressed areas based on "special need." The criteria align closely with special need criteria used by the Department of Commerce's Economic Development Administration in its own grant programs, including factors such as actual or threatened business closures (including job loss thresholds), military base closures, and natural disasters or emergencies.

Department of Housing and Urban Development

Implemented Recommendation

To ensure housing agencies use the correct job calculation, we recommend that the Secretary of Housing and Urban Development clearly emphasize to housing agencies that they discontinue use of the outdated jobs calculator provided by HUD in the first round of recipient reporting.

Agency Actions

In response to our recommendation, HUD sent an e-mail to housing agencies on June 30, 2010, that explicitly instructed them not to use the outdated jobs-counting calculator, as it was not correctly computing the FTE calculation per updated OMB guidance. This e-mail also included a link to HUD's new online jobs-counting calculator and instructed housing agencies to use this calculator for the July and all future reporting periods.

Implemented Recommendation

To help clarify the recipient reporting responsibilities of housing agencies and to improve the consistency and completeness of jobs data reported by housing agencies, we recommend that the Secretary of Housing and Urban Development issue guidance that explains when FTEs attributable to subcontractors should be reported by the prime recipient.

Agency Actions

In response to our recommendation, HUD notified housing agencies in a June 30, 2010, e-mail that it had developed additional guidance for housing agencies to use when determining whether prime recipients should report FTEs for subcontractors and provided a link to the guidance on its Web site. The guidance noted that housing agencies should include Recovery

Act-funded hours that contractors and subcontractors worked as part of their FTE calculation.

Implemented Recommendation

To help HUD achieve Recovery Act objectives and address challenges with its continued administration of Recovery Act funds, we recommend that the Secretary of Housing and Urban Development develop a management plan to determine the adequate level of agency staff needed to administer both the Recovery Act funds and the existing Capital Fund program going forward, including identifying future resource needs and determining whether current resources could be better utilized to administer these funds.

Agency Actions

In response to our recommendation, HUD developed a management plan for administration of Recovery Act funds, including the need for an additional 11 FTEs to carry out Recovery Act responsibilities. In July 2010, HUD also provided us with its management plan for the Public Housing Capital Fund program. The plan summarized the key activities HUD undertakes to monitor and facilitate the use of these funds by program area, including rule and policy development, planning, program awards, program management, technical assistance, and reporting. The plan also included the specific activities, tasks, and resources used for each of these existing program areas, identifying approximately 91 existing FTEs in its headquarters and field offices to support these activities. According to HUD's management plan, HUD's current staffing level is sufficient to manage its existing Capital Fund program, but the agency could more efficiently utilize its current resources. As a result, HUD plans to realign current staff to focus on its core missions including Recovery Act responsibilities.

Implemented Recommendation

We recommended on March 3, 2010 that the Secretary of Housing and Urban Development instruct housing agencies to discontinue use of the jobs calculator provided by HUD in the first round of recipient reporting for subsequent rounds of reporting to ensure the correct job calculation is used.

Agency Actions

In a March 26, 2010, e-mail to housing agencies, HUD included instructions to discontinue use of the jobs calculator originally posted on the HUD Recovery Act Web site in October 2009. HUD reiterated these instructions in a subsequent e-mail it sent to housing agencies on March 31, 2010.

Implemented Recommendation

To enhance HUD's ability to prevent, detect, and correct noncompliance with the use of Recovery Act funds, we recommended in September 2009 that the Secretary of Housing and Urban Development expand the criteria for selecting housing agencies for on-site reviews to include housing agencies with open Single Audit findings that may affect the use of and reporting on Recovery Act funds.

Agency Actions

In October 2009, HUD expanded its criteria for selecting housing agencies for on-site reviews to include all housing agencies with open 2007 and 2008 Single Audit findings as of July 7, 2009, relevant to the administration of Recovery Act funds. HUD has identified 27 such housing agencies and planned to complete these on-site reviews by February 15, 2010.

Department of Education

Implemented Recommendation

To ensure that FTEs are properly accounted for over time, we recommend that the Secretary of Education clarify how LEAs and IHEs should report FTEs when additional Recovery Act funds are received in a school year and are reallocated to cover costs incurred in previous quarters, particularly when the definite term methodology is used.

Agency Actions

In response to our recommendation, Education issued clarifying guidance on August 26, 2010, that addressed how FTEs should be reported when funds are expended in one quarter to cover costs incurred in previous quarters.

Implemented Recommendation

To ensure that subrecipients do not underreport vendor FTEs directly paid with Recovery Act funds, we recommend that the Secretary of Education re-emphasize the responsibility of subrecipients to include hours worked by vendors in their quarterly FTE calculations to the maximum extent practicable.

Agency Actions

In response to our recommendation, Education issued clarifying guidance on August 26, 2010, that re-emphasized the responsibility of subrecipients to include hours worked by vendors in their quarterly FTE calculations.

Implemented Recommendation	To improve consistency in how FTEs generated using the definite term are calculated, we recommend that the Secretary of Education and the Director of OMB clarify whether IHE and LEA officials using this methodology should include the cost of benefits in their calculations.

Agency Actions

In response to our recommendation, Education issued clarifying guidance on August 26, 2010, that addressed whether benefits should be included in the calculation of jobs under the OMB guidance released December 18, 2009.

Implemented Recommendation	To improve the consistency of FTE data collected and reported, we recommend that the Secretary of Education and the Director of OMB provide clarifying guidance to recipients on how to best calculate FTEs for education employees during quarters when school is not in session.

Agency Actions

In response to our recommendation, Education issued clarifying guidance on August 26, 2010, that explained that the length of a full-time contract (i.e., 10 or 12 months) should not affect FTE calculations.

Implemented Recommendation	We recommended in September 2009 that the Secretary of Education take further action such as collecting and reviewing documentation of state monitoring plans to ensure that states understand and fulfill their responsibility to monitor subrecipients of SFSF funds and consider providing training and technical assistance to states to help them develop and implement state monitoring plans for SFSF.

Agency Actions

In February 2010, Education instructed states to submit to Education for review their plans and protocols for monitoring subrecipients of SFSF funds. Education also issued its plans and protocols for monitoring state implementation of the SFSF program. The plan includes on-site visits to about half the states and desk reviews of the other states to be conducted over the next year.

Implemented Recommendation	We recommended in November 2009 that the Secretary of Education take further action to enhance transparency by requiring states to include an explanation of changes to maintenance-of-effort levels in their SFSF funding application resubmissions.[2]

Agency Actions

Education notified states that, if states made changes to their maintenance-of-effort data in their State Fiscal Stabilization Fund applications, they must provide a brief explanation of the reason the data changed.

Department of the Treasury

Implemented Recommendation	In order to increase the likelihood that state Housing Finance Agencies (HFA) will comply with Treasury's requirements for recapturing funds, the Secretary of the Treasury should define what it considers appropriate actions by HFAs to recapture funds in order to avoid liability when they are unable to collect funds from project owners that do not comply.

Agency Actions

Treasury agreed with our recommendation and in response to our recommendation, Treasury provided additional guidance to state HFAs to clarify what constitutes appropriate actions by HFAs to recapture funds in order to avoid liability in the event of project owner noncompliance. Specifically, in August 2010, the agency developed and issued a Recapture Guidance for Recovery Act projects that receive Section 1602 Program funds that defines a recapture event, specifies the amount of funds owed in the event of recapture, describes an HFA's obligation and responsibilities in avoiding project owner noncompliance, sets forth the kinds of recapture actions an HFA may take in the event of noncompliance, and directs HFAs on how to report noncompliance.

---

[2]For more details on the maintenance-of-effort requirements, see GAO, *Recovery Act: Planned Efforts and Challenges in Evaluating Compliance with Maintenance of Effort and Similar Provisions*, GAO-10-247 (Washington, D.C.: Nov. 30, 2009).

Executive Office of the President: Office of Management and Budget (OMB)

Implemented Recommendation

We were concerned that since the scope of Single Audit workloads due to Recovery Act programs being subject to Single Audits will increase, consideration should be given to determining what funds can be used to support Single Audit efforts related to Recovery Act programs, including whether legislative changes are needed to specifically direct resources to cover incremental audit costs related to Recovery Act programs. We recommended that the Director of OMB develop mechanisms to help fund the additional Single Audit costs and efforts for auditing Recovery Act programs.

Agency Actions

OMB addressed our recommendation by issuing guidance[3] to executive departments and agencies to help states with various approaches to recover administrative costs associated with the wide range of activities to comply with the Recovery Act. Administrative costs include, but are not limited to, oversight and audit costs and the costs of performing additional Single Audits. OMB issued the guidance to clarify actions (within the existing legal framework for identifying allowable reimbursable costs) that states could take to recover administrative costs in a more timely manner. In addition to our recommendation to OMB, as we previously noted in our bimonthly reports, it is our view that, to the extent that additional audit coverage is needed to achieve accountability over Recovery Act programs, Congress should consider mechanisms to provide additional resources to support those charged with carrying out the Single Audit Act and related audits.

Implemented Recommendation

We reported in July 2009 that OMB was encouraging communication of weaknesses to management early in the audit process, but did not add requirements for auditors to take these steps. This step did not address our concern that internal controls over Recovery Act programs should be reviewed before significant funding is expended. Under the current Single

---

[3]OMB, *Payments to State Grantees for Administrative Costs of Recovery Act Activities*, M-09-18 (Washington, D.C., May 11, 2009), and OMB, *Payments to State Grantees for their Administrative Costs for Recovery Act Funding – Alternative Allocation Methodologies*, M-10-03 (Washington, D.C., Oct. 13, 2009).

Audit framework and reporting timelines, the auditor evaluation of internal control and related reporting will occur too late—after significant levels of federal expenditures have already occurred. As a result of our recommendation, OMB implemented a Single Audit Internal Control Project under which a limited number of voluntarily participating auditors performing the Single Audits for states would communicate in writing internal control deficiencies noted in the single audit within 6 months of the 2009 fiscal year-end, rather than the 9 months required by the Single Audit Act. We recommended that the Director of OMB take steps to achieve sufficient participation and coverage in OMB's Single Audit Internal Control Project that provides for early written communication of internal control deficiencies to achieve the objective of more timely accountability over Recovery Act funds.

Agency Actions

OMB implemented its Single Audit Internal Control Project in October 2009. The project called for a minimum of 10 participants. OMB solicited the 50 states, the District of Columbia, Puerto Rico, and Guam, from which 16 states volunteered to participate.[4] The volunteer states were diverse in geographic characteristics and population and included states that use auditors within state government as well as external auditors to conduct Single Audits. In addition, the volunteer states included California and Texas, which are among the top three states with the highest levels of Recovery Act obligations from the federal government. Each state selected at least two Recovery Act programs from a list of 11 high-risk Recovery Act programs for internal control testing. OMB designed the project to be voluntary and OMB officials stated that, overall, they were satisfied with the population and geographic diversity among the states that volunteered. Although the project's coverage could be more comprehensive to provide greater assurance over Recovery Act funding, the results of the project could provide meaningful insight for making improvements to the Single Audit process.

Implemented Recommendation

The Single Audit Act requires that recipients submit their financial reporting packages, including the Single Audit report, to the federal government no later than 9 months after the end of the period being

---

[4]The following 16 states elected to participate: Alaska, California, Colorado, Florida, Georgia, Louisiana, Maine, Missouri, Nevada, North Carolina, Ohio, Oklahoma, South Dakota, Tennessee, Texas, and Virginia.

audited. As a result, an audited entity may not receive feedback needed to correct an identified internal control or compliance weakness until the latter part of the subsequent fiscal year. The timing problem is exacerbated by the extensions to the 9-month deadline that are routinely granted by the awarding agencies, consistent with OMB guidance. We made two recommendations in this area. First, we recommended that the Director of OMB formally advise federal cognizant agencies to adopt a policy of no longer approving extensions of the due dates of Single Audit reporting package submissions beyond the 9-month deadline. Second, we also recommended that the Director of OMB widely communicate this revised policy to the state audit community and others who have responsibility for conducting Single Audits and submitting the Single Audit reporting package.

Agency Actions

On March 22, 2010, OMB addressed these two recommendations by issuing memorandum M-10-14, Updated Guidance on the American Recovery and Reinvestment Act. This guidance directed federal agencies to not grant any requests made to extend the Single Audit reporting deadlines for fiscal years 2009 to 2011. OMB further stated that to meet the criteria for a low-risk auditee in the current year, the auditee must have submitted the prior 2 years' audit reports by the required due dates. OMB communicated this revised policy though the OMB Web site, the American Institute of Certified Public Accountants, and the National Association of State Auditors, Comptrollers, and Treasurers.

Implemented Recommendation

OMB should work with the Recovery Accountability and Transparency Board (the Board) and federal agencies, building on lessons learned, to establish a formal and feasible framework for review of recipient changes during the continual update period and consider providing more time for agencies to review and provide feedback to recipients before posting updated reports on Recovery.gov.

Agency Actions

In our March 3, 2010 report, we recommended that OMB work with the Board and federal agencies to establish a formal and feasible framework for review of recipient changes during the new continuous review period and consider providing more time for federal agencies to review and provide feedback to recipients before posting updated reports on Recovery.gov. On March 22, 2010, OMB issued updated guidance which highlighted the steps federal agencies must take to review data quality of recipient reports during the continuous review period. The guidance specified that federal agencies must, at a minimum, conduct a final review of the data upon the close of the continuous corrections period. In addition, now the Recovery Board reflects corrected data on Recovery.gov approximately every 2 weeks, allowing federal agencies time to review and provide feedback in the interim period.

Implemented Recommendation

States have been concerned about the burden imposed by new requirements, increased accounting and management workloads, and strains on information systems and staff capacity at a time when they are under severe budgetary stress. We recommended in April 2009 that the Director of OMB clarify what Recovery Act funds can be used to support state efforts to ensure accountability and oversight, especially in light of enhanced oversight and coordination requirements.

Agency Actions

On May 11, 2009, OMB released M-09-18, *Payments to State Grantees for Administrative Costs of Recovery Act Activities*, clarifying how state grantees could recover administrative costs of Recovery Act activities.

Implemented Recommendation

States and localities are expected to report quarterly on a number of measures, including the use of funds and an estimate of the number of jobs created and the number of jobs retained as required by Section 1512 of the Recovery Act. We recommended in our July 2009 report that to increase consistency in recipient reporting of jobs created and retained, the Director of OMB should work with federal agencies to have them provide program-specific examples of the application of OMB's guidance on recipient reporting of jobs created and retained.

Agency Actions

OMB has issued clarifications and frequently asked questions (FAQ) on Recovery Act reporting requirements. During the first reporting period, OMB also deployed regional federal employees to serve as liaisons to state and local recipients in large population centers and established a call center for entities that did not have an on-site federal liaison. In addition, federal agencies issued additional guidance that builds on the OMB June 22 recipient reporting guidance for their specific programs. This guidance is in the form of FAQs, tip sheets, and more traditional guidance that builds on what was provided on June 22, 2009. Federal agencies have also taken steps to provide additional education and training opportunities for state and local program officials on recipient reporting, including Web-based seminars.

Implemented Recommendation

To foster timely and efficient communications, we recommended in April 2009 that the Director of OMB should continue to develop and implement an approach that provides easily accessible, real-time notification to (1) prime recipients in states and localities when funds are made available for their use and (2) states—where the state is not the primary recipient of funds but has a statewide interest in this information.

Agency Actions

In response to our recommendation, OMB has made important progress in notifying recipients when Recovery Act funds are available, communicating the status of these funds at the federal level through agency Weekly Financial Activity reports, and disseminating Recovery Act guidance broadly while actively seeking public and stakeholder input. OMB has taken the additional step of requiring federal agencies to notify Recovery Act coordinators in states, the District of Columbia, commonwealths, and territories within 48 hours of an award to a grantee or contractor in their jurisdiction.

Implemented Recommendation

Responsibility for reporting on jobs created and retained falls to nonfederal recipients of Recovery Act funds. As such, states and localities have a critical role in determining the degree to which Recovery Act goals are achieved. Given questions raised by many state and local officials about how best to determine both direct and indirect jobs created and retained under the Recovery Act, we recommended in April 2009 that the Director of OMB continue OMB's efforts to identify appropriate methodologies that can be used to (1) assess jobs created and retained from projects funded by the Recovery Act; (2) determine the impact of Recovery Act spending when job creation is indirect; and (3) identify those types of programs, projects, or activities that in the past have demonstrated substantial job creation or are considered likely to do so in the future. We also recommended that the Director of OMB consider whether the approaches taken to estimate jobs created and retained in these cases can be replicated or adapted to other programs.

Agency Actions

On June 22, 2009, OMB issued additional implementation guidance on recipient reporting of jobs created and retained, (OMB memoranda M-09-21, *Implementing Guidance for the Reports on Use of Funds Pursuant to the American Recovery and Reinvestment Act of 2009*). This guidance is responsive to much of what we recommended. The June 2009 guidance provided detailed instructions on how to calculate and report jobs as FTEs. It also describes in detail the data model and reporting system to be used for the required recipient reporting on jobs. It clarifies that the prime recipient and not the subrecipient is responsible for reporting information on jobs created or retained. Federal agencies have issued guidance that expanded on the OMB June 22 governmentwide recipient reporting guidance and provided education and training opportunities for state and local program officials. Agency-specific guidance includes FAQs and tip sheets. Additionally, agencies are expected to provide examples of recipient reports for their programs, which is also consistent with what we recommended. In addition to the federal agency efforts, OMB has issued FAQs on Recovery Act reporting requirements. The June 22 guidance and subsequent actions by OMB are responsive to much of what we said in our recommendation.

Implemented Recommendation

We have noted in prior reports that in order to achieve the delicate balance between robust oversight and the smooth flow of funds to Recovery Act programs, states may need timely reimbursement for these activities. We recommended in September 2009 that to the extent that the Director of OMB has the authority to consider mechanisms to provide additional flexibilities to support state and local officials charged with carrying out Recovery Act responsibilities, it is important to expedite consideration of alternative administrative cost reimbursement proposals.

Agency Actions

In response to this recommendation, OMB issued a memorandum on October 13, 2009, to provide guidance to address states' questions regarding specific exceptions to OMB Circular A-87, *Cost Principles for State, Local and Indian Tribal Governments.* In the memorandum, OMB provided clarifications for states regarding specific exceptions to OMB Circular A-87 that are necessary in order for the states to perform timely and adequate Recovery Act oversight, reporting, and auditing. We believe the October 2009 OMB guidance provides the additional clarification needed for states and localities to proceed with their plans to recoup administrative costs.

Implemented Recommendation

To improve the consistency of FTE data collected and reported, we recommended in November 2009 that OMB clarify the definition and standardize the period of measurement for the FTE data element in the recipient reports.

Agency Actions

After the first round of reporting by states on their use of Recovery Act funds in October 2009, OMB updated the recipient reporting guidance on December 18, 2009. According to the agency, this guidance aligns with GAO's recommendation by requiring recipients to report job estimates on a quarterly rather than a cumulative basis. As a result, recipients will no longer be required to sum various data on hours worked across multiple quarters of data when calculating job estimates. The December guidance incorporated lessons learned from the first round of recipient reporting and also addressed recommendations we made in our November 2009 report on recipient reporting.[5] According to OMB, the December guidance is intended to help federal agencies improve the quality of data reported under Section 1512 and simplifies compliance by revising the definitions and calculations needed to define and estimate the number of jobs saved.

Implemented Recommendation

To improve the consistency of FTE data collected and reported, we also recommended in November 2009 that OMB consider being more explicit that "jobs created or retained" are to be reported as hours worked and paid for with Recovery Act funds.

Agency Actions

In response to our recommendation, OMB issued guidance on December 18, 2009, that no longer requires recipients make a subjective judgment of whether jobs were created or retained as a result of the Recovery Act. Instead, recipients will more easily and objectively report on jobs funded with Recovery Act dollars.

Implemented Recommendation

To improve the consistency of FTE data collected and reported, we also recommended in our November 2009 report that OMB continue working with federal agencies to provide or improve program-specific guidance to assist recipients, especially as it applies to the full-time equivalent calculation for individual programs.

Agency Actions

In response to our recommendation, OMB issued guidance on December 18, 2009, that required federal agencies to submit their guidance

---

[5]GAO-10-223.

documents to OMB for review and clearance to ensure consistency
between federal agency guidance and the guidance released by OMB.

Implemented Recommendation

To improve the consistency of FTE data collected and reported, we
recommended in November 2009 that OMB work with the Recovery
Accountability and Transparency Board and federal agencies to re-
examine review and quality assurance processes, procedures, and
requirements in light of experiences and identified issues with the initial
round of recipient reporting and consider whether additional
modifications need to be made and if additional guidance is warranted.

Agency Actions

In response to our recommendation, on December 18, 2009, OMB issued
updated guidance on data quality, nonreporting recipients, and reporting
of job estimates. The agency stated that the updated guidance
incorporates lessons learned from the first reporting period and further
addresses GAO's recommendations. The guidance also provides federal
agencies with a standard methodology for effectively implementing
reviews of the quality of data submitted by recipients.

Implemented Recommendation

In our July 2009 report we recommended that to strengthen the effort to
track the use of funds, the Director of OMB should (1) clarify what
constitutes appropriate quality control and reconciliation by prime
recipients, especially for subrecipient data, and (2) specify who should
best provide formal certification and approval of the data reported.

Agency Actions

Although OMB clarified that the prime recipient is responsible for
FederalReporting.gov data in its June 22 guidance, no statement of
assurance or certification will be required of prime recipients on the
quality of subrecipient data. Moreover, federal agencies are expected to
perform data quality checks, but they are not required to certify or
approve data for publication. We continue to believe that there needs to be
clearer accountability for the data submitted and during the subsequent
federal review process. OMB agreed with the recommendation in concept
but questioned the cost/benefit of data certification given the tight
reporting time frames for recipients and federal agency reviewers. OMB
staff stated that grant recipients are already expected to comply with data
requirements appropriate to the terms and conditions of a grant.
Furthermore, OMB will be monitoring the results of the quarterly recipient
reports for data quality issues and would want to determine whether these

issues are persistent problems before concluding that certification is
needed.

Through issuance of additional guidance and clarification we are now
satisfied OMB has implemented this recommendation.

Implemented Recommendation

In consultation with the Recovery Accountability and Transparency Board
and states, the Director of OMB should evaluate current information and
data collection requirements to determine whether sufficient, reliable, and
timely information is being collected before adding further data collection
requirements. As part of this evaluation, OMB should consider the cost
and burden of additional reporting on states and localities against
expected benefits.

Agency Actions

OMB has taken steps to ensure data quality through issuance of additional
guidance. OMB has also worked with the states to minimize to the extent
possible the new reporting burdens under the Recovery Act.

Closed Recommendation

We recommended in our April report the addition of a master schedule for
anticipated, new, or revised federal Recovery Act program guidance and a
more structured, centralized approach to making this information
available, such as what is provided at Recovery.gov on recipient reporting.

Agency Actions

This recommendation is closed because it is no longer applicable.

Closed Recommendation

In addition to providing additional types of program-specific examples of
guidance, the Director of OMB should work with federal agencies to use
other channels to educate state and local program officials on reporting
requirements, such as Web- or telephone-based information sessions or
other forums.

Agency Actions

In addition to the federal agency efforts, OMB has issued FAQs on
Recovery Act reporting requirements. The June 22 guidance and
subsequent actions by OMB are responsive to much of what we said in our
April 2009 report. OMB deployed regional federal employees to serve as
liaisons to state and local recipients in large population centers. The
objective was to provide on-site assistance and, as necessary, direct

questions to appropriate federal officials in Washington, D.C. OMB established a call center for entities that do not have an on-site federal liaison. These actions by OMB, together with an overall increase in state and local program officials' knowledge of reporting requirements, have made this recommendation inapplicable.

Appendix III: Program Descriptions

Airport Improvement Program	Within the Department of Transportation, the Federal Aviation Administration's Airport Improvement Program provides formula and discretionary grants for the planning and development of public-use airports. The Recovery Act provides $1.1 billion for discretionary Grant-in-Aid for Airports under this program with priority given to projects that can be completed within 2 years. The Recovery Act requires that the funds must supplement, not supplant, planned expenditures from airport-generated revenues or from other state and local sources for airport development activities.
Assistance to Rural Law Enforcement to Combat Crime and Drugs Program	The Recovery Act Assistance to Rural Law Enforcement to Combat Crime and Drugs Program is administered by the Bureau of Justice Assistance (BJA), a component of the Office of Justice Programs, Department of Justice. The purpose of this program is to help rural states and rural areas prevent and combat crime, especially drug-related crime, and provides for national support efforts, including training and technical assistance programs strategically targeted to address rural needs. The Recovery Act provides $125 million for this program, and BJA has made 212 awards.
Brownfields Program	The Recovery Act provides $100 million to the Brownfields Program, administered by the Office of Solid Waste and Emergency Response within the Environmental Protection Agency, for cleanup, revitalization, and sustainable reuse of contaminated properties. The funds will be awarded to eligible entities through job training, assessment, revolving loan fund, and cleanup grants.
Broadband Technology Opportunities Program	The Broadband Technology Opportunities Program (BTOP), funded by the Recovery Act and administered by the Department of Commerce's National Telecommunications and Information Administration provides grants to increase broadband infrastructure in unserved and underserved areas of the country. BTOP grants fund projects for new or improved internet facilities in schools, libraries, hospitals, and public safety facilities, projects to establish or upgrade public computer facilities that provide broadband access to the general public or vulnerable populations, and projects that increase broadband internet usage among populations where broadband technology has been underutilized. Projects may include training and outreach activities that will increase broadband activities in people's everyday lives.

Build America Bonds	Build America Bonds (BAB) administered by the Internal Revenue Service within the Department of the Treasury are taxable government bonds created by the Recovery Act that can be issued with federal subsidies for a portion of the borrowing costs delivered either through nonrefundable tax credits provided to holders of the bonds (tax credit BAB) or as refundable tax credits paid to state and local governmental issuers of the bonds (direct payment BAB). Direct payment BABs are a new type of bond that provide state and local government issuers with a direct subsidy payment equal to 35 percent of the bond interest they pay. Tax credit BABs provide investors with a nonrefundable tax credit of 35 percent of the net bond interest payments (excluding the credit), which represents a federal subsidy to the state or local governmental issuer equal to approximately 25 percent of the total return to the investor. State and local governments may issue an unlimited number of BABs through December 31, 2010, and all BAB proceeds must be used for capital expenditures.
Capital Improvement Program	The Department of Health and Human Services' Health Resources and Services Administration has allocated $862.5 million in Recovery Act funds for Capital Improvement Program grants to health centers to support the construction, repair, and renovation of more than 1,500 health center sites nationwide, including purchasing health information technology and expanding the use of electronic health records.
Child Care and Development Block Grants	Administered by the Administration for Children and Families within the Department of Health and Human Services, Child Care and Development Block Grants, one of the funding streams comprising the Child Care and Development Fund, are provided to states, according to a formula, to assist low-income families in obtaining child care, so that parents can work or participate in education or training activities. The Recovery Act provides $1.9 billion in supplemental funding for these grants.
Clean Cities Program	The Department of Energy's Clean Cities program, administered by the Office of Energy Efficiency and Renewable Energy, is a government-industry partnership that works to reduce America's petroleum consumption in the transportation sector. The Department of Energy is providing nearly $300 million in Recovery Act funds for projects under the Clean Cities program, which provide a range of energy-efficient and advanced vehicle technologies, such as hybrids, electric vehicles, plug-in electric hybrids, hydraulic hybrids, and compressed natural gas vehicles, helping reduce petroleum consumption across the United States. The

program also supports refueling infrastructure for various alternative fuel vehicles, as well as public education and training initiatives, to further the program's goal of reducing the national demand for petroleum.

Clean and Drinking Water State Revolving Funds

The Recovery Act appropriated $4 billion for the Clean Water State Revolving Fund (SRF) programs and $2 billion for the Drinking Water SRF programs. These amounts are a significant increase compared to federal funds awarded as annual appropriations to the SRF programs in recent years. From fiscal years 2000 through 2009, annual appropriations averaged about $1.1 billion for the Clean Water SRF program and about $833 million for the Drinking Water SRF program. The Environmental Protection Agency (EPA) distributed the Recovery Act funds to the 50 states, the District of Columbia, and Puerto Rico to make loans and grants to subrecipients—local governments and other entities awarded Recovery Act funds—for eligible wastewater and drinking water infrastructure projects and "nonpoint source" pollution projects intended to protect or improve water quality by, for example, controlling runoff from city streets and agricultural areas.[1] The Clean Water and Drinking Water SRF programs, established in 1987 and 1996 respectively, provide states and local communities independent and permanent sources of subsidized financial assistance, such as low or no-interest loans, for projects that protect or improve water quality and that are needed to comply with federal drinking water regulations and protect public health.

In addition to providing increased funds, the Recovery Act included specific requirements for states beyond those that are part of base Clean Water and Drinking Water SRF programs. For example, states were required to have all Recovery Act funds awarded to projects under

---

[1]EPA allocated Recovery Act Clean Water SRF capitalization grants to states based on a statutory formula. The agency allocated Recovery Act Drinking Water SRF capitalization grants to states based on the 2003 Drinking Water Infrastructure Needs Survey. EPA allocates Clean Water and Drinking Water SRF funds to the District of Columbia and U.S. territories as direct grants for the same purposes.

contract within 1-year of enactment—which was February 17, 2010[2]—and EPA was directed to reallocate any funds not under contract by that date.[3]

Further, states were required to use at least 50 percent of Recovery Act funds to provide assistance in the form of principal forgiveness, negative interest loans, or grants.[4] States were also required to use at least 20 percent of funds as a "green reserve" to provide assistance for green infrastructure projects, water or energy efficiency improvements, or other environmentally innovative activities.

Communities Putting Prevention to Work

The Recovery Act provides $650 million to carry out evidence-based clinical and community-based prevention and wellness strategies authorized by the Public Health Service Act that deliver specific, measurable health outcomes that address chronic disease rates. In response to the act, the Department of Health and Human Services launched the Communities Putting Prevention to work initiative on September 17, 2009. The goals of the initiative, which is to be administered by the Centers for Disease Control and Prevention, are to increase levels of physical activity, improve nutrition, decrease obesity rates, and decrease smoking prevalence, teen smoking initiation, and exposure to second-hand smoke through an emphasis on policy and environmental change at both the state and local levels. Of the $650 million appropriated for this initiative, approximately $450 million will support community approaches to chronic disease prevention and control; $120 million will support the efforts of states and territories to promote wellness, prevent chronic disease, and increase tobacco cessation; $32.5 million is allocated

---

[2]In this report we use the word "project" to mean an assistance agreement, i.e. a loan or grant agreement made by the state SRF program to a subrecipient for the purpose of a Recovery Act project.

[3]The Recovery Act requires states to have all funds awarded to projects "under contract or construction" by the 1-year deadline. EPA interprets this as requiring states to have all projects under contract in an amount equal to the full value of the Recovery Act assistance agreement by the deadline, regardless of whether construction has begun, according to a September 2009 memorandum. Thus, in this report, we use "under contract" when referring to this requirement. Further, according to EPA's March 2, 2009, memorandum, the agency will deobligate any Recovery Act SRF funds that a state does not have awarded to projects under contract by the 1-year deadline and reallocate them to other states.

[4]Under the base Drinking Water SRF, Congress has authorized states to use an amount equal to up to 30 percent of their capitalization grant to provide additional subsidies to communities that meet state-defined criteria for being "disadvantaged." There is no such statutory authorization for the Clean Water SRF program.

for state chronic disease self-management programs; and $40 million is allocated to establish a National Prevention Media Initiative and a National Organizations Initiative to encourage the development of prevention and wellness messages and advertisements.

Community Development Block Grants

The Community Development Block Grant (CDBG) program, administered by the Office of Community Planning and Development within the Department of Housing and Urban Development, enables state and local governments to undertake a wide range of activities intended to create suitable living environments, provide affordable housing, and create economic opportunities, primarily for persons of low and moderate income. Most local governments use this investment to rehabilitate affordable housing and improve key public facilities. The Recovery Act includes $1 billion for the CDBG.

Community Services Block Grants

Community Services Block Grants (CSBG), administered by the Administration for Children and Families within the Department of Health and Human Services, provide federal funds to states, territories, and tribes for distribution to local agencies to support a wide range of community-based activities to reduce poverty. The Recovery Act appropriated $1 billion for CSBG.

Community Oriented Policing Services Hiring Recovery Program

The Recovery Act provided $1 billion through the Department of Justice's (DOJ) Community Oriented Policing Service's (COPS) Hiring Recovery Program (CHRP) for competitive grant funding to law enforcement agencies to create and preserve jobs and to increase community policing capacity and crime-prevention efforts. CHRP grants provide 100 percent funding for 3 years to cover approved entry-level salaries and benefits for newly-hired, full-time sworn officers, including those who were hired to fill positions previously unfunded, as well as rehired officers who had been laid off. CHRP funds can also be used in the same manner to retain officers who were scheduled to be laid off as a result of local budget cuts. There is no local funding match requirement for CHRP. When the grant term expires after 3 years, grantees must retain all sworn officer positions awarded under the CHRP grant for at least 1 additional year.

The DOJ COPS office selected local law enforcement agencies to receive funding based on fiscal health factors—such as changes in budgets for law enforcement, poverty, unemployment, and foreclosure rates—and reported crime and planned community policing activities. DOJ awards 50 percent of CHRP funds to local law enforcement agencies with populations greater than 150,000 and awards the remaining 50 percent to local law enforcement agencies with populations of less than 150,000. Awards were capped at no more than 5 percent of the applicant agency's actual sworn force strength (up to a maximum of 50 officers) and a minimum of $5 million was allocated to each state or eligible territory.

Diesel Emission Reduction Act Grants

The program objective of the Diesel Emission Reduction Act Grants, administered by the Office of Air and Radiation in conjunction with the Office of Grants and Debarment, within the U.S. Environmental Protection Agency (EPA), is to reduce diesel emissions. EPA will award grants to address the emissions of in-use diesel engines by promoting a variety of cost-effective emission reduction strategies, including switching to cleaner fuels, retrofitting, repowering or replacing eligible vehicles and equipment, and idle reduction strategies. The Recovery Act appropriated $300 million for the Diesel Emission Reduction Act Grants. In addition, the funds appropriated through the Recovery Act for the program are not subject to the State Grant and Loan Program Matching Incentive provisions of the Energy Policy Act of 2005.

Education

Elementary and Secondary Education Act of 1965, Title I, Part A

The Recovery Act provides $10 billion to help local educational agencies (LEA) educate disadvantaged youth by making additional funds available beyond those regularly allocated through Title I, Part A of the Elementary and Secondary Education Act of 1965 (ESEA), as amended.[5] These additional funds are distributed through states to LEAs using existing federal funding formulas, which target funds based on such factors as high concentrations of students from families living in poverty. In using the funds, LEAs are required to comply with applicable statutory and regulatory requirements and must obligate 85 percent of the funds by September 30, 2010.[6] The Department of Education is advising LEAs to use the funds in ways that will build the agencies' long-term capacity to serve

[5]For the purposes of this report, "Title I" refers to Title I, Part A of the Elementary and Secondary Education Act of 1965 (ESEA), as amended.

[6]LEAs must obligate at least 85 percent of their Recovery Act ESEA Title I, Part A funds by September 30, 2010, unless granted a waiver, and must obligate all of their funds by September 30, 2011. This will be referred to as a carryover limitation.

disadvantaged youth, such as through providing professional development to teachers. The Recovery Act also appropriated $3 billion for ESEA Title I School Improvement Grants (SIG), which provides funds to states for use in ESEA Title I schools identified for improvement[7] in order to substantially raise the achievement of their students.[8] These funds are awarded by formula to states, which will then make competitive grants to LEAs. State applications for the $3 billion in Recovery Act SIG funding, as well as an additional $546 million in regular fiscal year 2009 SIG funding, were due to the Department of Education on February 28, 2010. SIG regulatory requirements effective in February 2010,[9] prioritize the use of SIG funds in each state's persistently lowest-achieving Title I schools.[10]

To receive funds, states must identify their persistently lowest-achieving schools, and an LEA that wishes to receive SIG funds must submit an application to its state educational agency (SEA) identifying which schools it commits to serve and how it will use school improvement funds to implement one of four school intervention models: (1) turnaround model, which includes replacing the principal and rehiring no more than 50 percent of the school's staff; (2) restart model, in which an LEA converts the school or closes and reopens it as a charter school or under an education management organization; (3) school closure, in which an LEA closes the school and enrolls the students who attended the school in other, higher-achieving schools in the LEA; or (4) the transformation model, which addresses four specific areas intended to improve schools.

Individuals with Disabilities Education Act, Parts B and C

The Recovery Act provided supplemental funding for programs authorized by Part B and C of the Individuals with Disabilities Education Act (IDEA) as amended, the major federal statute that supports early intervention and special education and related services for children and youth with disabilities. Part B funds programs that ensure preschool and school-age

---

[7] Under ESEA, schools in improvement have failed to meet adequate yearly progress for at least 2 consecutive years.

[8] School Improvement Grants are authorized under Section 1003(g) of ESEA.

[9] Final requirements for SIG were published in Dec. 2009 (74 Fed. Reg. 65618 (Dec. 10, 2009)), and were amended by interim final requirements published in Jan. 2010 (75 Fed. Reg. 3375 (Jan. 21, 2010)).

[10] To identify the persistently lowest-achieving schools in the state, a state educational agency must take into account both the performance of all students in a school on the state's assessments in reading/language arts and mathematics combined and the lack of progress by all students on those assessments over a number of years.

children with disabilities access to a free and appropriate public education and is divided into two separate grants—Part B grants to states (for school-age children) and Part B preschool grants. Part C funds programs that provide early intervention and related services for infants and toddlers with disabilities—or at risk of developing a disability—and their families.

State Fiscal Stabilization Fund

The State Fiscal Stabilization Fund (SFSF) included approximately $48.6 billion to award to states by formula and up to $5 billion to award to states as competitive grants. The Recovery Act created the SFSF in part to help state and local governments stabilize their budgets by minimizing budgetary cuts in education and other essential government services, such as public safety. Stabilization funds for education distributed under the Recovery Act must first be used to alleviate shortfalls in state support for education to LEAs and public institutions of higher education (IHE). States must use 81.8 percent of their SFSF formula grant funds to support education (these funds are referred to as education stabilization funds) and must use the remaining 18.2 percent for public safety and other government services, which may include education (these funds are referred to as government services funds). The SFSF funds are being provided to states in two phases. Phase 1 funds—at least 67 percent of education stabilization funds and all government services funds—were provided to each state after the Department of Education (Education) approved the state's Phase 1 application for funds. Phase 2 funds are being awarded to states as Education approves each state's Phase 2 application. The Phase 1 application required each state to provide several assurances, including that the state will meet maintenance-of-effort requirements (or will be able to comply with the relevant waiver provisions); will meet requirements for accountability, transparency, reporting, and compliance with certain federal laws and regulations; and that it will implement strategies to advance four core areas of education reform.[11] The Phase 2 application requires each state to explain the information the state makes available to the public related to the four core areas of education reform or provide plans for making information related to the education reforms

---

[11]The four core areas of education reform, as described by Education, are: (1) increase teacher effectiveness and address inequities in the distribution of highly qualified teachers; (2) establish a pre-K-through-college data system to track student progress and foster improvement; (3) make progress toward rigorous college- and career-ready standards and high-quality assessments that are valid and reliable for all students, including students with limited English proficiency and students with disabilities; and (4) provide targeted, intensive support and effective interventions to turn around schools identified for corrective action or restructuring.

publicly available no later than September 30, 2011. States must use education stabilization funds to restore state funding to the greater of fiscal year 2008 or 2009 levels for state support to LEAs and public IHEs. When distributing these funds to LEAs, states must use their primary education funding formula, but they can determine how to allocate funds to public IHEs. In general, LEAs maintain broad discretion in how they can use education stabilization funds, but states have some ability to direct IHEs in how to use these funds.

Edward Byrne Memorial Justice Assistance Grant Program

The Recovery Act provided $2 billion through the Department of Justice's (DOJ) Edward Byrne Memorial Justice Assistance Grant (JAG) Program for grants to state and local governments for law enforcement and criminal justice activities. JAG funds can be used to support a range of activities in seven broad program areas: (1) law enforcement; (2) prosecution and courts; (3) crime prevention and education; (4) corrections; (5) drug treatment and enforcement; (6) program planning, evaluation, and technology improvement; and (7) crime victim and witness programs. Within these areas, JAG funds can be used for state and local initiatives, training, personnel, equipment, supplies, contractual support, research, and information systems for criminal justice.

Although each state is guaranteed a minimum allocation of JAG funding, states and localities therein must apply to DOJ's Bureau of Justice Assistance (BJA) to receive their grant awards. BJA applies a statutory formula based on population and violent crime statistics to determine annual funding levels. After applying the formula, BJA distributes each state's allocation in two ways:

- BJA awards 60 percent directly to the state, and the state must in turn allocate a formula-based share of these funds—considered a "variable pass-through," to its local governments; and

- BJA awards the remaining 40 percent directly to eligible units of local government within the state.

Electronic Baggage Screening Program

Administered by the Transportation Security Administration (TSA) of the Department of Homeland Security, the Electronic Baggage Screening Program provides funding to strengthen screening of checked baggage in airports. The Recovery Act provided approximately $1 billion to invest in the procurement and installation of checked baggage explosives detection systems and checkpoint explosives detection equipment. According to

TSA, it has allocated over $700 million to its Electronic Baggage Screening Program for purposes that include facility modifications; equipment purchase and installation; and programmatic, maintenance, and technological support.

Emergency Food and Shelter Program	The Emergency Food and Shelter Program (EFSP), which is administered by the Federal Emergency Management Agency (FEMA) within the Department of Homeland Security, was authorized in July 1987 by the Stewart B. McKinney Homeless Assistance Act to provide food, shelter, and supportive services to the homeless.[12] The program is governed by a National Board composed of a representative from FEMA and six statutorily designated national nonprofit organizations.[13] Since its first appropriation in fiscal year 1983, EFSP has awarded over $3.4 billion in federal aid to more than 12,000 local private, nonprofit and government human service entities in more than 2,500 communities nationwide.

Energy Efficiency and Conservation Block Grants	The Energy Efficiency and Conservation Block Grants (EECBG), administered by the Office of Energy Efficiency and Renewable Energy within the Department of Energy, provides funds through competitive and formula grants to units of local and state government and Indian tribes to develop and implement projects to improve energy efficiency and reduce energy use and fossil fuel emissions in their communities. The Recovery Act includes $3.2 billion for the EECBG. Of that total, $400 million is to be awarded on a competitive basis to grant applicants.

Green Capacity Building Grants	Under the Recovery Act, the Green Capacity Building Grants program, administered by the Employment and Training Administration within the Department of Labor, provides funds to build the green training capacity of current Department of Labor (Labor) grantees. Grants will help individuals in targeted groups acquire the skills needed to enter and advance in green industries and occupations by building the capacity of

---

[12]Pub. L. No. 100-77, 101 Stat. 482 (July 22, 1987).

[13]Under the Act, the members of the EFSP National Board are to be the Director of the Federal Emergency Management Agency (Chair) and six members appointed by the Director from individuals nominated by the following organizations: American Red Cross, Catholic Charities USA, National Council of Churches of Christ in the USA, The Salvation Army, The Council of Jewish Federations, Inc. (now known as The Jewish Federations of North America), and the United Way of America (now known as United Way Worldwide).

active Labor-funded training programs. Grantees are required to give priority to targeted groups, including workers impacted by national energy and environmental policy, individuals in need of updated training related to energy-efficiency and renewable energy industries, veterans, unemployed individuals, and individuals with criminal records.

Health Information Technology Extension Program	The Department of Health and Human Services' Health Information Technology Extension Program, administered by the Office of the National Coordinator for Health Information Technology, allocated $643 million to establish 60 Health Information Technology Regional Extension Centers (REC) and $50 million to establish a national Health Information Technology Research Center (HITRC). The first cycle of awards, announced February 12, 2010, provided $375 million to create 32 RECs, while the second cycle of awards, announced April 6, 2010, provided $267 million to establish 28 RECs. RECs offer technical assistance, guidance, and information on best practices for the use of Electronic Health Records (EHR) to health care providers. The HITRC supports RECs' efforts by collecting information on best practices from a wide variety of sources across the country and by acting as a virtual community for RECs to collaborate with one another and with relevant stakeholders to identify and share best practices for the use of EHRs. The goal of the RECs and HITRC is to enable nationwide health information exchange through the adoption and meaningful use of secure EHRs.
Head Start/Early Head Start	The Head Start program, administered by the Office of Head Start of the Administration for Children and Families within the Department of Health and Human Services, provides comprehensive early childhood development services to low-income children, including educational, health, nutritional, social, and other services, intended to promote the school readiness of low-income children. Federal Head Start funds are provided directly to local grantees, rather than through states. The Recovery Act provided an additional $2.1 billion in funding for Head Start and Early Head Start programs. The Early Head Start program provides family-centered services to low-income families with very young children designed to promote the development of the children, and to enable their parents to fulfill their roles as parents and to move toward self-sufficiency.
High-Speed Intercity Passenger Rail Program	The High-Speed Intercity Passenger Rail Program (HSIPR) is administered by the Federal Railroad Administration, within the Department of Transportation (DOT). The purpose of the HSIPR Program is to build an

efficient, high-speed passenger rail network connecting major population centers 100 to 600 miles apart. In the near-term, the program will aid in economic recovery efforts and lay the foundation for this high-speed passenger rail network through targeted investments in existing intercity passenger rail infrastructure, equipment, and intermodal connections. In addition to the $8 billion provided in the Recovery Act, the HSIPR Program also included approximately $92 million in fiscal year 2009 and remaining fiscal year 2008 funds appropriated under the existing State Grant Program (formally titled, Capital Assistance to States—Intercity Passenger Rail Service). The fiscal year 2010 DOT appropriation included $2.5 billion for high speed rail and intercity passenger rail projects.

Homelessness Prevention and Rapid Re-Housing Program

The Homelessness Prevention and Rapid Re-Housing Program, administered by the Office of Community Planning and Development within the Department of Housing and Urban Development, awards formula grants to states and localities to prevent homelessness and procure shelter for those who have become homeless. Funding for this program is being distributed based on the formula used for the Emergency Shelter Grants program. According to the Recovery Act, program funds should be used for short-term or medium-term rental assistance; housing relocation and stabilization services, including housing search, mediation or outreach to property owners, credit repair, security or utility deposits, utility payments, and rental assistance for management; or appropriate activities for homeless prevention and rapid re-housing of persons who have become homeless. The Recovery Act includes $1.5 billion for this program.

Highway Infrastructure Investment Program

The Recovery Act provides funding to states for restoration, repair, and construction of highways and other activities allowed under the Federal Highway Administration's Federal-Aid Highway Surface Transportation Program and for other eligible surface transportation projects. The Recovery Act requires that 30 percent of these funds be suballocated, primarily based on population, for metropolitan, regional, and local use. Highway funds are apportioned to states through federal-aid highway program mechanisms, and states must follow existing program requirements. While the maximum federal fund share of highway infrastructure investment projects under the existing federal-aid highway program is generally 80 percent, under the Recovery Act, it is 100 percent.

Funds appropriated for highway infrastructure spending must be used in accordance with Recovery Act requirements. States were given a 1-year deadline (March 2, 2010) to ensure that all apportioned Recovery Act funds—including suballocated funds—were obligated.[14] The Secretary of Transportation was to withdraw and redistribute to eligible states any amount that was not obligated by that time.[15] Additionally, the governor of each state was required to certify that the state would maintain its level of spending for the types of transportation projects funded by the Recovery Act it planned to spend the day the Recovery Act was enacted. As part of this certification, the governor of each state was required to identify the amount of funds the state planned to expend from state sources from February 17, 2009, through September 30, 2010.[16]

On March 2, 2009, the Federal Highway Administration apportioned $799.8 million in Recovery Act funds to states for its Transportation Enhancement program. States may use program funds for qualifying surface transportation activities, such as constructing or rehabilitating off-road shared use paths for bicycles and pedestrians; conducting landscaping and other beautification projects along highways, streets, and waterfronts; and rehabilitating and operating historic transportation facilities such as historic railroad depots.[17] The Recovery Act requires that 3 percent of Highway Infrastructure Investment funds provided to states must be used for Transportation Enhancement activities. Additionally, states may decide to use additional Recovery Act Transportation Enhancement funds, beyond the 3 percent requirement, for qualifying activities such as those mentioned above. States determine the share of federal funds used for qualifying Transportation Enhancement projects up to 100 percent of the projects' costs.

Increased Demand for Services

The Department of Health and Human Services' Health Resources and Services Administration (HRSA) has allocated Recovery Act funds for Increased Demand for Services (IDS) grants to health centers to increase health center staffing, extend hours of operations, and expand existing

---

[14]For the Highway Infrastructure Investment program, DOT has interpreted the term "obligation of funds" to mean the federal government's commitment to pay for the federal share of the project. This commitment occurs at the time the federal government signs a project agreement.

[15]Recovery Act, div. A, title XII, 123 Stat. 206.

[16]Recovery Act, div. A, title XII, § 1201(a).

[17]The full list of qualifying Transportation Enhancement activities is defined in 23 U.S.C. § 101(a)(35).

services. The Recovery Act provided $500 million for health center operations. HRSA has allocated $343 million for IDS grants to health centers.[18]

Internet Crimes Against Children Initiatives	Internet Crimes Against Children Initiatives (ICAC), administered by the Department of Justice, Office of Justice Programs' Office of Juvenile Justice and Delinquency Prevention, seeks to maintain and expand state and regional ICAC task forces to address technology-facilitated child exploitation. This program provides funding to states and localities for salaries and employment costs of law enforcement officers, prosecutors, forensic analysts, and other related professionals. The Recovery Act appropriated $50 million for ICAC.
Lead-Based Paint Hazard Control Grants and Lead Hazard Reduction Demonstration Grant Program	The Recovery Act provided approximately $78 million to the Lead-Based Paint Hazard Control Grant Program through the Department of Housing and Urban Development to assist states and localities in undertaking programs to identify and control lead-based paint hazards in eligible privately owned housing for rental or owner-occupants. Funds will be used to perform lead-based paint inspections, soil and paint-chip testing, risk assessments, and other activities that are in support of lead hazard abatement work. An additional $2.6 million was provided for the Lead Hazard Reduction Demonstration Grant Program which will assist urban areas with the greatest lead paint abatement needs to identify and control lead-based paint hazards in eligible privately owned single- family housing units and multifamily buildings occupied by low-income families.
Local Energy Assurance Planning Initiative	The Recovery Act provided funding to support Local Energy Assurance Planning (LEAP) Initiatives to help communities prepare for energy emergencies and disruptions. The Department of Energy will award funds to cities and towns to develop or expand local energy assurance plans that will improve electricity reliability and energy security in their communities. LEAP aims to facilitate recovery from disruptions to the

---

[18]The Recovery Act provided $2 billion to HRSA for grants to health centers. Of this total, $1.5 billion is for the construction and renovation of health centers and the acquisition of Health Information Technology systems, and the remaining $500 million is for operating grants to health centers. Of the $500 million for health center operations, HRSA has allocated $157 million for New Access Point grants to support health centers' new service delivery sites, and $343 million for IDS grants.

energy supply and enhance reliability and quicker repairs following energy supply disruptions.

Medicaid Federal Medical Assistance Percentage

Medicaid is a joint federal-state program that finances health care for certain categories of low-income individuals, including children, families, persons with disabilities, and persons who are elderly. The federal government matches state spending for Medicaid services according to a formula based on each state's per capita income in relation to the national average per capita income. The Centers for Medicare and Medicaid Services, within the Department of Health and Human Services, approves state Medicaid plans, and the amount of federal assistance states receive for Medicaid service expenditures is determined by the Federal Medical Assistance Percentage (FMAP). The Recovery Act's temporary increase in FMAP funding will provide all 50 states and the District with approximately $87 billion in assistance. Federal legislation was recently enacted amending the Recovery Act to provide for an extension of increased FMAP funding through June 30, 2011, but at a lower level.

National Clean Diesel Funding Assistance Projects

The Recovery Act provided $156 million in new funding to the National Clean Diesel Funding Assistance Program to support the implementation of verified and certified diesel emission reduction technologies. The competitive grant program funded projects that would achieve significant reductions in diesel emissions, especially from fleets operating in areas designated as having poor air quality. This is one of the Recovery Act-funded National Clean Diesel Campaign programs which have the goal to accelerate emission reductions from older diesel engines to provide air quality benefits and improve public health.

National Endowment for the Arts Recovery Act Grants

The Recovery Act provides $50 million to be distributed in direct grants by the National Endowment for the Arts to fund arts projects and activities that preserve jobs in the nonprofit arts sector threatened by declines in philanthropic and other support during the current economic downturn.

Neighborhood Stabilization Program 2

The Neighborhood Stabilization Program (NSP), administered by the Office of Community Planning and Development within the Department of Housing and Urban Development, provides assistance for the redevelopment of abandoned and foreclosed homes and residential properties in order that such properties may be returned to productive use or made available for redevelopment purposes. The $2 billion in NSP2 funds appropriated in the Recovery Act are competitively awarded to states, local governments, and nonprofit organizations.[19] NSP is considered to be a component of the Community Development Block Grant (CDBG) program and basic CDBG requirements govern NSP.

Port Security Grant Program

The Port Security Grant Program (PSGP) provides grant funding to port areas for the protection of critical port infrastructure from terrorism. The Recovery Act provides $150 million in stimulus funding for the PSGP administered by the Federal Emergency Management Agency (FEMA), an agency of the Department of Homeland Security. PSGP funds are primarily intended to assist ports in enhancing maritime domain awareness, enhancing risk management capabilities to prevent, detect, respond to, and recover from attacks involving improvised explosive devices, weapons of mass destruction and other nonconventional weapons, as well as training and exercises and Transportation Worker Identification Credential implementation. Ports compete for funds and priority is given to cost-effective projects that can be executed expeditiously and have a significant and near-term impact on risk mitigation.

Public Housing Capital Fund

The Public Housing Capital Fund provides formula-based grant funds directly to public housing agencies to improve the physical condition of their properties; to develop, finance, and modernize public housing developments; and to improve management. Under the Recovery Act, the Office of Public and Indian Housing within the Department of Housing and Urban Development (HUD) allocated nearly $3 billion through the Public Housing Capital Fund to public housing agencies using the same formula for amounts made available in fiscal year 2008 and obligated these funds to housing agencies in March 2009.

HUD was also required to award nearly $1 billion to public housing agencies based on competition for priority investments, including investments that leverage private sector funding or financing for renovations and energy conservation retrofitting. In September 2009, HUD

---

[19]NSP, a term that references the NSP funds authorized under Division B, Title III of the Housing and Economic Recovery Act of 2008, provides grants to all states and selected local governments on a formula basis. Under NSP, the Department of Housing and Urban Development allocated $3.92 billion on a formula basis to states, territories, and selected local governments. The term "NSP2" references the NSP funds authorized under the Recovery Act on a competitive basis.

awarded competitive grants for the creation of energy-efficient communities, gap financing for projects stalled due to financing issues, public housing transformation, and improvements addressing the needs of the elderly or persons with disabilities.

Public Transportation Program	The Recovery Act appropriated $8.4 billion to fund public transit throughout the country through existing Federal Transit Administration (FTA) grant programs, including the Transit Capital Assistance Program, and the Fixed Guideway Infrastructure Investment Program. Under the Transit Capital Assistance Program's formula grant program, Recovery Act funds were apportioned to large and medium urbanized areas—which in some cases include a metropolitan area that spans multiple states—throughout the country according to existing program formulas. Recovery Act funds were also apportioned to states for small urbanized areas and nonurbanized areas under the Transit Capital Assistance Program's formula grant programs using the program's existing formula. Transit Capital Assistance Program funds may be used for such activities as vehicle replacements, facilities renovation or construction, preventive maintenance, and paratransit services. Recovery Act funds from the Fixed Guideway Infrastructure Investment Program[20] were apportioned by formula directly to qualifying urbanized areas, and funds may be used for any capital projects to maintain, modernize, or improve fixed guideway systems.[21] As they work through the state and regional transportation planning process, designated recipients of the apportioned funds— typically public transit agencies and metropolitan planning organizations—develop a list of transit projects that project sponsors (typically transit agencies) submit to FTA for approval.[22]

---

[20]Fixed guideway systems use and occupy a separate right-of-way for the exclusive use of public transportation services. They include fixed rail, exclusive lanes for buses and other high-occupancy vehicles, and other systems.

[21]Generally, to qualify for funding under the applicable formula grant program, an urbanized area must have a fixed guideway system that has been in operation for at least 7 years and is more than 1 mile in length.

[22]Metropolitan planning organizations (MPO) are federally mandated regional organizations, representing local governments and working in coordination with state departments of transportation, that are responsible for comprehensive transportation planning and programming in urbanized areas. MPOs facilitate decision making on regional transportation issues, including major capital investment projects and priorities. To be eligible for Recovery Act funding, projects must be included in the region's Transportation Improvement and State Transportation Improvement Programs.

Funds appropriated for the Transit Capital Assistance Program and the Fixed Guideway Infrastructure Investment Program must be used in accordance with Recovery Act requirements. States were given a 1-year deadline (March 5, 2010) to ensure that all apportioned Recovery Act funds were obligated.[23] The Secretary of Transportation was to withdraw and redistribute to each state or urbanized area any amount that was not obligated within these time frames.[24] Additionally, the governor of each state was required to certify that the state would maintain its level of spending for the types of transportation projects funded by the Recovery Act it planned to spend the day the Recovery Act was enacted. As part of this certification, the governor of each state was required to identify the amount of funds the state planned to expend from state sources from February 17, 2009, through September 30, 2010.[25]

The Transit Investments for Greenhouse Gas and Energy Reduction (TIGGER) Grant program, administered by FTA within the Department of Transportation, is a discretionary program to support transit capital projects that result in greenhouse gas reductions or reduced energy use. The Recovery Act provides $100 million for the TIGGER program, and each submitted proposal must request a minimum of $2 million.

Race to the Top Fund

The Recovery Act includes up to $5 billion for the Race to the Top Fund, administered by the Office of Elementary and Secondary Education within the Department of Education (Education). According to Education, awards in Race to the Top will go to states that are leading the way with ambitious yet achievable plans for implementing coherent, compelling, and comprehensive educational reform. Through Race to the Top, Education asks states to advance reforms in four specific areas: adopting standards and assessments that prepare students to succeed in college and the workplace and to compete in the global economy; building data systems that measure student growth and success, and inform teachers and principals about how they can improve instruction; recruiting,

---

[23]For the Transit Capital Assistance Program and Fixed Guideway Infrastructure Investment Program, the Department of Transportation has interpreted the term obligation of funds to mean the federal government's commitment to pay for the federal share of the project. This commitment occurs at the time the federal government signs a grant agreement.

[24]Recovery Act, div. A, title XII,123 Stat. 210.

[25]Recovery Act, div. A, title XII, § 1201(a).

developing, rewarding, and retaining effective teachers and principals, especially where they are needed most; and turning around our lowest-achieving schools.

Recovery Act Assistance to Firefighters Fire Station Construction Grants	The Recovery Act Assistance to Firefighters Fire Station Construction Grants, also known as fire grants or the FIRE Act grant program, is administered by the Department of Homeland Security, Federal Emergency Management Agency, Assistance to Firefighters Program Office. The program provides federal grants directly to fire departments on a competitive basis to build or modify existing nonfederal fire stations in order for departments to enhance their response capability and protect the communities they serve from fire and fire-related hazards. The Recovery Act includes $210 million for this program and provides that no grant shall exceed $15 million.
Recovery Act Impact on Child Support Incentives	The Child Support Enforcement (CSE) Program (Title IV-D of the Social Security Act) is a joint federal-state program administered by the Administration for Children and Families (ACF), within the Department of Health and Human Services. The program provides federal matching funds to states to carry out their child support enforcement programs, which enhance the well-being of children by, among other things, establishing paternity, establishing child support orders, and collecting child support. Furthermore, ACF makes additional incentive payments to states based in part on their child support enforcement programs meeting certain performance goals. States must reinvest their incentive fund payments into the CSE program or an activity to improve the CSE program; however, incentive funds reinvested in the CSE program are not eligible for federal matching funds. Funds for the federal matching payments and incentive payments are appropriated annually, and the Recovery Act does not appropriate funds for either of them. However, the Recovery Act temporarily provides for incentive payments expended by states for child support enforcement to count as state funds eligible for the federal match. This change is effective October 1, 2008, through September 30, 2010.
Recovery Zone Bonds	Recovery Zone Bonds are administered by the Internal Revenue Service within the Department of the Treasury and come in two types: Recovery Zone Economic Development Bonds (RZEDB) and Recovery Zone Facility Bonds. RZEDB are a type of direct payment Build America Bond (BAB), created under the Recovery Act. Direct payment BABs allow issuers the option of receiving a federal payment instead of allowing a federal tax

exemption on the interest payments. RZEDBs provide a 45 percent credit instead of a 35 percent credit like other types of BABs and must meet certain requirements. RZEDBs are targeted to economically distressed areas meeting certain criteria and are to be used for qualified forms of economic development. Recovery Zone Facility Bonds are exempt facility bonds which may be used to finance certain designated recovery zone property. The Recovery Act authorized up to $10 billion for RZEDBs and up to $15 billion for Recovery Zone Facility Bonds to be allocated to states, the District of Columbia, and territories, based to the their employment declines in 2008.

Renewable and Distributed Systems Integration

The Renewable and Distributed Systems Integration (RDSI) program, administered by the Office of Electricity Delivery and Energy Reliability within the Department of Energy (DOE), focuses on integrating renewable and distributed energy technologies into the electric distribution and transmission system. In April 2008, DOE announced plans to invest up to $50 million over 5 years (fiscal years 2008 to 2012) in nine projects aimed at demonstrating the use of RDSI technologies to reduce peak load electricity demand by at least 15 percent at distribution feeders—the power lines delivering electricity to consumers. The program goal is to reduce peak load electricity demand by 20 percent at distribution feeders by 2015.

Retrofit Ramp-Up Program

The Recovery Act's Retrofit Ramp-Up program will provide funding to projects to "ramp-up" energy efficiency building retrofits. The program will target community-scale retrofit projects that make significant, long-term impacts on energy use and can serve as national role models for energy-efficiency efforts. These programs should result in retrofits that lead to significant efficiency improvements to a large number of buildings in communities or neighborhoods. The retrofits must reduce the total monthly operating costs of the buildings including any repayments of loans. The Retrofit Ramp-Up projects are the competitive portion of DOE's Energy Efficiency and Conservation Block Grant Program and are part of the Recovery Act investment in clean energy and energy efficiency.

Senior Community Service Employment Program

The Senior Community Service Employment Program (SCSEP), administered by the Employment and Training Administration within the Department of Labor, is a community service and work-based training program which serves low-income persons who are 55 years or older and have poor employment prospects by placing them in part-time community service positions and by assisting them to transition to unsubsidized employment. The Recovery Act provides $120 million for SCSEP.

Senior Nutrition Programs	The Recovery Act provides $100 million to the Senior Nutrition Programs, administered by the Administration on Aging (AoA) within the Department of Health and Human Services. AoA distributed funds to 56 States and Territories and 246 tribes and Native Hawaiian organizations to fund three programs at senior centers and other community sites. The Recovery act awarded $65 million for congregate nutrition services provided at senior centers and other community sites, $32 million for home-delivered nutrition services delivered to elders at home, and $3 million for Native American nutrition programs. The Congregate Nutrition Services and Home-delivered Nutrition Services programs specifically targets vulnerable seniors, such as low-income minorities and those residing in rural areas, and aims to help elderly individuals avoid hospitalization and nursing home placement by maintaining their health through meals. The Nutrition Services for Native Americans provides congregate and home-delivered meals and related nutrition services to American Indian, Alaskan Native, and Native Hawaiian elders.
Services*Training*Officers *Prosecutors Violence Against Women Formula Grants Program	Under the Services*Training*Officers*Prosecutors (STOP) Violence Against Women Formula Grants Program, the Office on Violence Against Women within the Department of Justice, has awarded over $139 million in Recovery Act funds to promote a coordinated, multidisciplinary approach to enhance services and advocacy to victims, improve the criminal justice system's response, and promote effective law enforcement, prosecution, and judicial strategies to address domestic violence, dating violence, sexual assault, and stalking.
Smart Grid Investment Grant Program	Under the Recovery Act, states will receive $3.4 billion to deploy and integrate advanced digital technology to modernize the electric delivery network through the Smart Grid Investment Grant Program, administered by the Office of Electricity Delivery and Energy Reliability within the Department of Energy. The program funds a broad range of projects aimed at applying smart grid technologies to existing electric system equipment, consumer products and appliances, meters, electric distribution and transmission systems, and homes, offices, and industrial facilities.

Staffing for Adequate Fire and Emergency Response

The Staffing for Adequate Fire and Emergency Response (SAFER) grants program, administered by the Federal Emergency Management Agency within the Department of Homeland Security, was created to provide funding directly to volunteer, combination, and career fire departments[26] to help them increase staffing and enhance their emergency deployment capabilities. The goal of SAFER is to ensure departments have an adequate number of trained, frontline active firefighters capable of safely responding to and protecting their communities from fire and fire-related hazards. SAFER provides 2-year grants to fire departments to pay the salaries of newly hired firefighters or to rehire recently laid-off firefighters. Fire departments using SAFER funding to hire new fire fighters commit to retaining the SAFER-funded firefighters for 1 full year after the 2-year grant has been expended. The retention commitment does not extend to previously laid-off firefighters who have been rehired. In addition, volunteer and combination firefighter departments are eligible to apply for SAFER funding to pay for activities related to the recruitment and retention of volunteer firefighters.[27]

State Broadband Data and Development Program

The Recovery Act appropriated $7.2 billion to extend access to broadband throughout the United States. Of the $7.2 billion, $4.7 billion was appropriated to the Department of Commerce's National Telecommunications and Information Administration (NTIA) and $2.5 billion to the Department of Agriculture's Rural Utilities Service. Of the $4.7 billion, up to $350 million was available pursuant to the Broadband Data Improvement Act (BDIA) for the purpose of developing and maintaining a nationwide map featuring the availability of broadband service. BDIA directs the Secretary of Commerce to establish the State Broadband Data and Development Grant Program and to award grants to eligible entities to develop and implement statewide initiatives to identify

---

[26]Per FEMA's definition, a "volunteer fire department is composed entirely of members who do not receive compensation other than a length of service retirement program (LSOP) and insurance. A career department is one in which all members are compensated for their services. A combination department has at least one volunteer, with the balance being career members, or one career member with the balance being volunteers. Also, if a volunteer fire department provides stipends to their members or provides pay-on-call for their members, the department is considered to be combination."

[27]Volunteer fire departments are eligible to apply for both Hiring and Recruitment and Retention grants. Combination fire departments are eligible to apply for both Hiring/Rehiring of Firefighters and Recruitment and Retention of volunteer firefighters SAFER grants. Career fire departments are only eligible to apply for SAFER Hiring/Rehiring of firefighters grants.

and track the adoption and availability of broadband services within each state. To accomplish the joint purposes of the Recovery Act and BDIA, NTIA has developed the State Broadband Data and Development projects that collect comprehensive and accurate state-level broadband mapping data, develop state-level broadband maps, aid in the development and maintenance of a national broadband map, and fund statewide initiatives directed at broadband planning.

State Energy Program

Under the Recovery Act, states will receive $3.1 billion for energy projects through the State Energy Program (SEP), administered by the Office of Energy Efficiency and Renewable Energy within the Department of Energy (DOE). States should prioritize the grants toward funding energy-efficiency and renewable energy programs, including expanding existing energy-efficiency programs, renewable energy projects, and joint activities between states. The SEP's 20 percent cost match is not required for grants made with Recovery Act funds. DOE estimates that SEP funding will have an annual costs savings of $256 million.

State Health Information Exchange Cooperative Agreement Program

Under the Department of Health and Human Services' State Health Information Exchange (HIE) Cooperative Agreement Program, $564 million has been allocated to support states' efforts to develop the capacity among health care providers and hospitals in their jurisdiction to exchange health information across health care systems through the meaningful use of Electronic Health Records (EHR). The meaningful use of EHRs aims to improve the quality and efficiency of patient care. In order to ensure secure and effective use of HIE technology within and across state borders, grant recipients are expected to use their authority and resources to implement HIE privacy and security requirements, coordinate with Medicaid and state public health programs in using HIE technology, and enable interoperability through the creation of state-level directories and technical services and the removal of barriers. The state HIE program uses a cooperative agreement, or partnership between the grant recipient and the federal government, to administer the awards (when the federal government has a substantial stake in the outcomes or operation of the program). The state HIE cooperative agreements are 4-year agreements and recipients will be required to match grant awards beginning in the second year of the award, 2011.

Statewide Longitudinal Data Systems	The Statewide Longitudinal Data Systems grant program, administered by the Department of Education's Institute of Education Sciences, awards competitive grants to state educational agencies for the design, development, and implementation of statewide longitudinal data systems. These systems are intended to enhance the ability of states to efficiently and accurately manage, analyze, and use education data, including individual student records, while protecting student privacy. The first grants were awarded to 14 states in November 2005; 12 states and the District of Columbia were awarded grants in 2007, and 27 states were awarded grants in 2009. The Recovery Act appropriated $250 million for this program.
Supplemental Nutrition Assistance Program (formerly the Food Stamp Program)	The Supplemental Nutrition Assistance Program (SNAP), administered by the Food and Nutrition Service within the Department of Agriculture, serves more than 35 million people nationwide each month. SNAP's goal, in part, is to help raise the level of nutrition and alleviate the hunger of low-income households. The Recovery Act provides for a monthly increase in benefits for the program's recipients. The increases in benefits under the Recovery Act are estimated to total $20 billion over the next 5 years.
Tax Credit Assistance Program (TCAP) and Section 1602 Program	The Tax Credit Assistance Program administered by the Department of Housing and Urban Development (HUD) provides gap financing to be used by state Housing Finance Agencies (HFA) in the form of grants or loans for capital investment in low-income housing tax credits (LIHTC) projects through a formula-based allocation to HFAs.
	HUD obligated $2.25 billion in TCAP funds to HFAs. The HFAs were to award the funds competitively according to their qualified allocation plans, which explain selection criteria and application requirements for housing tax credits (as determined by the states and in accordance with Section 42 of the Internal Revenue Code). Projects that were awarded low-income housing tax credits in fiscal years 2007, 2008, or 2009 were eligible for TCAP funding, but HFAs had to give priority to projects that were "shovel-ready" and expected to be completed by February 2012. Also, TCAP projects had to include some low-income tax credits and equity investment. HFAs must commit 75 percent of their TCAP awards by February 2010 and disburse 75 percent by February 2011. Project owners must spend all of their TCAP funds by February 2012. HUD can recapture TCAP funds from any HFA whose projects do not comply with TCAP requirements. In these cases, HFAs are responsible for recapturing funds

from project owners. Furthermore, because TCAP funds are federal financial assistance, they are subject to certain federal requirements, such as Davis-Bacon and the National Environmental Policy Act (NEPA). These acts, respectively, require that projects receiving federal funds pay prevailing wages and meet federal environmental requirements.

The Section 1602 Program allows HFAs to exchange returned and unused tax credits for a payment from Treasury at the rate of 85 cents for every tax credit dollar. HFAs can exchange up to 100 percent of unused 2008 credits and 40 percent of their 2009 allocation. HFAs may award Section 1602 Program funds to finance the construction or acquisition and rehabilitation of qualified low-income buildings in accordance with the HFA's Qualified Allocation Plan, which establishes criteria for selecting LIHTC projects. Section 1602 Program funds may be committed to project owners that have not sold their LIHTC allocation to private investors, as long as the project owner has made good faith efforts to find an investor. However, some HFAs have required Section 1602 Program projects to include some tax credit equity from private investors. Section 1602 Program funds are subject to the same requirements as the standard LIHTC program, and like TCAP funds, may be recaptured if a project does not comply with the requirements. HFAs may submit applications to Treasury for Section 1602 Program funds through 2010. The last day for HFAs to commit funds to project owners is December 31, 2010, but they can continue to disburse funds for committed projects through December 31, 2011, provided that the project owners paid or incurred at least 30 percent of eligible project costs by the end of 2010. Congress appropriated 'such sums as may be necessary' for the operation of the Section 1602 Program. The Joint Committee on Taxation originally estimated the budget impact of this program at $3 billion. As of the end of April 2010, however, Treasury had obligated more than $5 billion to HFAs in Section 1602 Program funds. Section 1602 Program funds are not considered by Treasury to be federal financial assistance and, therefore, the Section 1602 Program is not subject to many of the requirements placed on TCAP.

Title IV-E Adoption Assistance and Foster Care Programs

Administered by the Administration for Children and Families within the Department of Health and Human Services, the Foster Care Program helps states to provide safe and stable out-of-home care for children until the children are safely returned home, placed permanently with adoptive families, or placed in other planned arrangements for permanency. The Adoption Assistance Program provides funds to states to facilitate the timely placement of children, whose special needs or circumstances would otherwise make placement difficult, with adoptive families. Federal

Title IV-E funds are paid to reimburse states for their maintenance payments using the states' respective Federal Medical Assistance Percentage (FMAP) rates.[28] The Recovery Act temporarily increased the FMAP rate effective October 1, 2008, through December 31, 2010, resulting in an estimated additional $806 million that will be provided to states for the Adoption Assistance and Foster Care Programs.

Transportation Investment Generating Economic Recovery Discretionary Grants

Administered by the Department of Transportation's Office of the Secretary, the Recovery Act provides $1.5 billion in competitive grants, generally between $20 million and $300 million, to state and local governments and transit agencies. These grants are for capital investments in surface transportation infrastructure projects that will have a significant impact on the nation, a metropolitan area, or a region. Projects eligible for funding provided under this program include, but are not limited to, highway or bridge projects, public transportation projects, passenger and freight rail transportation projects, and port infrastructure investments.

Water and Waste Disposal Loan and Grant Program

The Water and Environmental Programs administered by the Department of Agriculture's Rural Development, provides loans, grants, and loan guarantees for drinking water, sanitary sewer, solid waste, and storm drainage facilities in rural areas and cities and towns of 10,000 or less. The Recovery Act provided nearly $3.3 billion in Rural Water and Waste Disposal funding for these programs. Loans, grants and loan guarantees to rural water and waste systems will be used to construct, improve, rehabilitate, or expand existing water and waste disposal systems to areas initially excluded because service was not economically feasible.

Water Quality Management Planning Grants

The Environmental Protection Agency (EPA) awarded $39.3 million in Recovery Act funding for Water Quality Management Planning Grants to assist states in water quality management planning. Funds are used to determine the nature and extent of point and nonpoint source water pollution and to develop water quality management plans. Funded activities also include green infrastructure planning and integrated water resources planning. The fund is administered by the Office of Water, EPA.

---

[28]See the Medicaid Federal Medical Assistance Percentage (FMAP) description in this appendix.

Weatherization Assistance Program	The Recovery Act appropriated $5 billion for the Weatherization Assistance Program, which the Department of Energy (DOE) is distributing to each of the states, the District of Columbia, and seven territories and Indian tribes, to be spent by March 31, 2012. The program, administered by the Office of Energy Efficiency and Renewable Energy within DOE, enables low-income families to reduce their utility bills by making long-term energy-efficiency improvements to their homes by, for example, installing insulation; sealing leaks; and modernizing heating equipment, air circulation fans, and air conditioning equipment. Over the past 33 years, the Weatherization Assistance Program has assisted more than 6.2 million low-income families. By reducing the energy bills of low-income families, the program allows these households to spend their money on other needs, according to DOE. The Recovery Act appropriation represents a significant increase for a program that has received about $225 million per year in recent years. DOE has approved the weatherization plans of the 16 states and the District of Columbia that are in our review and has provided at least half of the funds to those areas.
Wildland Fire Management Program	The Department of Agriculture's Forest Service administers the Wildland Fire Management Program funding for projects on federal, state, and private land. The goals of these projects include ecosystem restoration, research, and rehabilitation; forest health and invasive species protection; and hazardous fuels reduction. The Recovery Act provided $500 million for the Wildland Fire Management program.
Workforce Investment Act of 1998 Title I-B Grants	The Workforce Investment Act of 1998 (WIA) Youth, Adult, and Dislocated Worker Programs, administered by the Employment and Training Administration within the Department of Labor (Labor), provide job training and related services to unemployed and underemployed individuals. The Recovery Act provides an additional $2.95 billion in funding for Youth, Adult, and Dislocated Worker employment and training activities under Title I-B of WIA. These funds are allotted to states, which in turn allocate funds to local entities pursuant to formulas set out in WIA. The adult program provides training and related services to individuals ages 18 and older, the youth program provides training and related services to low-income youth ages 14 to 21, and dislocated worker funds

provide training and related services to individuals who have been laid off or notified that they will be laid off.[29]

Recovery Act funds can be used for all activities allowed under WIA, including core services, such as job search and placement assistance; intensive services, such as skill assessment and career counseling; and training services, including occupational skills training, on-the-job training, registered apprenticeship, and customized training. For the youth program, Labor encouraged states and local areas to use as much of these funds as possible to expand summer youth employment opportunities. In addition, Labor advised states that training for adults and dislocated workers should be a significant focus for Recovery Act funds, and encouraged states to establish policies to make supportive services and needs-related payments available for individuals who need these services to participate in job training. To facilitate increased training for high-demand occupations, the Recovery Act expanded the methods for providing training under WIA and allowed local workforce boards to directly enter into contracts with institutions of higher education and other training providers, if the local board determines that it would facilitate the training of multiple individuals and the contract does not limit customer choice.

---

[29]In general, a dislocated worker is an individual who has been terminated or laid off, or who has received a notice of termination or layoff, from employment; was self-employed but is unemployed as a result of general economic conditions in the community in which the individual resides or because of natural disasters; or is a displaced homemaker who is no longer supported by another family member. In addition, the Recovery Act provides that youth up to age 24 may be served with Recovery Act funds.

Appendix IV: Entities Visited by GAO in Selected States and the District of Columbia

Table 15: Education Entities Visited by GAO

States and the District of Columbia	City/county	Entity
California	Elk Grove	Elk Grove Unified School District
	Mountain View	Mountain View-Whisman School District
	Moreno Valley	Moreno Valley Unified School District
	San Bernardino	San Bernardino City Unified School District
	Los Angeles	Los Angeles Unified School District
	Stockton	Stockton Unified School District
	Sacramento	Sacramento City Unified School District
District of Columbia	Washington	District of Columbia Public Schools
	Washington	Center City Public Charter School
	Washington	Friendship Public Charter School
Iowa	Des Moines	Des Moines Independent Community School District
	Marshalltown	Marshalltown Community School District
Massachusetts	Boston	Boston Public Schools
	Boston	Massachusetts Dept. of Elementary and Secondary Education
	Revere	Revere Public Schools
Michigan	Detroit	Detroit Public Schools
	Detroit	Plymouth Educational Center
	Kingston	Kingston Community School District
New York	Syracuse	Syracuse City School District

Source: GAO.

Note: Total education entities visited by GAO is 19.

Table 16: Head Start Entities Visited by GAO

States and the District of Columbia	City/county	Entity
Georgia	Athens	Clarke County School District
	Columbus	Enrichment Services Program, Inc.
Florida	Miami	Miami-Dade County Community Action Agency
	Sarasota	Children First, Inc.
North Carolina	Greensboro	Guilford Child Development
	Smithfield	Johnston-Lee-Harnett Community Action Agency, Inc.
Ohio	Columbus	Child Development Council of Franklin County
	Dayton	Miami Valley Child Development Centers
	Circleville/Pickaway County	Pickaway County Community Action Organization

Source: GAO.

Note: Total head start entities visited by GAO is 9.

Table 17: Transit Entities Visited by GAO

States and the District of Columbia	City/county	Entity
Massachusetts	Boston	Massachusetts Bay Transportation Authority
Michigan	Lansing	Michigan Department of Transportation

Source: GAO.

Note: Total transit entities visited by GAO is 2.

Table 18: State Energy Program Entities Visited by GAO

States and the District of Columbia	City/county	Entity
Arizona	Phoenix	Energy Office, Arizona Department of Commerce
California	Sacramento	California Energy Commission
District of Columbia	Washington	District Department of the Environment
Iowa	Des Moines	Iowa Office of Energy Independence
	West Des Moines	Sun Prairie/Vista Court Apartments
	Ankeny	Iowa Association of Municipal Utilities
New York	Albany	New York State Energy Research and Development Authority (NYSERDA)
Pennsylvania	Carlisle	Carlisle Area School District
	Harrisburg	Department of Environmental Protection

Source: GAO.

Note: Total State Energy Program entities visited by GAO is 9.

Table 19: Energy Efficiency Conservation Block Grant Entities Visited by GAO

States and the District of Columbia	City/county	Entity
Arizona	Phoenix	City of Phoenix
	Phoenix	Energy Office, Arizona Department of Commerce
	Casa Grande	City of Casa Grande
California	Sacramento County	Sacramento County
	Redding	City of Redding
	San Jose	City of San Jose
Colorado	Colorado Springs	City of Colorado Springs
	Weld County	Weld County
District of Columbia	Washington	District Department of the Environment
Florida	Tampa	City of Tampa
	Jacksonville	City of Jacksonville
	Miami	City of Miami
	Miami-Dade County	Miami-Dade County
Georgia	Columbus/Muscogee County	Columbus Consolidated Government
	Cobb County	Cobb County
	Warner Robins	City of Warner Robins
Iowa	Des Moines	Iowa Office of Energy Independence
	Iowa city	City of Iowa City
	Warren County	County of Warren
	Ankeny	Des Moines Area Community College in Ankeny, Iowa
Massachusetts	Boston	City of Boston
	Everett	City of Everett
Michigan	City of Farmington Hills	Suburb
	Kent County	Kent County
	Lansing	Michigan Department of Energy, Labor & Economic Growth, Bureau of Energy Systems
Mississippi	Tupelo	City of Tupelo
New Jersey	Newark	State of New Jersey Board of Public Utilities
	Morris County	County of Morris
	Jersey City	City of Jersey city
	Woodbridge Township	Woodbridge Township
New York	Albany	New York State Energy Research and Development
	Orange County	Orange County
	Town of Brookhaven	Town of Brookhaven

States and the District of Columbia	City/county	Entity
Pennsylvania	Lancaster	Thaddeus Stevens College of Technology
	Philadelphia	City of Philadelphia
	Berks County	County of Berks
	Harrisburg	Department of Environmental Protection
Texas	Austin	City of Austin
	Round Rock	Round Rock
	Bryan	City of Bryan
	Austin	State Energy Conservation Office (SECO)

Source: GAO.

Note: Total Energy Efficiency Conservation Block Grant entities visited by GAO is 41.

Table 20: Weatherization Entities Visited by GAO

States and the District of Columbia	City/county	Entity
Arizona	Phoenix	Arizona Department of Commerce
	Apache, Coconino, Navajo, and Yavapai Counties	Northern Arizona Council of Governments
	Tucson and South Tucson	Tucson Urban League
California	Roseville	Project GO, Inc.
	Santa Fe Springs	Maravilla Foundation
	Fountain Valley	Community Action Partnership of Orange County
	Redding	Self Help Home Improvement Project
	Sacramento	California Department of Community Services and Development
District of Columbia	Washington	District Department of the Environment
	Washington	United Planning Organization
	Washington	African Heritage Dancers and Drummers
	Washington	Prosperity Media Enterprise
Florida	Miami-Dade	Miami-Dade County Community Action Agency
	Tampa/Hillsborough	Tampa-Hillsborough Action Plan
Iowa	Des Moines	Division of Community Action Agencies, Iowa Department of Human Rights
	Des Moines	Polk County Public Works Department
	Ottumwa	Southern Iowa Economic Development Association
Pennsylvania	York County	York County Planning Commission

Source: GAO.

Note: Total weatherization entities visited by GAO is 18.

Table 21: Housing Entities Visited by GAO

States and the District of Columbia	City/county	Entity
Arizona	Flagstaff	Housing Authority of the City of Flagstaff
	Phoenix	City of Phoenix Housing Department
	South Tucson	South Tucson Housing Authority
	Phoenix	Department of Housing and Urban Development Phoenix Field Office
California	San Francisco	San Francisco Housing Authority
	San Francisco	U.S. Department of Housing and Urban Development, San Francisco Regional Office
Georgia	Athens	Housing Authority of the City of Athens
	Macon	Housing Authority of the City of Macon
	Atlanta	Housing Authority of the City of Atlanta
Illinois	Chicago	Chicago Housing Authority
	Chicago	U.S. Department of Housing and Urban Development, Chicago Regional Office
Iowa	Des Moines	City of Des Moines Municipal Housing Agency
Massachusetts	Boston	Boston Housing Authority
		U.S. Department of Housing and Urban Development, Boston Regional Office
Mississippi	Picayune	Picayune Housing Authority
	Gulfport	Mississippi Regional Housing Authority No. VIII
	Meridian	Meridian Housing Authority
	Jackson	U.S. Department of Housing and Urban Development, Jackson Field Office
New Jersey	Newark	Newark Housing Authority
Pennsylvania	Philadelphia	Philadelphia Housing Authority
	Harrisburg	Harrisburg Housing Authority
	Philadelphia	Department of Housing and Urban Development Philadelphia Office
Texas	San Antonio	San Antonio Housing Authority
	San Antonio	U.S. Department of Housing and Urban Development, San Antonio Field Office, Region VI, Office of Public Housing
	Fort Worth	U.S. Department of Housing and Urban Development, Fort Worth Regional Office, Region VI, Office of Public Housing

Source: GAO.

Note: Total housing entities visited by GAO is 24.

Table 22: Tax Credit Assistance Program and Section 1602 Program Entities Visited by GAO

States and the District of Columbia	City/county	Entity
Florida	Winter Haven	Cypress Cove
	Lakeland	Bonnett Shores
Georgia	Dublin	Riverview Heights
	Sandersville	Camellia Lane L.P.
Mississippi	Jackson	Mississippi Home Corporation
	Pickens	Caffey Apartments
	Pascagoula	Bayside Village
Ohio	Coshocton	Kno-Ho-Co Ashland Community Action Commission
	Dayton	Oberer Residential Construction
	Columbus	Buckeye Community Hope Foundation
	Columbus	Ohio Capital Corporation for Housing (OCCH)
	Columbus	Ohio Housing Finance Agency
	Knox County	Heart of Ohio Homes
	Knox County	Mount Vernon Senior Village
	Montgomery County	East End Twin Towers Crossing
Pennsylvania	Stewartstown	Hopewell Courtyard
	City of Allentown	Greystone Apartments
	Northumberland	Cannery Point
	Philadelphia	Presser Senior Apartments
	Philadelphia	Mantua Square
	Harrisburg	Pennsylvania Housing Finance Agency

Source: GAO.

Note: Total Tax Credit Assistance Program and Section 1602 Program entities visited by GAO is 21.

Table 23: Local Government Entities Visited by GAO

States	Local government	Type of local government	Population	Unemployment Rate
Arizona	Phoenix	City	1,601,587	10.3
California	Redding	City	90,521	13.4
	San Jose	City	964,695	12.5
Colorado	Colorado Springs	City	399,827	8.9
	Weld	County	254,759	9.6
Florida	Miami-Dade	County	2,500,625	12.8
Georgia	Columbus Consolidated Government	Consolidated city/county	190,414	9.7
	The Unified Government of Athens-Clarke County	Consolidated city/county	116,342	8.3
Illinois	Chrisman	City	1,219	10.5
	Steward	Village	258	11.1
Iowa	Des Moines	City	198,460	7.4
	Marshalltown	City	25,645	7.5
Massachusetts	Boston	City	645,169	9.0
Michigan	Farmington Hills	City	78,675	11.0
Mississippi	Tupelo	City	36,336	12.3
New Jersey	Jersey City	City	242,503	11.5
New York	Brookhaven	Town	490,416	6.9
	Steuben	County	96,552	9.0
North Carolina	Wilmington	City	101,350	8.6
Ohio	Cincinnati	City	333,013	10.6
Pennsylvania	Berks	County	407,125	9.8
	Philadelphia	City	1,547,297	11.9
Texas	Austin	City	786,382	6.9
	Round Rock	City	105,412	6.7

Source: U.S. Census Bureau and U.S. Department of Labor, Bureau of Labor Statistics (BLS), Local Area Unemployment Statistics (LAUS) data.

Notes: Population data are from the latest available estimate, July 1, 2009. Unemployment rates are preliminary estimates for June 2010 and have not been seasonally adjusted. Rates are a percentage of the labor force. Estimates are subject to revisions.

Total local government entities visited by GAO is 24.

Total entities visited is 167.

Appendix V: GAO Contacts and Staff Acknowledgments

GAO Contacts

J. Christopher Mihm, Managing Director for Strategic Issues, (202) 512-6806 or mihmj@gao.gov

For issues related to SFSF and other education programs: Barbara D. Bovbjerg, Managing Director of Education, Workforce, and Income Security, (202) 512-7215 or bovbjergb@gao.gov

For issues related to Medicaid programs: Dr. Marjorie Kanof, Managing Director of Health Care, (202) 512-7114 or kanofm@gao.gov

For issues related to highways, transit, and other transportation programs: Katherine A. Siggerud, Managing Director of Physical Infrastructure, (202) 512-2834 or siggerudk@gao.gov

For issues related to State Energy Program (SEP), Energy Efficiency and Conservation Block Grant (EECBG), and weatherization: Patricia Dalton, Managing Director of Natural Resources and Environment, (202) 512-3841 or daltonp@gao.gov

For issues related to public housing, Tax Credit Assistance Program (TCAP), and Section 1602 Program: Richard J. Hillman, Managing Director of Financial Markets and Community Investment, (202) 512-9073 or hillmanr@gao.gov

For issues related to internal controls and Single Audits: Jeanette Franzel, Managing Director of Financial Management and Assurance, (202) 512-2600 or franzelj@gao.gov

For issues related to contracting and procurement: Paul Francis, Managing Director of Acquisition and Sourcing Management, (202) 512-4841 or francisp@gao.gov

For issues related to fraud, waste, and abuse: Gregory D. Kutz, Managing Director of Forensic Audits and Special Investigations, (202) 512-6722 or kutzg@gao.gov

Staff Acknowledgments

The following staff contributed to this report: Stanley Czerwinski, Denise Fantone, Susan Irving, and Yvonne Jones, (Directors); Thomas James, and Michelle Sager, (Assistant Directors); Sandra Beattie (Analyst-in-Charge); and Marie Ahearn, David Alexander, Judith Ambrose, Peter Anderson, Thomas Beall, Noah Bleicher, Jessica Botsford, Anthony Bova, Richard Cambosos, Ralph Campbell Jr., Virginia Chanley, Tina Cheng, Andrew

Ching, Marcus Corbin, Robert Cramer, Fran Davison, Michael Derr, Helen Desaulniers, Ruth "Eli" DeVan, Alexandra Dew, David Dornisch, Kevin Dooley, Abe Dymond, Holly Dye, Janet Eackloff, Lorraine Ettaro, James Fuquay, Alice Feldesman, Alexander Galuten, Ellen Grady, Anita Hamilton, Geoffrey Hamilton, Tracy Harris, Kristine Hassinger, Lauren Heft, David Hooper, Bert Japikse, Mitchell Karpman, Karen Keegan, John Krump, Jon Kucskar, Hannah Laufe, Jean K. Lee, Natalie Maddox, Stephanie May, Sarah M. McGrath, John Mc Grail, Jean McSween, Donna Miller, Kevin Milne, Marc Molino, Mimi Nguyen, Ken Patton, Anthony Pordes, Brenda Rabinowitz, Carl Ramirez, James Rebbe, Beverly Ross, Sylvia Schatz, Sidney Schwartz, Don Springman, Andrew J. Stephens, Esther Toledo, Alyssa Weir, Crystal Wesco, Craig Winslow, Elizabeth Wood, William T. Woods, and Kimberly Young.

Program Contributors

Federal Medical Assistance Percentage (FMAP)	Susan Anthony, Laura Brogan, Ted Burik, Julianne Flowers, Martha Kelly, Zachary Levinson, and Carolyn Yocom
Education—SFSF, ESEA Title I, and IDEA	Jaime Allentuck, James Ashley, Cornelia M. Ashby, Edward Bodine, Jessica Botsford, Amy Buck, Karen Febey, Alex Galuten, Mark Glickman, Bryon Gordon, Sonya Harmeyer, Ying Long, Jean McSween, Elizabeth Morrison, Luann Moy, Karen O'Conor, Mimi Nguyen, Kathy Peyman, James M. Rebbe, Crystal Robinson, Scott Spicer, Michelle Verbrugge, Charles Willson, and Sarah Wood
Federal-Aid Highway Surface Transportation and Transit Capital Assistance Programs	Aisha Cabrer, Steve Cohen, Philip Herr, Joah Iannotta, Les Locke, Lisa Shibata, Raymond Sendejas, and David Wise
State Energy Program (SEP) and Energy Efficiency Conservation Block Grant (EECBG)	Nicholas Weeks, Kristen Massey, Jessica Bryant-Bertail, Mark Gaffigan, Kim Gianopoulos, and Stuart Ryba
Public Housing Capital Fund	Rebecca Rose, Aimee Elivert, May Lee, John McGrail, Marc Molino, Deena Richart, Paul Schmidt, Barb Roesmann, and Mathew Scire
Tax Credit Assistance Program (TCAP) and Section 1602 Program	Jennifer Alpha, Heather Chartier, Swetha Doraiswamy, Andrew Finkel, John McGrail, Marc Molino, Roberto Piñero, Carl Ramirez, Barbara Roesmann, and Mathew Scire.
Weatherization	Jessica Bryant-Bertail, Mark Gaffigan, Kim Gianopoulos, Stuart Ryba, and Jason Trentacoste, and Stephanie Gaines
Recipient reporting	Yvonne Jones, Judith Kordahl, Carol Patey, Patricia Norris, Steve Punto, and Jon Stehle
Safeguarding/Single Audit	Phyllis Anderson, Marcia Buchanan, Eric Holbrook, Jason Kelly, Maria Morton, Laura Pacheco, Susan Ragland, Sandra Silzer, and Glenn Slocum
State and local budget	Sandra Beattie, Anthony Bova, Stanley J. Czerwinski, Michelle Sager, and Esther Toledo

Contributors to the Selected States and the District

The names of GAO staff contributing to the selected states and the District are as follows:

Arizona	Karyn Angulo, Rebecca Bolnick, Tom Brew, Lisa Brownson, Steven Calvo, Eileen Larence, Roy Judy, Radha Seshagiri, and Jeff Schmerling
California	Linda Calbom, Emily Eischen, Guillermo Gonzalez, Richard Griswold, Susan Lawless, Gail Luna, Heather MacLeod, Emmy Rhine, Eddie Uyekawa, and Lacy Vong
Colorado	Paul Begnaud, Kathy Hale, Kay Harnish-Ladd, Susan Iott, Jennifer Leone, Brian Lepore, Robin Nazzaro, Tony Padilla, Leslie Pollock, Kathleen Richardson, and Dawn Shorey
District of Columbia	Laurel Beedon, Labony Chakraborty, Sunny Chang, Nagla'a El-Hodiri, Mattias Fenton, Nicole Harris, Adam Hoffman, William O. Jenkins, Jr., and Leyla Kazaz
Florida	Michael Armes, Susan Aschoff, Patrick di Battista, Sabur Ibrahim, Kevin Kumanga, Frank Minore, Maria Morton, Daniel Ramsey, Brenda Ross, Andy Sherrill, Bernard Ungar, Margaret Weber, and James Whitcomb
Georgia	Alicia Puente Cackley, Waylon Catrett, Chase Cook, Marc Molino, Daniel Newman, John H. Pendleton, Nadine Garrick Raidbard, Barbara Roesmann, Paige Smith, and David Shoemaker
Illinois	Silvia Arbelaez-Ellis, Josh Bartzen, Dean Campbell, James Cosgrove, Cory Marzullo, Paul Schmidt, Roberta Rickey, and Rosemary Torres Lerma
Iowa	Richard Cheston, Thomas Cook, Daniel Egan, Christine Kehr, Ronald Maxon, Mark Ryan, Raymond Smith, Jr., Lisa Shames, and Carol Herrnstadt Shulman
Massachusetts	Stanley J. Czerwinski, Laurie Ekstrand, Anthony Bova, Nancy J. Donovan, Kathleen M. Drennan, Anna M. Kelley, David Lin, Keith C. O'Brien, Kathryn O'Dea, Carol Patey, and Robert Yetvin
Michigan	Ranya Elias, Patrick Frey, Henry Malone, Giao N. Nguyen, Robert Owens, Laura Pacheco, Susan Ragland, Tejdev Sandhu, Regina Santucci, and Amy Sweet
Mississippi	James Elgas, Barbara Haynes, John K. Needham, Norman J. Rabkin, William C. Allbritton, James Kim, Gary Shepard, and Erin Stockdale
New Jersey	Gene Aloise, Kisha Clark, Anne Doré, Diana Glod, Alexander Lawrence Jr., Nancy Lueke, Tarunkant Mithani, and David Wise
New York	Christopher Farrell, Susan Fleming, Kendall Helm, Dave Maurer, Tiffany Mostert, Summer Pachman, Frank Putallaz, and Ronald Stouffer
North Carolina	Laura G. Acosta, Cornelia M. Ashby, Sandra Baxter, Sarah Jane Brady, Bonnie Derby, Bryon Gordon, Sara S. Kelly, Tahra Nichols, Anthony Patterson, Paula Rascona, and Connie W. Sawyer
Ohio	Debra Cottrell, Matthew Drerup, Bill J. Keller, Jeffrey G. Miller, Tranchau Nguyen, George A. Scott, Brian Smith, David C. Trimble, and Myra Watts-Butler
Pennsylvania	Eleanor Cambridge, Mark Gaffigan, John Healey, Phillip Herr, Richard Mayfield, Jodi M. Prosser, Matthew Rosenberg, MaryLynn Sergent, and Stephen Ulrich
Texas	Fredrick D. Berry, Danny Burton, K. Eric Essig, Erinn Flanagan, Michael O'Neill, Gloria Proa, Bob Robinson, and Lorelei St. James

Related GAO Products

Recovery Act: Further Opportunities Exist to Strengthen Oversight of Broadband Stimulus Programs. GAO-10-823. Washington, D.C.: August 4, 2010.

Recovery Act: States Could Provide More Information on Education Programs to Enhance the Public's Understanding of Fund Use. GAO-10-807. Washington, D.C.: July 30, 2010.

Recovery Act: Most DOE Cleanup Projects Appear to Be Meeting Cost and Schedule Targets, but Assessing Impact of Spending Remains a Challenge. GAO-10-784. Washington, D.C.: July 29, 2010.

Recovery Act: Contracting Approaches and Oversight Used by Selected Federal Agencies and States. GAO-10-809. Washington, D.C.: July 15, 2010.

GAO Review of LEA Controls over and Uses of Recovery Act Education Funds (Avery County Schools). GAO-10-746R. Washington, D.C.: July 9, 2010.

GAO Review of LEA Controls over and Uses of Recovery Act Education Funds (Winston-Salem/Forsyth County Schools). GAO-10-747R. Washington, D.C.: July 9, 2010.

Independent Oversight of Recovery Act Funding for Mississippi's Weatherization Assistance Program. GAO-10-796R. Washington, D.C.: June 30, 2010.

High Speed Rail: Learning From Service Start-ups, Prospects for Increased Industry Investment, and Federal Oversight Plans. GAO-10-625. Washington, D.C.: June 17, 2010.

Federal Energy Management: GSA's Recovery Act Program Is on Track, but Opportunities Exist to Improve Transparency, Performance Criteria, and Risk Management. GAO-10-630. Washington, D.C.: June 16, 2010.

GAO Proactive Testing of ARRA Tax Credits for COBRA Premium Payments. GAO-10-804R. Washington, D.C.: June 14, 2010.

Temporary Assistance for Needy Families: Implications of Recent Legislative and Economic Changes for State Programs and Work Participation Rates. GAO-10-525. Washington, D.C.: May 28, 2010.

Recovery Act: Increasing the Public's Understanding of What Funds Are Being Spent on and What Outcomes Are Expected. GAO-10-581. Washington, D.C.: May 27, 2010.

Recovery Act: Clean Water Projects Are Underway, but Procedures May Not Be in Place to Ensure Adequate Oversight. GAO-10-761T. Washington, D.C.: May 26, 2010.

Recovery Act: States' and Localities' Uses of Funds and Actions Needed to Address Implementation Challenges and Bolster Accountability. GAO-10-604. Washington, D.C.: May 26, 2010.

Recovery Act: States' and Localities' Uses of Funds and Actions Needed to Address Implementation Challenges and Bolster Accountability (Appendixes). GAO-10-605SP. Washington, D.C.: May, 26, 2010.

Head Start: Undercover Testing Finds Fraud and Abuse at Selected Head Start Centers. GAO-10-733T. Washington, D.C.: May 18, 2010.

Health Coverage Tax Credit: Participation and Administrative Costs. GAO-10-521R. Washington, D.C.: April 30, 2010.

2010 Census: Plans for Census Coverage Measurement Are on Track, but Additional Steps Will Improve Its Usefulness. GAO-10-324. Washington, D.C.: April 23, 2010.

Energy Star Program: Covert Testing Shows the Energy Star Program Certification Process Is Vulnerable to Fraud and Abuse. GAO-10-470. Washington, D.C.: March 5, 2010.

Recovery Act: California's Use of Funds and Efforts to Ensure Accountability. GAO-10-467T. Washington, D.C.: March 5, 2010.

Recovery Act: Factors Affecting the Department of Energy's Program Implementation. GAO-10-497T. Washington, D.C.: March 4, 2010.

Recovery Act: One Year Later, States' and Localities' Uses of Funds and Opportunities to Strengthen Accountability. GAO-10-437. Washington, D.C.: March 3, 2010.

State and Local Governments' Fiscal Outlook March 2010 Update. GAO-10-358. Washington, D.C.: March 2, 2010.

Recovery Act: Officials' Views Vary on Impacts of Davis-Bacon Act Prevailing Wage Provision. GAO-10-421. Washington, D.C.: February 24, 2010.

Electronic Personal Health Information Exchange: Health Care Entities' Reported Disclosure Practices and Effects on Quality of Care. GAO-10-361. Washington, D.C.: February 17, 2010.

Recovery Act: Project Selection and Starts Are Influenced by Certain Federal Requirements and Other Factors. GAO-10-383. Washington, D.C.: February 10, 2010

Recovery Act: IRS Quickly Implemented Tax Provisions, but Reporting and Enforcement Improvements Are Needed. GAO-10-349. Washington, D.C.: February 10, 2010.

Status of the Small Business Administration's Implementation of Administrative Provisions in the American Recovery and Reinvestment Act of 2009. GAO-10-298R. Washington, D.C.: January 19, 2010.

Recovery Act: States' Use of Highway and Transit Funds and Efforts to Meet the Act's Requirements. GAO-10-312T. Washington, D.C.: December 10, 2009.

Recovery Act: Status of States' and Localities' Use of Funds and Efforts to Ensure Accountability. GAO-10-231. Washington, D.C.: December 10, 2009.

Recovery Act: Status of States' and Localities' Use of Funds and Efforts to Ensure Accountability (Appendixes). GAO-10-232SP. Washington, D.C.: December 10, 2009.

Recovery Act: Planned Efforts and Challenges in Evaluating Compliance with Maintenance of Effort and Similar Provisions. GAO-10-247. Washington, D.C.: November 30, 2009.

Recovery Act: Contract Oversight Activities of the Recovery Accountability and Transparency Board and Observations on Contract Spending in Selected States. GAO-10-216R. Washington, D.C.: November 30, 2009.

Recovery Act: Recipient Reported Jobs Data Provide Some Insight into Use of Recovery Act Funding, but Data Quality and Reporting Issues Need Attention. GAO-10-223. Washington, D.C.: November 19, 2009.

Recovery Act: Recipient Reported Jobs Data Provide Some Insight into Use of Recovery Act Funding, but Data Quality and Reporting Issues Need Attention. GAO-10-224T. Washington, D.C.: November 19, 2009.

Recovery Act: Agencies Are Addressing Broadband Program Challenges, but Actions Are Needed to Improve Implementation. GAO-10-80. Washington, D.C.: November 16, 2009.

Recovery Act: Preliminary Observations on the Implementation of Broadband Programs. GAO-10-192T. Washington, D.C.: October 27, 2009.

First-Time Homebuyer Tax Credit: Taxpayers' Use of the Credit and Implementation and Compliance Challenges. GAO-10-166T. Washington, D.C.: October 22, 2009.

Federal Energy Management: Agencies Are Taking Steps to Meet High-Performance Federal Building Requirements, but Face Challenges. GAO-10-22. Washington, D.C.: October 30, 2009.

High Speed Passenger Rail: Developing Viable High Speed Rail Projects under the Recovery Act and Beyond. GAO-10-162T. Washington, D.C.: October 14, 2009.

Tax Administration: Opportunities Exist for IRS to Enhance Taxpayer Service and Enforcement for the 2010 Filing Season. GAO-09-1026. Washington, D.C.: September 23, 2009.

Recovery Act: Funds Continue to Provide Fiscal Relief to States and Localities, While Accountability and Reporting Challenges Need to Be Fully Addressed. GAO-09-1016. Washington, D.C.: September 23, 2009.

Recovery Act: Funds Continue to Provide Fiscal Relief to States and Localities, While Accountability and Reporting Challenges Need to Be Fully Addressed (Appendixes). GAO-09-1017SP. Washington, D.C.: September 23, 2009.

Recovery Act: States' and Localities' Current and Planned Uses of Funds While Facing Fiscal Stresses. GAO-09-908T. Washington, D.C.: September 10, 2009.

Recovery Act: States' Use of Highway Infrastructure Funds and Compliance with the Act's Requirements. GAO-09-926T. Washington, D.C.: July 31, 2009.

Unemployment Insurance Measures Included in the American Recovery and Reinvestment Act of 2009, as of July 2009. GAO-09-942R. Washington, D.C.: July 27, 2009.

Grants Management: Grants.gov Has Systematic Weaknesses That Require Attention. GAO-09-589. Washington, D.C.: July 15, 2009.

Recovery Act: States' and Localities' Current and Planned Uses of Funds While Facing Fiscal Stresses. GAO-09-829. Washington, D.C.: July 8, 2009.

Recovery Act: States' and Localities' Current and Planned Uses of Funds While Facing Fiscal Stresses. GAO-09-831T. Washington, D.C.: July 8, 2009.

Recovery Act: States' and Localities' Current and Planned Uses of Funds While Facing Fiscal Stresses (Appendixes). GAO-09-830SP. Washington, D.C.: July 8, 2009.

Recovery Act: The Department of Transportation Followed Key Federal Requirements in Developing Selection Criteria for Its Supplemental Discretionary Grants Program. GAO-09-785R. Washington, D.C.: June 30, 2009.

High Speed Passenger Rail: Effectively Using Recovery Act Funds for High Speed Rail Projects. GAO-09-786T. Washington, D.C.: June 23, 2009.

Recovery Act: GAO's Efforts to Work with the Accountability Community to Help Ensure Effective and Efficient Oversight. GAO-09-672T. Washington, D.C.: May 5, 2009.

Recovery Act: Consistent Policies Needed to Ensure Equal Consideration of Grant Applications. GAO-09-590R. Washington, D.C.: April 29, 2009.

Recovery Act: Initial Results on States' Use of and Accountability for Transportation Funds. GAO-09-597T. Washington, D.C.: April 29, 2009.

Recovery Act: As Initial Implementation Unfolds in States and Localities, Continued Attention to Accountability Issues Is Essential. GAO-09-580. Washington, D.C.: April 23, 2009.

Recovery Act: As Initial Implementation Unfolds in States and Localities, Continued Attention to Accountability Issues Is Essential. GAO-09-631T. Washington, D.C.: April 23, 2009.

Small Business Administration's Implementation of Administrative Provisions in the American Recovery and Reinvestment Act. GAO-09-507R. Washington, D.C.: April 16, 2009.

American Recovery and Reinvestment Act: GAO's Role in Helping to Ensure Accountability and Transparency for Science Funding. GAO-09-515T. Washington, D.C.: March 19, 2009.

American Recovery and Reinvestment Act: GAO's Role in Helping to Ensure Accountability and Transparency. GAO-09-453T. Washington, D.C.: March 5, 2009.

Estimated Adjusted Medicaid Funding Allocations Related to the Proposed American Recovery and Reinvestment Act. GAO-09-371R. Washington, D.C.: February 5, 2009.

Estimated Temporary Medicaid Funding Allocations Related to Section 5001 of the American Recovery and Reinvestment Act. GAO-09-364R. Washington, D.C.: February 4, 2009.

GAO's Mission	The Government Accountability Office, the audit, evaluation, and investigative arm of Congress, exists to support Congress in meeting its constitutional responsibilities and to help improve the performance and accountability of the federal government for the American people. GAO examines the use of public funds; evaluates federal programs and policies; and provides analyses, recommendations, and other assistance to help Congress make informed oversight, policy, and funding decisions. GAO's commitment to good government is reflected in its core values of accountability, integrity, and reliability.
Obtaining Copies of GAO Reports and Testimony	The fastest and easiest way to obtain copies of GAO documents at no cost is through GAO's Web site (www.gao.gov). Each weekday afternoon, GAO posts on its Web site newly released reports, testimony, and correspondence. To have GAO e-mail you a list of newly posted products, go to www.gao.gov and select "E-mail Updates."
Order by Phone	The price of each GAO publication reflects GAO's actual cost of production and distribution and depends on the number of pages in the publication and whether the publication is printed in color or black and white. Pricing and ordering information is posted on GAO's Web site, http://www.gao.gov/ordering.htm.
	Place orders by calling (202) 512-6000, toll free (866) 801-7077, or TDD (202) 512-2537.
	Orders may be paid for using American Express, Discover Card, MasterCard, Visa, check, or money order. Call for additional information.
To Report Fraud, Waste, and Abuse in Federal Programs	Contact:
	Web site: www.gao.gov/fraudnet/fraudnet.htm E-mail: fraudnet@gao.gov Automated answering system: (800) 424-5454 or (202) 512-7470
Congressional Relations	Ralph Dawn, Managing Director, dawnr@gao.gov, (202) 512-4400 U.S. Government Accountability Office, 441 G Street NW, Room 7125 Washington, DC 20548
Public Affairs	Chuck Young, Managing Director, youngc1@gao.gov, (202) 512-4800 U.S. Government Accountability Office, 441 G Street NW, Room 7149 Washington, DC 20548